The New Politics of Transnational Labor

THE NEW POLITICS OF TRANSNATIONAL LABOR

Why Some Alliances Succeed

MARISSA BROOKES

ILR PRESS
AN IMPRINT OF CORNELL UNIVERSITY PRESS
ITHACA AND LONDON

First published 2019 by Cornell University Press

Library of Congress Cataloging-in-Publication Data
Names: Brookes, Marissa, author.
Title: The new politics of transnational labor : why some alliances
    succeed / Marissa Brookes.
Description: Ithaca [New York] : ILR Press, an imprint of Cornell
    University Press, 2019. | Includes bibliographical references and index.
Identifiers: LCCN 2018047431 (print) | LCCN 2018052484 (ebook) |
    ISBN 9781501733208 (pdf) | ISBN 9781501733215 (ret) |
    ISBN 9781501733192 | ISBN 9781501733192 (cloth) |
    ISBN 9781501739309 (pbk.)
Subjects: LCSH: International labor activities. | Labor movement—
    International cooperation. | Labor and globalization. | Labor
    unions—Political activity. | Transnationalism.
Classification: LCC HD6475.A1 (ebook) | LCC HD6475.A1 B76 2019
    (print) | DDC 331.88091—dc23
LC record available at https://lccn.loc.gov/2018047431

Contents

Acknowledgments

This book emerged out of a decade-long process of listening and learning that began in Chicago but came to encompass a tremendous variety of people and places scattered across four continents. It owes its existence first and foremost to the workers, union representatives, and labor activists who took the time to talk with me about their activism, jobs, and lives. Though here they remain unnamed, I give these workers and unionists my deepest gratitude.

I owe much of my intellectual development to my time at Northwestern University and to my advisers, Kathleen Thelen and James Mahoney. I thank Kathy for pushing me beyond what I thought were my limits and supporting my work well after she left Northwestern for MIT. Kathy taught me that only by tackling tough questions and seeking to solve challenging puzzles does one become an independent scholar. I owe much of my drive and ambition to her. I am equally grateful to Jim, who mentored me and believed in me from my earliest days in graduate school. Jim's incisive feedback, spot-on criticism, and genuine enthusiasm have strengthened my work beyond measure. I cannot thank him enough for his guidance. I thank Ben Page for always reminding me of the big picture in our discussions about unions and globalization. Jeffrey Winters shaped my thinking on the concept of power and stimulated my interest in Southeast Asia. For his sharp thinking and candid advice, I owe him my sincere thanks.

My colleagues at the University of California, Riverside, have provided a tremendous amount of inspiration and support. I am especially indebted to David Pion-Berlin for his steady mentorship and practical advice, as well as to John W. Cioffi for his encouragement and helpful guidance. For demystifying the book-writing process and assisting me through various stages of this project, I thank Ben Bishin, Shaun Bowler, Farah Godrej, Bronwyn Leebaw, John Medearis, and Georgia Warnke. For keeping my mind on track and my spirits high, Liz Davis and Megan Robbins deserve special thanks. I am also thankful for the vibrant energy of my graduate and undergraduate students, who mean the world to me.

Others also helped me develop this book through a mix of conversation, comment, and critique. Mike Fichter gave many useful comments on my manuscript, as did the anonymous reviewers, to whom I express sincere gratitude. I learned a great deal from Teri Caraway, whose knowledge of Indonesia helped me refine parts of an early version of this book. Lowell Turner and Lance Compa generously hosted my first visit to Cornell University, where I received feedback on an early iteration of this book's theoretical framework from folks at the School of Industrial and Labor Relations. Chris Tilly at UCLA likewise provided a venue in which to present my book-in-progress and receive valuable feedback. Back at Boston University, it was Cathie Jo Martin who built the core of my knowledge of political economy and labor politics, and it was Peter J. Schwartz who first sharpened my capacity for critical thinking in ways that still inspire my scholarship. I also had the good fortune to participate in numerous conferences and workshops over the years that forced my ideas to evolve and mature, and for this I thank the Labor and Employment Relations Association, the Society for the Advancement of Socio-Economics, the International Studies Association, the Interuniversity Research Centre on Globalization and Work, and the American Political Science Association. Informal conversations on the subject of labor transnationalism with Mark Anner, Jamie McCallum, Sabrina Zajak, and many others also deserve acknowledgment here.

With the generous support of the US Fulbright Program, I spent a year conducting fieldwork for this project in Australia. Bradon Ellem, who hosted my stay at the University of Sydney Business School, went above and beyond in supporting my research. He read and commented on early drafts of my theory chapter, enhanced my comprehension of labor politics, and welcomed me into the community of scholars at Work and Organisational Studies. I owe Bradon deep gratitude. Peter Fairbrother, who hosted my stay at the Royal Melbourne Institute of Technology, likewise went out of his way to help develop my theoretical framework, converse about labor transnationalism, and connect me with a global network of scholars. Peter pushed me to read and think deeply about power. I am glad that he did.

Others in Australia contributed to this book's development. Michele Ford shared with me her expertise on Indonesia and taught me a lot about labor politics in Southeast Asia. Also in Australia, I thank Marian Baird, Ruth Barton, Verity Burgmann, Rae Cooper, Leanne Cutcher, Victor Gekara, Angela Knox, Russell Lansbury, Susan McGrath-Champ, Al Rainnie, and Darryn Snell. I owe a special thanks to Charlotte Yates from McMaster University, whom I met while we were both visiting in Melbourne and who introduced me to opportunities I otherwise would not have had. Alex McCallum and Mary Ann Gibson were of enormous help in ensuring that my fieldwork in Australia got off to a great start. I think Alex would have quite liked this book if he were still with us today. In the United Kingdom, I thank the many folks who facilitated my fieldwork in London and Manchester and offered good advice in the very early stages of this project. I am thankful to everyone who hosted me at what was then the Employment Relations and Organisational Behaviour Group at the London School of Economics, especially Virginia Doellgast. Ian Greer was encouraging and connected me with key contacts. Tom Hazeldine was a solid guide in London.

Several sources of funding made fieldwork for this project possible. I am grateful to the Institute of International Education for the Fulbright Postgraduate Scholarship. I am also grateful to have received a Dispute Resolution Research Center Grant from the Kellogg School of Management, a Graduate Research Grant from Northwestern University, and a Summer Research Grant from the Buffett Center for International and Comparative Studies. Additionally, a Resident Fellowship from the Center for Ideas and

Society at UC Riverside afforded me time and space to develop my theory of labor coordination in transnational campaigns, while a generous grant from the Hellman Fellows Fund allowed me to collect additional data.

I thank those at Cornell University Press for their excellent work in the publishing process. Most especially I thank Fran Benson, who backed this project from the proposal stage. The enthusiasm and encouragement she expressed about my book proposal in our very first phone call meant so much to me as an early-career scholar writing my first book. Although this book greatly benefited from the skills and talents of those at Cornell, I alone am responsible for any errors in fact or analysis found in the pages of this book.

To my family, I give my most heartfelt thanks. Together my parents, sisters, cousin, aunt, nieces, and nephew instilled in me strong values, cheered me on through every finish line, and have always believed in me completely. My parents, Melinda Encinares Brookes and Daniel J. Brookes, continue to inspire me with their wisdom and powerful love of learning. Above all, I am eternally grateful for the love, understanding, and encouragement of my best friend, Kenton McMillin. He has stood by my side throughout more challenges than I can begin to recount. With humor, patience, and a steadfast belief in me, Kenton has been more generous and supportive than I ever thought possible of anyone. He worked hard to make sure I had everything I needed to finish this book. He has worked hard his entire life. This book is dedicated to him.

Abbreviations

AC	arbitration council
ACTU	Australian Council of Trade Unions
AFL-CIO	American Federation of Labor and Congress of Industrial Organizations
AGM	annual general meeting
AMWU	Australian Manufacturing Workers' Union
CCAP	coordination and context-appropriate power
CTSWF	Cambodian Tourism and Service Workers Federation
ETUC	European Trade Union Confederation
EWC	European Works Council
FSPM	Federasi Serikat Pekerja Mandiri (Federation of Independent Unions)
G4S	Group 4 Securicor
GFA	global framework agreement
GMB	General, Municipal, Boilermakers and Allied Trade Union
GUF	global union federation

GVC	global value chain
IDC	International Dockworkers Council
ILA	International Longshoremen's Association
ILO	International Labour Organisation
ILWU	International Longshore and Warehouse Union
IRI	International Republican Institute
ITF	International Transport Workers' Federation
ITUC	International Trade Union Confederation
IUF	International Union of Food, Agricultural, Hotel, Restaurant, Catering, Tobacco and Allied Workers' Associations
LHMU	Liquor, Hospitality, and Miscellaneous Workers' Union
MDHC	Mersey Docks and Harbour Company
MUA	Maritime Union of Australia
NCP	National Contact Point
NGO	nongovernmental organization
NPR	National Public Radio
OECD	Organisation for Economic Co-operation and Development
P4P	Panitia Penyelesaian Perselisihan Perburuhan Pusat
SEIU	Service Employees International Union
SPMS	Serikat Pekerja Mandiri Shangri-La (Shangri-La Independent Workers' Union)
TAN	transnational advocacy network
TGWU	Transport and General Workers' Union
TLA	transnational labor alliance
TNC	transnational corporation
TUAC	Trade Union Advisory Committee
UFCW	United Food and Commercial Workers
UNI	Union Network International
USDAW	Union of Shop, Distributive and Allied Workers
USINDO	United States–Indonesia Society

The New Politics of Transnational Labor

Chapter 1

The New Politics of
Transnational Labor

For decades, labor scholars saw a one-way relationship between global-ization and workers' rights: freer trade and more mobile capital devastated unions, decreased incomes, and destroyed jobs. According to this narrative, starvation wages, unsafe conditions, erratic hours, and unpredictable shifts swept across workplaces in the global South as countries desperate to attract investment restrained workers' rights and suppressed labor movements, sometimes violently. Meanwhile, waves of corporate restructuring and off-shore outsourcing upended whole industries in the global North, forcing workers to endure varying combinations of low wages, worsening conditions, restricted rights, and vanishing jobs. At the close of the twentieth century, it seemed fair to conclude that workers, organized or otherwise, simply lacked the capacity to steer economic globalization toward more equitable ends.

In the 2000s and 2010s, however, a surge of strategic cooperation among workers from a wide range of countries offered evidence of a reverse rela-tionship: labor can actively shape economic globalization and, in doing so, push back against precarious employment, poor working conditions, and growing global inequality. In particular, transnational labor alliances (TLAs)—defined as active collaborations of organized workers (such as unions, works councils, or even informal groups) based in two or more countries—have used strategic campaigns to convince employers to improve wages, working conditions, and labor rights in workplaces worldwide. Adidas, H&M, Tesco, Carrefour, Sheridan, Hyatt, Volkswagen, Ford, Daimler, Nestlé, Chiquita, Unilever, Tetley, T-Mobile, IKEA, Group 4 Securicor (G4S), the United Parcel Service, DHL, Rio Tinto, and Samsung are among the scores of companies targeted by TLAs in just the past fifteen years. Given dramatic declines in unionization across the Organisation for Economic Co-operation and Development (OECD) countries and the rapid expansion of corporate power globally since the 1970s, it is surprising that activist campaigns spearheaded by organized labor have succeeded at all, let alone without assistance from powerful states. And yet success stories continue to appear.

One of the most successful and high-profile TLA campaigns to date concluded in 2009 with a global framework agreement (GFA) signed by UNI Global Union and security services corporation G4S, the second-largest private-sector employer on the planet. The agreement bolstered union organizing and collective bargaining rights for over half a million security guards worldwide.[1] In 2015 a TLA helped workers in Guatemala unionize every Coca-Cola bottling plant in the country with help from the International Union of Food, Agricultural, Hotel, Restaurant, Catering, Tobacco and Allied Workers' Associations (IUF). In 2014 transportation unions from Germany, New Zealand, and Norway helped a Turkish union win higher wages and bonuses from logistics company DHL, along with permanent jobs for 750 subcontracted workers and social security for over two thousand DHL employees. That same year, workers in an export-processing zone in the Philippines won reinstatement and a 12 percent wage increase from semiconductor manufacturer NXP with support from unions in Australia, Finland, Sweden, and the United States. A transnational campaign focused on food and beverage corporation Nestlé helped fifty-three workers in Indonesia win their jobs back and sign a collective bargaining agreement in 2011. Also in 2011, workers employed by an IKEA subsidiary in the United States successfully formed a union and entered into collective bargaining after unions from more than twenty-five countries put pressure on the Swedish furniture company to cease antiunion practices at a plant in Danville, Virginia. In 2009 a TLA campaign focused on Anglo-Dutch corporation Unilever increased salaries and ended abusive casual labor practices at a Lipton tea factory in Khanewal, Pakistan. Dozens more success stories have appeared in recent years. Though they involved different unions, companies, and countries, all are similar in that workers won clear material or capacity-enhancing gains without incurring losses substantial enough to outweigh them.

In a world of winners and losers, labor need not always be the latter. Successful TLAs demonstrate not only that labor has agency in the global economy but also that transnational activism matters, as the gains from successful campaigns—whether in the form of better pay, job security, or guarantees of safety, dignity, and democracy in the workplace—concretely improve people's lives. TLAs also matter in a broader sense, as the future of secure, stable, and gainful employment comes to depend less on the domestic policy decisions of self-contained nation-states and more on the decisions of transnational corporations and other nonstate actors. TLA campaigns thus highlight the growing importance of transnational actors in an international system still dominated but by no means entirely controlled by states.

Acknowledging that labor has agency as a transnational actor does not mean, however, that TLAs always and everywhere have a significant impact. Surely, some succeed. Yet far more numerous and far less publicized are the scores of TLAs that have faltered, broken down, dissipated, or collapsed.[2] Even TLAs that remain intact might not ever execute an effective transnational campaign, as their attempts to take on major corporations end in uncertain stand-offs or total defeat. Despite rapidly expanding interest in what scholars have called "the new labor internationalism," there are still no systematic analyses of the causes of success and failure in TLA campaigns. Why are some TLAs more effective than others in altering the behaviors and practices of corporations, even without the backing of international organizations or powerful states? Which strategies, under what conditions, enable a TLA to generate material gains for workers and increase their capacity without risking significant losses over the long run?

In this book I answer these questions through the development of a new theoretical framework that identifies the necessary conditions for successful labor transnationalism. I argue that TLA campaigns only succeed if they feature three key conditions: *intraunion coordination*, *interunion coordination*, and *context-appropriate power*. Intraunion coordination means that individual workers involved in the TLA are coordinated internally, within their own organizations, and therefore capable of taking concrete action at the local level. Interunion coordination means that the unions that form the TLA as a whole are coordinated among themselves, across national borders, and have agreed on goals and tactics for the transnational campaign. Context-appropriate power means that the TLA's actions directly threaten the core material interests of the employer with whom it is in conflict. Intra- and interunion coordination both facilitate collective action, while context-appropriate power is what compels the employer to alter its labor practices. Absent any of these three conditions, a TLA will not succeed.

Central to this analysis is the concept of workers' power, which I argue takes three forms: *structural power*, the capacity to physically disrupt an employer's operations through strikes, slowdowns, and other forms of industrial action; *institutional power*, the capacity to hold an employer accountable through laws, regulations, and other formal or informal rules; and *coalitional power*, the capacity to mobilize nonlabor stakeholders to whom the employer must respond.[3] These three power types derive from workers' and employers' embeddedness in, respectively, international economic structures such as global value chains (GVCs) or production networks; national- and international-level institutions; and transnational networks of consumers, investors, and other stakeholders beyond the labor movement. Because companies depend on these economic structures, institutional frameworks, and nonlabor stakeholders for their profitability and long-term viability, workers can compel a corporation to do something it otherwise would not do by strategically disrupting one of these three relationships—that is, by exercising structural, institutional, or coalitional power. As just noted, however, in order to effectively exercise any power type on the international scale, workers must first coordinate both internally (within individual unions) and externally (across national borders).

Six in-depth case studies—spanning the stevedoring, retail, security services, and luxury hotel industries in Australia, Britain, Cambodia, Indonesia, and the United States between 1995 and 2010—test this causal hypothesis. The case studies are organized into three pairs, each featuring an empirical puzzle in the form of two highly similar TLA campaigns that nonetheless had different outcomes (one success, one failure). These matched-pair comparisons make it possible to control for potentially confounding variables, allowing for the rigorous application of both within- and cross-case qualitative methods of causal analysis. Original interview data collected over several years of field research, in addition to news archives and other documentation, inform the in-depth analysis of each campaign, as well as a broader analysis of patterns prevailing across all six cases. Evidence from these case studies not only links intraunion coordination, interunion coordination, and context-appropriate power to the outcome in each successful campaign but also demonstrates that the absence of any one of these conditions is sufficient for a campaign to fail.

Ultimately, I identify both the structural conditions that make successful labor transnationalism possible and the consequences of strategic choices that workers and employers make as actors within those structures. My findings reveal that processes of conflict and compromise among nonstate actors on the international scale can have an immediate impact on labor rights, regardless of limited state involvement. Nevertheless, it is only possible to convince a corporation to change under certain conditions, and even then, TLAs must not only coordinate effectively but also choose the correct power strategy to succeed.

In the remainder of this chapter I consider TLAs in historical context and define key concepts before outlining the main theoretical framework, research methods, and core findings. I begin by providing some background on the TLA phenomenon and the so-called new labor internationalism. Following that is a discussion of what it means for a TLA campaign to succeed or fail. This sets the stage for a discussion of theories that shed light on but do not fully explain the outcomes of TLA campaigns. I then articulate the coordination and context-appropriate power (CCAP) theory, which posits that successful labor transnationalism hinges not only on TLAs' capacities to exercise power in ways that threaten employers' core interests but also on effective worker coordination both internally (within workers' local organizations) and externally (across national borders), which are prerequisites for exercising power on the international scale. Next I explain the methods of causal analysis and data sources informing this book's six case studies. The chapter ends by previewing the findings from the case studies and the evidence supporting the CCAP theory.

Labor Transnationalism: When and Why?

In the late 1990s, academics began writing about "the new internationalism" to distinguish trade unions' contemporary efforts at cross-national cooperation from practices that prevailed before and during the Cold War (Harrod and O'Brien 2002; Munck 2002; Lambert and Webster 2001; Waterman 2001; Moody 1997). Spanning the late nineteenth through the late twentieth centuries, the "old" internationalism was marked by formalized and hierarchical relationships among allied unions (mainly from Western Europe and North America), actions directed primarily at states and intergovernmental organizations, sharp communist/anticommunist divides, and the relative marginalization of workers in the global South. Insiders and observers alike have long criticized the first century of transnational labor cooperation as heavily bureaucratic, high on rhetoric, and low on results. In contrast, the "new" internationalism emerged at the close of the twentieth century in the context of rapid worldwide economic integration, the global spread of neoliberalism, and the rise of transnational corporations with increasingly complex structures and supply chains. The new transnational labor activists sought to rely less on the state to secure labor rights and attempted instead to engage directly with employers through research-based "corporate campaigns" (Bronfenbrenner 2007). The new internationalism also entailed a greater proclivity of unions to form coalitions with human rights organizations, environmental activists, women's rights organizations, and other groups, as well as a shift from an "aid mentality" to substantial solidarity actions with more potential to bridge the North-South divide, such as international strikes, demonstrations, and protests (Munck 2002; Waterman 2001).

Strictly speaking, the transition from the old to the new has been neither clear cut nor homogenizing across the labor movement. Elements of the old persist in the new (Lambert and Gillan 2007; Hodkinson 2005), and in practice the actions of transnational labor activists still range widely from thinly veiled "solidarity" campaigns intended to secure parochial interests to more lofty attempts aimed at leveling labor rights worldwide. Furthermore, despite its salience as a buzzword of the 1990s and early 2000s, economic globalization—the growing economic interdependence of countries through increased international flows of trade and investment—began much earlier than popular narratives imply. The rise of transnational corporations (TNCs) as influential actors in the global economy dates back at least to the early 1970s. Why, then, has there only been talk of a new internationalism—and, consequently, revived academic interest in labor transnationalism—in the past twenty years?

The short answer is that global economic integration does not automatically and deterministically give rise to a renewed international consciousness on the part of labor (Evans 2010, 359; Waterman 2001, 53). It took time, trial, and error for trade union officials and rank-and-file workers to grasp the implications of new economic trends for their collective future, let alone act to meet these new challenges. As the twentieth century was coming to a close, disruptive forces were dramatically altering the nature of employment relations and the relationship of workers to the state, as governments dismantled welfare states and embraced, to varying extents, a slew of pact-shattering neoliberal reforms. Labor leaders in the advanced industrialized democracies saw austere macroeconomic policies and broken social pacts as a sign of the declining capacity and willingness of states to secure social protections. In the developing countries, labor movements likewise sought new strategies to secure labor rights without relying on unresponsive states. Transnational activism looked like a solution to some, so as the twenty-first century commenced, more and more TLAs formed to challenge TNCs head-on.

Today's TLAs are thus a response to the structural pressures imposed on labor in the current era of economic globalization (Schulze-Cleven 2017; Mc-Callum 2013). Still, it is impossible to predict whether TLAs will succeed based only on an analysis of structural conditions. This is evident in the puzzling fact that similar TLA campaigns emerging and operating under the same structural conditions can produce totally different results. In order to understand how highly similar campaigns can have such divergent outcomes, one must analyze not only structural conditions but also interactions among TLA members and the strategic interplay between TLAs and the employers they engage. Before exploring those factors that lead TLAs to succeed, however, we must first begin with a more basic question: How does one define success in a TLA campaign?

Dimensions of Success: Evaluating Losses and Gains in TLA Campaigns

What does it mean for a transnational labor campaign to succeed? What exactly is at stake when workers challenge corporate practices on the international scale? Most analyses of labor transnationalism do not clearly define success, though many make the excellent point that what matters most are long-run outcomes: the revitalization of the labor movement, transformations in corporate governance, and long-term institutional change. I agree—but argue that immediate impacts matter as well. Political scientists have long examined a variety of initial outcomes—such as transitions to democracy, electoral victories, alliance formations, military coups, investment inflows, laws passed, treaties signed, ceasefires, and the onset of war—whose separate explanations illuminate the origins of subsequent changes that only unfold over time, such as the consolidation of democratic institutions, the implementation of policy goals, economic development, or lasting peace. In a similar vein, understanding what caused a TLA campaign's initial outcome is essential for comprehending its eventual impact. Moreover, initial outcomes are significant apart from their later developments. The initial impacts of democratic transitions, economic crises, laws, coups, and ceasefires can be as serious as life or death. The same is true for the immediate results of TLA campaigns that determine whether workers are reemployed, better paid, safer, and more secure or unemployed, unsafe, and destitute. In this book I therefore give special attention to initial outcomes in defining success and failure in TLA campaigns.

In conceptualizing success, it is helpful to think in terms of two types of gains: material and capacity enhancing. *Material gains* are tangible improvements in wages, benefits, and working conditions, such as higher pay, better safety equipment, shorter workweeks, or paid leave. *Capacity gains* enhance workers' prospects of obtaining and retaining material gains in the future. Examples include collective bargaining rights, official union recognition, and union membership growth.[4] Material and capacity gains need not dramatically shift the balance of power between labor and capital to count; they can be modest and piecemeal and still meaningfully impact workers' lives. Successful labor transnationalism is therefore defined as a campaign outcome that yields a material improvement for any of the workers involved *or* meaningfully increases workers' capacity to obtain future gains—as long as the workers do not suffer any losses significant enough to outweigh those gains. In this conceptualization, gains and losses refer only to the immediate aftermath of a TLA campaign, so that gains or losses experienced well after a campaign's conclusion do not count in assessing the initial outcome, even if those later gains or losses can be traced back to the campaign. Figure 1 displays a three-level chart diagramming the concept of a successful TLA campaign using conceptualization tools developed by Goertz (2006). Table 1

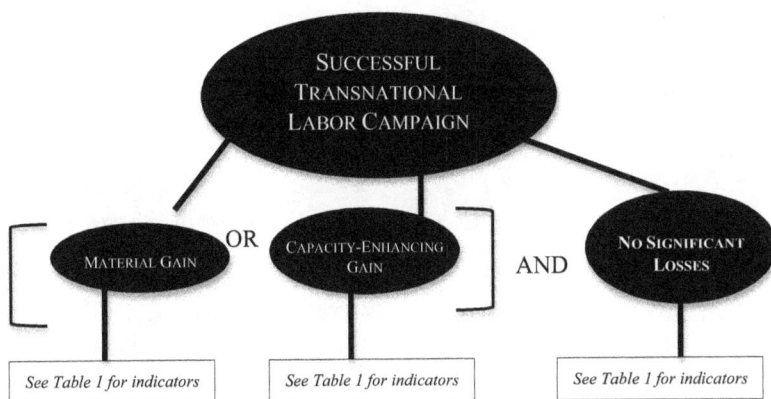

Figure 1. This concept chart summarizes the ontology of the concept "successful labor transnationalism" using the logical OR and AND from Boolean algebra to indicate, respectively, the sufficiency and necessity of its constitutive elements.

elaborates on the third-level indicators of each of the concept's basic (second-level) components.

The opposite of successful campaigns are, of course, failures, which are marked not merely by a lack of gains but also by significant losses, such as lower pay, longer hours, benefit cuts, dismissals, or deunionization.[5] One example of failed labor transnationalism is the 2005 campaign to unionize workers at the largest almond-processing facility in the world, the Blue Diamond plant in Sacramento, California. Led by the International Longshore and Warehouse Union (ILWU), a TLA comprising unions from Australia, Canada, Japan, New Zealand, South Korea, and the United States staged demonstrations in support of the Blue Diamond workers, rallied outside several almond purchasers' headquarters, and sent petitions and letters to Blue Diamond's head offices. Management fought back by firing pro-union workers, intimidating others, and threatening to shut down the plant. This not only squelched the campaign but also entrenched antiunion sentiment among the employees, who voted 353 to 142 against unionization (*Sacramento Business Journal*, November 20, 2008). This campaign was a failure not only because it did not achieve its aims but also because it left workers worse off.

Not all failed campaigns end as devastatingly as that at Blue Diamond, nor does every successful campaign conclude in complete victory. Correctly

Table 1. Third-level indicators for successful transnational labor campaign

Material gain *(need at least one of these indicators to count a material gain)*	Higher wages, better working conditions, more full-time jobs, shorter working hours, reinstatement of terminated workers, vacation days, health and safety measures, improved work hours, health care, childcare, pensions and other retirement provisions, more comfortable work environment, overtime pay, bonuses
Capacity-enhancing gain *(need at least one of these indicators to count a capacity-enhancing gain)*	GFA, union membership growth, more full-time jobs, strengthened union identity, enhanced networking capacity, enhanced learning capabilities, collective bargaining rights, strengthened community ties, favorable labor legislation, official union recognition, more workplace democracy, improved communication capacity, better leader-member relationship within a union
Significant losses *(campaign must not result in any of the following)*	Lower pay, worsened working conditions, mandatory overtime, decreased union membership, job losses, benefit cuts, replacement of collective bargaining with individual contracts, severely depleted financial resources, union's loss of political support, union decertification, significant union member attrition, loss of worker control over workplace practices, legal limits on industrial action

coding campaign outcomes thus depends on the accuracy with which one weighs the balance of losses and gains in a campaign's immediate aftermath. Doing so, in turn, requires close contextual knowledge of the circumstances surrounding that campaign. Moreover, since gains and losses are relative to the status quo, comprehending the full context in which a TLA campaign played out, including the material situation and capacity of the workers just before its launch, is essential. Also important is discerning whether a campaign was proactive or reactive. In proactive campaigns, TLAs initiate engagement with employers, whereas TLAs respond defensively to employers' actions in reactive campaigns. What constitutes the status quo, and what therefore counts as a loss or a gain, hinges on this distinction. In a proactive campaign, the maintenance of existing wage levels or the continued existence of a union does not count as a gain. If a campaign is reactive, however, then the reinstatement of previously fired workers at existing wage levels or a successful defense against attempts to dismantle an existing union would count as a gain since the status quo is the situation workers would have faced had the employer's actions gone unchallenged.

Since campaign outcomes are rarely clear cut, I have taken great care to gather multiple perspectives from primary sources, including personal interviews and news reports, for each of the TLA campaigns analyzed in this book. Nevertheless, disagreements inevitably arose over the significance of gains and the severity of losses, even among campaign participants on the same side. Hence, it is important to acknowledge that some subjective element almost always shapes the ultimate coding of cases. At the same time, formalizing the criteria used to conceptualize outcomes at least offers some assurance to the reader that these distinctions, though contested, are not arbitrary.

Bringing Labor Back In: TLAs through the Lens of GVCs, Institutions, and Transnational Advocacy Networks

If defining success is difficult, determining how success comes about may be even more so. Absent from the analysis of TLA campaigns is a generalizable causal theory of their success and failure. Part of the problem is an undertheorization of labor as a transnational actor. As national governments lost their abilities to discipline corporations amid the rapid globalization of production at the close of the twentieth century, new theories of corporate governance arose to examine how firms might be regulated on the international scale. Initially, however, theories of GVCs and international institutions viewed labor mainly as a factor of production, not an actor with agency (see critique in Rainnie, Herod, and McGrath-Champ [2011], 156), while early theories of transnational advocacy acknowledged labor's agency but dismissed labor transnationalism as "transitory" (Keck and Sikkink 1998, 15). Scholars thus made great progress in analyzing firms and advocacy networks as both actors and structures but for the most part left labor as an afterthought.

By the mid-2000s, scholars were making more significant strides in theorizing labor as a strategic actor. An expanding, multidisciplinary literature on "the new labor internationalism," alongside a handful of mainstream social science theories, explored labor's active role in corporate governance. Scattered across several subfields—including labor geography, international and comparative political economy, labor sociology, and international relations—these studies shed light on the specific strategies workers and unions have used to confront the growing power of TNCs. Especially insightful are three key areas of research—on GVCs, international institutions, and transnational activism—that offer evidence that workers can influence employer behavior by, respectively, exploiting vulnerabilities in global economic structures, strengthening institutions on the international scale, and becoming more like social movements.

Yet even with these theoretical developments, it remains unclear why workers are only occasionally effective in changing employers' practices through transnational campaigns. Hence, taken separately, each strand of scholarship falls short of a full explanation for why some TLA campaigns succeed. Combining their insights, however, provides a promising route to the development of a comprehensive theoretical framework for understanding the causes of success and failure in TLA campaigns.

GVC Vulnerabilities

One of the defining features of twenty-first-century economic globalization is the growing interconnection of lead and supplier firms through geographically dispersed networks of production and investment, referred to as global value chains. While earlier examinations of labor and GVCs mainly emphasized GVCs' detrimental impact on workers' rights, more recent works have highlighted labor's active contributions to value chain governance (Anner 2012; Riisgaard and Hammer 2011; Davies et al. 2011; Rainnie, Herod, and McGrath-Champ 2011). Since the early 2000s, scholars have examined ways in which workers are able to extract concessions from employers by exploiting GVCs' structural weaknesses (Coe and Jordhus-Lier 2011; Anderson 2009; Wills 2008; Silver 2003), advancing E. Wright's (2000) concept of structural power (discussed later). Herod (2001, 1997, 1995), for example, offered evidence that manufacturing unions can change the behavior of

TNCs by striking at specific choke points within segments of supply chains. Similarly, Selwyn (2011, 2007) showed how agricultural workers enhance their bargaining positions by deliberately varying the speed at which they pick fresh fruit, thus reducing its value further down the chain, given the short shelf life of export-quality produce. GVCs' key features—such as extended chains of offshoring, just-in-time production, overnight shipping guarantees, and global product markets—have thus exacerbated firms' vulnerabilities to labor unrest by feeding into customers' expectations of the abundance and near-instant availability of goods.

One take-home message of these analyses, which often infuse GVC theories from international political economy with labor geographers' concepts of place, space, and scale, is that traditional industrial action still works—at least sometimes, under selective conditions. Following this line of logic, several unions have even attempted to research and map out complex logistics networks in transportation, garments, and other industries in hopes of enhancing labor's leverage (Anderson, Hamilton, and Wills 2010; Croucher and Cotton 2009; Juravich 2007). Yet not all workers are in a position, literally, to disrupt a whole production network. Moreover, in many parts of the world, employers exercise severe forms of labor control precisely to prevent such disruptions, since the firms they supply prioritize predictable production flows even over low labor costs (Anner 2015). Hence, some scholarship has been criticized for showcasing strategies dependent on spatial specificities and therefore inapplicable to the majority of workers. Still, these analyses contribute the valuable insight that industrial action not only remains viable but also has the potential to be magnified throughout entire logistics networks as an unintended consequence of the structure of GVCs.

The Influence of International Institutions

While the expansion of production across far-flung GVCs has in many ways empowered workers, the structure of the global economy has simultaneously diminished the capacity and political will of states to protect labor rights on the national scale. Constant corporate restructuring, mutating production methods, accelerated trade, and hypermobile capital all impose structural constraints on national governments, enhancing what Lindblom (1977) referred to as "the privileged position of business." Some scholars and activists therefore see solutions in international institutions, specifically codes, guidelines, and agreements that promote adherence to core labor standards or otherwise advance workers' rights. Examples include the UN Guiding Principles on Business and Human Rights, the OECD Guidelines for Multinational Enterprises, the UN Global Compact, the Ethical Trading Initiative, and a growing number of GFAs. While some international institutions are endorsed directly by states, others either also include or are formed entirely from the formal input of nonstate actors, including organized labor, nongovernmental organizations (NGOs), and other stakeholder groups. While not necessarily intended to replace national-level labor protections (Ruggie 2004), institutions of private governance have sometimes substituted for states in practice, especially in countries with weakly enforced labor laws (Locke, Rissing, and Pal 2013).

Unions in particular can play a role in constructing and implementing international institutions (Ford and Gillan 2015, 11). Most prominently, the global unions (also known as global union federations or GUFs)—which are organized by industry and formally link together national and subnational unions around the world—have encouraged numerous corporations to commit to core standards by signing GFAs. Some, such as the Daimler GFA, have proved effective at strengthening union power, even in supplier firms (Evans 2014, 267; Fichter and Helfen 2011, 99–100). Other GFAs have been mixed in their impact or even highly problematic (Williams, Davies, and Chinguno 2015). For example, McCallum's (2013) extensive investigation of the G4S framework agreement contrasts its facilitation of union organization in South Africa with the intractable issues inhibiting its implementation in India. Others have likewise found that without supportive national-level institutions, GFAs are only as strong as the workers they purport to protect (Niforou 2014; Locke 2013).

Suggestions that labor should strengthen institutions on the international scale thus have several limitations. States rarely enforce the core labor standards set forth in major international institutions, unless it is in their direct interest to do so (Zajak 2017; Kang 2012). And although private governance at times appears promising, it is not always effective (Locke 2013; Vogel 2010). Hence, while TLAs have at times invoked GFAs, the OECD guidelines, and other international institutions with great success, there are many more instances in which international institutions have not helped. Still, one should not discount entirely labor's potential to influence corporate practices by invoking institutions on the international scale.

Social Movement Strategies

Despite their different points of departure, analyses of labor transnationalism that focus on GVCs and international institutions share a common focus on how workers strategically leverage aspects of the employment relationship. In contrast, scholars of social movements and transnational advocacy examine dynamics beyond the employment relationship by focusing on the mobilization of actors and activists from a variety of backgrounds and positions. Scholars of social movement unionism in particular have emphasized organized labor's long history of uniting in common cause with community leaders, environmentalists, human rights advocates, students, and other actors on issues relevant but not limited to labor rights (Tattersall 2010). Some have argued that labor is most effective when workers embrace grassroots organizing, active coalition building, and goals that transcend workplace issues (Wills 2008; Milkman 2006; Moody 1997). While many such studies focus on the local or national scale, others have suggested that social movement unionism can and should translate into transnationalism (Munck 2002, 154; Waterman 2001; Gordon and Turner 2000).

Likewise, the rich literature on transnational advocacy networks (TANs) based on Keck and Sikkink's (1998) boomerang model has inspired a wealth of scholarship relevant to TLAs. In the original boomerang model, local actors blocked from political action in their home state activate an international network of NGOs, activist groups, and other supporters who pressure more powerful states to intervene in the first state's domestic affairs. In the process, TANs use ideas, values, and norms to persuade states to reformulate their interests and alter their behavior. More recent works apply the boomerang model to nonstate targets such as TNCs (den Hond and de Bakker 2012; McAteer and Pulver 2009; Seidman 2008) and show how TANs can change targeted actors' behavior without necessarily convincing them to internalize international norms (Kang 2012; Nolan García 2011). Although TLAs do not exactly fit the definition of TANs, these theories still offer valuable insights on TLA campaigns. Transnational cross-movement coalitions are becoming more common (Zajak 2017), and cross-border campaigns featuring the incorporation of multiple stakeholders have seen success. For instance, numerous transnational campaigns aimed at garment factories and the clothing companies they supply have successfully combined workers' actions with consumer pressure to improve sweatshop conditions (Anner 2015; C. Wright and Kaine 2015, 10; Donaghey et al. 2014; Riisgaard and Hammer 2011; Merk 2009; Armbruster-Sandoval 2005; Sadler 2004).

While theories of social movements and TANs shed some light on the causes of success and failure in TLA campaigns, they cannot explain campaigns that utilized TAN-like tactics yet ended unsuccessfully or those that succeeded without the boomerang model's signature "name-and-shame" strategy. As Locke pointed out, "naming and shaming" is based on the assumption that the TNC targeted is so dependent on its brand name and positive image that it will change in response to public pressure (Locke 2013, 28–29). Yet not all TNCs are equally sensitive to reputational damage; some are more "shameable" than others (Bartley and Child 2014, 662). There are therefore limits to transnational coalition building. Nevertheless, that workers can at times influence corporate practices by forming coalitions with stakeholders beyond the labor movement remains a valuable insight.

New Insights: Embeddedness, Interdependence, and Power

The studies just cited advance our knowledge of the tactics available to TLAs. Nevertheless, it remains difficult to predict when each of these strategies—exploiting GVCs' vulnerabilities, invoking international institutions, and mobilizing public pressure—will actually be effective. What is missing from all of these analyses is a comprehensive theory of workers' power in transnational campaigns. Despite recent developments in the theorization of labor's power resources (Webster 2015; Brookes 2013; Fairbrother, Lévesque, and Hennebert 2013; McCallum 2013; Silver 2003; E. Wright 2000), the term *power* is often deployed without precise definition and without consideration of how the exercise of power relates to various coordination issues or the interests of other actors involved. These considerations are indispensable for the analysis of the mechanisms through which workers' actions affect employers' behavior.

Following Knight (1992, 41) and Dahl (1961), I define power generally as the capacity of an actor A to make another actor B do something B otherwise would not do.[6] Contrary to the classic pluralist perspective (Dahl 1961), which viewed power as evident only after an actor prevails in a conflict, I conceptualize power not as that which produces an outcome but, rather, as a capacity that can remain latent indefinitely. As Lukes (2005, 69) argued, "Power is a potentiality, not an actuality—indeed a potentiality that may never be actualized." Moreover, in contrast to existing power resource frameworks, I conceive of power as inherently relational. It is therefore only meaningful to discuss A's power with reference to actor B, as well as the economic, political, and social contexts in which both are embedded (Piven 2008; Lukes 2005, 1994; Knight 1992).

A relational definition of power is crucial for the analysis of TLA campaigns, which unfold in the context of complex interdependencies created by the expansion of production and investment across national borders. The present analysis thus answers the call for "new theoretical tools and frameworks to address these new interdependencies" (Jackson, Kuruvilla, and Frege 2013, 427), specifically by identifying the two factors that interact to produce workers' power in the global economy: the external environment in which workers are embedded—namely, economic structures such as GVCs, national and international institutional frameworks, and networks of non-labor stakeholders—and the extent to which employers depend on these same structures, institutions, and networks to fulfill their core interests. I argue that these two factors—workers' embeddedness and employers' dependence—interact to produce three types of labor power: structural power, institutional power, and coalitional power (Brookes 2015, 2013). I further argue that the potential effectiveness of each power type depends crucially on context, as an employer will only alter its behavior if the tactics deployed directly threaten the structures, institutions, or networks vital to its core interests. These three power types, inspired respectively by the three bodies of scholarship reviewed earlier, are discussed in greater detail in the sections that follow.

Structural Power

First, workers and employers are embedded in complex economic structures. While extensive offshoring and far-flung distribution networks afford firms considerable flexibility, the globalization of production has also increased employers' vulnerabilities to disruptions caused by workers who produce and deliver goods and services. The embeddedness of workers and employers in GVCs and other economic structures, combined with the dependence of employers on those workers for the smooth functioning of production and distribution networks, creates workers' capacity for *structural power.*

Structural power is the capacity of workers to physically disrupt the production or delivery of goods and services through their own, direct action, including strikes, walkouts, and go-slows; it entails the actual or threatened withdrawal of labor. Coined by E. Wright (2000) and developed by Silver (2003), the concept of structural power is well known and widely used. As noted earlier, scholars of GVCs and global production networks have shown how extended chains of offshoring, just-in-time production, overnight shipping guarantees, and global product markets have exacerbated TNCs' vulnerabilities to disruption; hence, the present era of economic globalization offers far more opportunities for "a small disruption at one point in a supply chain [to become] increasingly magnified further up or down the chain" (Selwyn 2007, 549). In some instances a small number of strikes or slowdowns can temporarily debilitate a firm or even ripple through an entire distribution network, as when UPS workers from different countries simultaneously halted deliveries in support of the 1997 Teamsters strike in the United States (Urata 2010, 61; Banks and Russo 1998).

Less well understood, however, is what makes structural power effective in some instances but not others. To be clear, structural power is not a characteristic of industries but rather a capacity that workers have as a function of their employer's dependence on their labor and the specific ways in which both actors are embedded in the economic system. Hence, to predict whether workers' structural power will be effective, it is not enough to analyze an industry in isolation; one must also situate specific sets of workers and employers in relation to each other. Because production processes vary, so too do the interdependencies that create vulnerabilities, which in turn determine the contexts in which structural power is effective. For example, a manufacturer that can endure a brief disruption to its operations or easily replace its existing workforce is less vulnerable to structural power than one that relies on just-in-time production or cannot replace its workforce because of high skill requirements or tight labor markets.

Institutional Power

Second, workers and employers are embedded in a variety of national, subnational, and supranational institutions. Institutions are defined as laws, regulations, practices, procedures, and other formal or informal rules that persist over time, structure actors' incentives, channel their preferences, and create rational expectations of each other's behavior. Both workers and employers depend on various sets of institutions for the governance of labor markets, vocational training, employment relations, and other realms of activity that not only make particular business practices possible but also maintain the basic functioning of capitalism. Even the most mobile TNCs are still subject to several forms of regulation, whether through traditional command-and-control structures or informal institutions of private governance (Locke 2013; Vogel 2010). Workers can thus exercise *institutional power* by invoking the formal or informal rules on which employers depend. Exercising institutional power does not mean creating new rules of the game, which is the goal of what McCallum (2013, 11) calls "governance struggles." Rather, institutional power involves taking advantage of existing rules or repurposing those rules to work in labor's favor.

Institutions are of special significance to understanding power dynamics because they are themselves the product of past and ongoing power struggles (Mahoney and Thelen 2010; Streeck and Thelen 2005; Thelen 1999; Hall 1986). Historically, workers' abilities to organize into unions, bargain collectively, and participate in corporate decision making have varied across countries as states developed different regulatory capacities, social commitments, and approaches to managing production, finance, and trade. Today, disparities in workers' institutional power persist not only along North–South lines but also among the advanced, industrialized economies, some of which afford workers far greater decision-making capacity within firms, positive relationships with employers, and substantially better labor rights protections than in other countries.

Workers who lack institutional protections and enforceable rights in their home country might therefore seek support from workers abroad who are embedded in a more advantageous national institutional framework, especially when both sets of workers are employed by the same TNC (Evans 2014, 272). The relatively advantaged workers would then draw on the rules and regulations of their home country—and often, their home union relationship with the employer in question—to pressure the company into changing its behavior in the other country. In 2001, for instance, the Brazilian union federation Central Única dos Trabalhadores convinced its union allies in Germany to negotiate directly with Volkswagen managers in order to resolve a dispute at a VW plant in Sao Paulo (Anner 2011, 128).

What makes institutional power effective in some instances but not others? The key component of institutional power is the extent to which an employer depends on the specific law, rule, regulation, regularized interaction, or other institution that workers have invoked. If the employer cannot ignore or subvert that institution without consequently inviting harm to its core interests, then institutional power is likely to be effective. One obvious example is a firm facing direct sanctions for failing to comply with national labor laws backed by the coercive power of the state. Less obvious, but equally important, are institutions that lack overt enforcement yet are just as valued by the employer. For instance, a manufacturing firm whose production strategy depends on a positive relationship with and constant input from a stable, unionized workforce with accumulated shop floor knowledge would be more likely to negotiate with its workers in ways that maintain that relationship than a firm that can afford to shed labor for short-term gain (Hall and Soskice 2001). Even legally nonbinding international institutions such as the UN Guiding Principles on Business and Human Rights or the OECD Guidelines for Multinational Enterprises can be invoked to alter an employer's behavior. This is because TNCs that commit to such agreements have signaled to the international community a willingness to meet certain expectations, and if these expectations are not met, then there are grounds for raising the matter with an international regulatory body or other third party with the capacity to pressure (but not coerce) the company into compliance.

Coalitional Power

Third, workers and employers are embedded in widespread networks of actors beyond the employment relationship. For workers, these networks are a product of engaging in the world in their various and overlapping roles as citizens, consumers, neighbors, activists, volunteers, and members of religious, political, cultural, and other associations in civil society. Workers also have formal ties to other stakeholders through organizational relationships such as those between unions and NGOs or TANs. Firms, in turn, depend on many of these nonlabor actors for the smooth and profitable functioning of business. As TNCs expand, they increasingly come to depend on new groups of investors, consumers, journalists, and others who provide capital, purchase goods, generate media attention, shape public perceptions of corporate practices, create long-term brand loyalty, and otherwise secure the TNC's prospects for profit making. When workers use their embeddedness in social networks to mobilize the influence of nonlabor stakeholders on whom an employer depends, they are exercising *coalitional power*.

Unlike structural and institutional power, coalitional power does not depend on workers' own capacities to withdraw their labor or on rules specific to employment relations; rather, coalitional power is rooted in nonlabor actors' abilities to boycott, divest, or otherwise impact a company's current or future profits. Coalitional power entails more than just forging ties with sympathetic stakeholders or disseminating information that appeals to international norms. The exercise of coalitional power necessarily entails actions on the part of workers to convince nonlabor actors—meaning groups or individuals outside the employment relationship—to leverage their position as stakeholders in ways that threaten an employer's core interests. Although nonlabor stakeholders, by definition, cannot threaten to withdraw labor, they can threaten to withdraw investment, damage a brand name, or cease purchasing goods and services. Only when nonlabor stakeholders take such actions has a TLA exercised coalitional power.

How effective coalitional power is depends on how dependent a given employer is on the stakeholders mobilized by the TLA. A company that depends directly on its brand name and public image for drawing in customers—such as a restaurant, hotel chain, or airline—will be more vulnerable to negative publicity from a worker-consumer coalition than a company for whom image and brand are less essential, such as an oil company or defense contractor. Likewise, a worker-investor coalition obviously has more potential to affect a publicly traded company that is subject to shareholder scrutiny rather than a privately held company that is not. And while a location-dependent firm might respond to pressure from a coalition of workers and local politicians, a relatively more mobile TNC, less fearful of losing political favor, might not.

Context-Appropriate Power in TLA Campaigns

As the foregoing discussion reveals, the extent to which an employer depends on particular structures, institutions, or actors for its present and future profitability determines whether workers' structural, institutional, or coalitional power has potential to threaten that employer's core, material interests and thus alter its behavior. Therefore, from the workers' perspective, each power type is only appropriate in certain contexts. The concept of *context-appropriate power* does not assume that the core interests of an employer can be simply read off the sector or the industry in which that employer is located. Rather, comprehending "context" means assessing that employer's specific priorities, business strategies, and long-term goals.

In other words, employers' cores interests—and therefore their vulnerabilities—can be specified *ex ante* by analyzing not just the industry in which an employer operates but also that specific employer's dependence on particular production methods, specific institutional frameworks, and key stakeholders. One can define workers' exercise of power as context appropriate when it threatens to undermine the physical structures, institutional frameworks, or nonlabor stakeholder relationships on which the target employer depends to fulfill its core interests. Not all employers depend on the same structures, institutions, and stakeholders to be profitable; hence, context can mean something different for two employers in the same industry. At the same time, context is not so specific that one cannot generalize across cases or group similar contexts together.

When workers exercise context-appropriate power, this compels an employer to weigh the costs of standing its ground against those of conceding to labor's demands. In the language of bargaining, context-appropriate power alters the reversion outcome so that the consequences of an ongoing dispute become far worse for the employer than they were before the campaign. The employer then becomes inclined to compromise with the workers, if not outright accept their demands. The exercise of context-appropriate power can be difficult, however, especially when the target employer is owned by, controlled by, or a supplier to a major TNC. Because TNCs typically operate across complex GVCs, in multiple institutional contexts, and among shifting sets of stakeholders, effectively exercising power might necessitate actions across multiple contexts at once, even when workers wish only to resolve a dispute in one workplace. Workers thus turn to TLAs to enhance the impact of their actions on TNCs.

TLAs enhance workers' structural, institutional, and coalitional power by affording workers access to multiple leverage points across different spaces and on multiple scales at once. In particular, TLAs enhance structural power by increasing the number of nodes in a GVC through which workers can cause disruptions. Dockworkers refusing to unload cargo at a single port are unlikely to gain as much attention as a mass-scale, coordinated effort by dockers in dozens of countries that halts shipments at several ports around the world. TLAs enhance institutional power by facilitating the strategic relocation of conflict from one national institutional context to a more favorable national institutional context or from a strictly national setting to one in which international institutions are more influential. Finally, TLAs enhance coalitional power by multiplying workers' opportunities to tap into different stakeholder networks, as when workers in various nations help mobilize consumers to boycott a retail chain in several different countries at once.

Solving the Double Coordination Problem

While workers form TLAs to embrace the strategic advantages of multiscalar campaigns, merely forming a transnational alliance is insufficient for the exercise of power on several scales simultaneously. Because power is, by definition, a capacity, there is a difference between merely possessing structural, institutional, or coalitional power and actually putting that power to use. In other words, power must be "activated" in order to be exercised.

The key to activation is coordination. First, and most obviously, a TLA cannot exist unless at least one group of workers actively cooperates with another group of workers in a different country. This cross-border coordination—which I refer to as *interunion coordination*—is not just necessary for a TLA's existence; it is also essential for sustaining workers' multiscalar exercise of power over the duration of a transnational campaign. Second, workers must also coordinate internally—that is, mobilize themselves within their own organizations—in order to exercise structural, institutional, or coalitional power in the first place. This internal type of coordination— which I refer to as *intraunion coordination*—is what enables a group of workers to exercise power collectively through a union or other organization. Because both inter- and intraunion coordination facilitate the exercise of power in transnational campaigns, a TLA cannot succeed absent one or the other coordination type. Understanding why workers strive to coordinate both across borders and within their own organizations is relatively straightforward. Understanding *how* workers actually achieve the coordination necessary for TLAs to function, however, requires deeper consideration.

Interunion Coordination: Issues and Obstacles

Interunion coordination refers to two or more unions from different countries coalescing around common goals and cooperating on tangible efforts to attain those goals. While scholars have analyzed labor cooperation in formal organizations such as the International Trade Union Confederation (ITUC), the European Trade Union Confederation (ETUC), and various European Works Councils (EWCs) (Larsson 2012; Hardy and Fitzgerald 2010; Jensen, Madsen, and Due 1995), we know less about the factors facilitating interunion coordination in TLAs, which are not always tied to preexisting networks or established international organizations. Moreover, because cooperation in a TLA campaign requires an explicit commitment by allied unions to take direct action against an employer, TLA campaigns almost always entail greater risk than cooperation aimed only at information sharing, coordinated collective bargaining, or social dialogue. Hence, common obstacles to interunion coordination in general—including conflicting interests, collective action problems, and practical constraints—appear even more daunting in the context of TLA campaigns.

The most obvious barrier to interunion coordination is a conflict of material interests. Corporate restructuring and capital mobility have rendered workers increasingly vulnerable to dislocation, encouraging some unions to embrace protectionist strategies that exacerbate international divides (Johns 1998). The perception that states have lost much of their power to regulate capital and provide social safety nets in the advanced economies (Thelen 2014; Pierson 2001; Scharpf and Schmidt 2000) and the fact that states have little history of offering such protections in most developing countries (Piven and Cloward 2000, 418) further heighten workers' sense of vulnerability, which can breed intraclass distrust just as easily as it can incentivize transnational cooperation (Silver 2003).

Nevertheless, these competitive pressures affect some sectors more severely than others. Because the threat of capital flight is particularly strong in the manufacturing industries, manufacturing workers are often hesitant to help those with whom they are competing for jobs. Unions in service industries—such as education, health care, and property services—may be more open to labor transnationalism since many service jobs cannot be offshored (Evans 2010, 358). Still, these broad generalizations obscure the fact that several manufacturing unions, such as the United Steelworkers in the United States and IG Metall in Germany, have been active in TLAs, while there are plenty of service-sector unions that have not, in part because not all service jobs are immune to offshoring. Unions' proclivities toward transnationalism are therefore only partly a function of economic sector.

Whether and how workers coordinate across borders also depends on the national institutional frameworks in which they are embedded (Larsson 2012; Lillie and Martinez Lucio 2004). Cross-national differences in labor rights and employment relations institutions can create conflicting interests. For instance, institutions of codetermination and social partnership give unions and works councils in some countries not only more power to negotiate with management but also incentives to maintain their positive relationships with employers (Greven 2008, 6; Bronfenbrenner 2007, 6). Even in the absence of formal codetermination, a union that has a good relationship with an employer might rationally prioritize the interests of the employer over those of other workers abroad (Young and Sierra Becerra 2014). This is especially true for the home union, which represents employees of a TNC within that company's home country. On one hand, the home union has great potential to assist in TLA campaigns, given its close relationship with the employer, close understanding of the legal and political institutions to which that employer is accountable, and—if embedded in institutions of codetermination or social partnership—direct access to information and channels of influence. Some home unions have in fact played a significant role in convincing employers to sign GFAs (Fichter, Helfen, and Sydow 2011, 81) and to support labor organizing in host countries, as IG Metall has done with Daimler and Volkswagen in the United States. On the other hand, close relationships with employers have led other home unions to prioritize national-, firm-, or even plant-level interests over transnational solidarity (Dufour and Hege 2010;

Lindberg 2010, 212). For example, in 2007 employees of the Turkish pharmaceutical manufacturer Novamed requested help from the German union IG Bergbau, Chemie, Energie in pressuring Fresenius Medical Care, the German owner of Novamed, to negotiate a GFA. The German union, however, refused to put pressure on the company. The union focused on "social partnership and dialogue" rather than support "a more adversarial campaign aimed at pushing FMC to negotiate and sign such an agreement" (Fougner and Kurtoglu 2010, 112).

In addition to conflicting interests, national institutional differences also lead to some simple misunderstandings. When Colombian employees of the Swedish company Ericsson asked a union in Sweden to approach corporate leaders about Ericsson's labor rights abuses in Colombia, the Swedish union rather unhelpfully suggested the Colombian workers first affiliate with a union, join the ITUC, then negotiate with management through those channels (Sjolander 2010). "While this may have been logical in a Swedish context, it made no sense in Columbia [sic]," a country in which violence and death threats against unionists tend to dampen the prospects for productive negotiations (Bieler and Lindberg 2010, 222).

Potentially allied unions might also face collective action problems. Just as two or more states can sign a human rights treaty or an environmental accord yet never cooperate enough to follow through on implementation (Hathaway 2007), so too can a TLA form without workers taking action. Like states, TLA members are subject to collective action problems insofar as their goals—such as industry-wide safety standards or universal respect for union rights by a TNC—constitute public goods (Olson 1965). In other words, when the benefits of successful transnationalism cannot be excluded from and are not diminished when utilized by unions that did not participate in gaining them, it is rational for TLA members to attempt to free ride on each other's efforts. Hence, even after a TLA is assembled, and even if members' interests align, interunion coordination is still not guaranteed.

Finally, it is possible that interunion coordination is simply subject to practical constraints such as language barriers, limited finances, lack of access to technology, or unstable political climates that put labor activists at physical or legal risk. Although Larsson (2012) found that practical problems such as language barriers and cultural differences do far less to inhibit interunion coordination than material differences or divergent national labor market institutions, his investigation is limited to union cooperation under the

ETUC. It is possible that practical constraints play a larger role in TLAs not tied to an established organization.

SOLUTIONS FOR INTERUNION COORDINATION: INTERESTS, OUTLOOKS, AND RECIPROCITY

Conflicting material interests, collective action problems, and practical constraints all inhibit interunion coordination. Of these three challenges, those rooted in seemingly incompatible interests are arguably the most pernicious because they indicate a fundamental *unwillingness* on the part of potential union allies to engage in cooperative efforts, as opposed to a situation in which unions *wish to* cooperate but have rational incentives to free ride (collective action problems) or a situation in which unions *wish to* cooperate *and are also willing to put in equal effort* yet nonetheless encounter obstacles in the political or institutional settings in which they seek to act (practical constraints). Essentially, if potential TLA members cannot focus on common interests, then the other two interunion coordination problems are irrelevant.

Hence, the first step in effective interunion coordination is fostering shared interests among potential labor allies. Building a TLA around straightforward material goals enables unions to focus on clearly shared interests. Nevertheless, cooperation based solely on material goals might be too weak a foundation of coordination for something as complex and drawn out as a transnational campaign. Even closely matched material interests among unions are unlikely to completely overlap, and without some deeper basis for long-term commitment, a campaign can fall apart. Beyond just focusing on immediate shared goals, then, unions need more sophisticated incentives for active cooperation.

The strongest possible basis for interunion coordination is having a history of genuine reciprocity among unions, which develops as unions establish a track record of taking action in support of each other over time. More than just an acknowledgment of long-term mutual interests, reciprocity is about unions internalizing norms of solidarity based not just on shared interests but on the experience of active support and mutual expectations of future assistance. Unions that have established a track record of taking direct, sometimes altruistic, actions in support of other unions time and time again tend to place immense value on international solidarity, which effectively deters free riding, even in campaigns that make great demands on unions' resources.

Shipping and stevedoring unions are the epitome of reciprocity, with a history of international solidarity that is practically legendary (Ahlquist and Levi 2013; Lillie 2006). Describing the relationship between the ILWU in the United States and the Maritime Union of Australia (MUA), an ILWU official explained, "We have a more expansive view of self-interests. We don't want to let that first domino fall. And we have good personal relationships— our folks go out with people on picket lines and even represent us overseas. Once you've worked with somebody on a struggle, some day, the next time, they'll pick up the phone and take your call" (personal interview, August 18, 2010).

Even in the fiercely competitive automotive industry, there is evidence that a history of reciprocity among unions can be the basis of strong interunion coordination. As Greer and Hauptmeier (2008, 88) illustrated, "Even though the Zaragossa plant [in Spain] was the direct beneficiary of the transfer of production, the local unions did not hesitate to organize a strike in solidarity with their Portuguese colleagues. This act of solidarity, *which went against the economic self-interest of the Spanish unions*, showed to what extent worker representatives had developed and internalized the common norms to resist plant closures and dismissals in Europe. *After co-operating for more than 10 years, the Spanish unions believed that they could count on their European colleagues in a similar crisis*" (emphasis added).

Nevertheless, reciprocity does not develop overnight. As the foregoing quote suggests, a sense of genuine reciprocity among unions from different countries requires repeated instances of active support over time; "solidarity is shaped in action" (Lindberg 2010, 206). While shared labor identities can enhance reciprocity (Anner 2011, 14), as can the personal ideological orientation of union leaders (Ahlquist and Levi 2013; McCallum 2013, 158), reciprocity is not simply a matter of identity or ideology. A TLA focused on Mercedes-Benz and DaimlerChrysler, for instance, which ultimately "sustained and developed transnational labour solidarity," took two full decades of unions "working together to slowly develop the trust and shared understandings that later allowed the unionists to participate in solidarity strikes" (Anner 2011, 131).

This is a problem for TLAs. As Lillie, following Ramsay (1997), pointed out, "One of the major problems unions encounter when asking for international solidarity is that by the time the need for such solidarity is evident, it is too late to develop the long term relationships solidarity implies" (Lillie 2006, 78). It is not practical for unions seeking to cooperate across borders to first spend decades demonstrating their commitment to mutual support through piecemeal displays of transnational solidarity. Hence, most unions wishing to achieve interunion coordination soon after forming a TLA need a more efficient means of signaling reciprocity.

Shared strategic outlooks can solve this problem. When unions focus on long-term issues of mutual concern that extend beyond immediate material goals, they are more likely to put effort into transnational cooperation. Though no substitute for a long history of genuine reciprocity, emphasis on a shared strategic outlook can serve as a strong basis for interunion coordination in a TLA campaign. Such outlooks develop through unions' conscious efforts to project others' perspectives onto big-picture, long-term issues of mutual concern. Maritime unions' participation in the successful Flags of Convenience campaign, for example, was "a result of an organizational interest in maintaining the resources to resist globalization, liberalization and de-unionization in the port industry" (Lillie 2006, 78). Similarly, the Driving Up Standards alliance between the American Service Employees International Union (SEIU) and the British Transport and General Workers' Union (TGWU) that targeted British bus company First Group rested on "a broad, long-term strategic outlook. As such, the relationship has proved able to absorb tensions arising within particular campaigns and it has served as a platform for a variety of global initiatives" (Anderson, Hamilton, and Wills 2010, 389). Shared strategic outlooks encourage unions to participate in TLAs with longer time horizons in mind and to devote resources to transnational campaigns for which there might be few, if any, benefits in the short run.

A SPECIAL ROLE FOR THE GLOBAL UNIONS?

The global unions can help potential TLA members develop shared strategic outlooks. Global unions seek to promote unions' shared interests, regularize their communication, provide financial resources and logistical support for campaigns, and afford their affiliates some measure of mutual accountability (Ford and Gillan 2015; Croucher and Cotton 2009, 8; Lillie 2006, 125; Goodman 2004, 112). Global unions have their own staff who can present themselves as relatively neutral actors in order to ease tensions among unions with seemingly conflicting interests. For example, global union leaders can act as bridge builders who ensure that the voices of developing-country unionists are not drowned out by those of their labor allies from the North. Global unions can also address the home union problem by emphasizing shared long-term goals over home unions' more immediate concerns. They therefore have the potential to create interunion coordination by helping unions reconcile conflicting interests, overcome collective action problems, and move past practical constraints.

The extent to which global unions can solve the interunion coordination problem depends, however, on how well they promote genuine reciprocity among their affiliates. It is possible for power imbalances within the global unions to bias their agendas and resource commitments. Global unions are controlled by their national affiliates, which fund them, govern them, and appoint their staff. Power in each of the global unions weighs on the side of unions from the advanced industrialized countries, which derive clout not only from their substantial financial contributions but also from what Croucher and Cotton (2009, 44) call "political authority," which comes "from the perceived political importance of an affiliate's country and its trade union movement."

Still, power imbalances do not entirely preclude the development of the type of long-term, strategic outlooks that promote reciprocity-based interunion coordination. Croucher and Cotton (2009), following Ruggie (1993), argue that global unions facilitate a type of reciprocity based not on direct give-and-take but on multilateralism, "an institutional form that coordinates relations among three or more states [or in this case unions] on the basis of generalized principles of conduct . . . without regard to the particularist interests of the parties or the strategic exigencies that may exist in any specific occurrence" (Ruggie 1993, 77). The "diffuse reciprocity" (Keohane 1986, 4) fostered by global unions means that affiliate unions "do not expect short-term payoffs for their membership," which is instead "expected to yield a rough equivalence of benefits between members in the aggregate and over time" (Croucher and Cotton 2009, 50). Contrary to the argument that global unions cannot produce solidaristic outcomes (cf. Lillie 2006, 128), this view suggests that they do in fact help unions overcome the core challenges outlined earlier by fostering a form of coordination based on actual expectations of reciprocity, albeit a diffuse reciprocity.

The extent to which the multilateral nature of global unions can compensate for power imbalances within them nevertheless remains debatable. Global unions may be key to maintaining interunion coordination in TLA campaigns led by unions that lack a long history of solidarity. Yet only a case-by-case examination of global unions' internal power dynamics can determine the extent to which the involvement of a particular global union truly enhances prospects for effective interunion coordination.

In sum, TLAs can achieve interunion coordination even without a history of reciprocity. Focusing on shared short-term interests can help but is a relatively weak basis for coordination because it does not solve collective action problems or address practical constraints. The strongest basis for interunion coordination is a long-standing history of genuine reciprocity among unions, which is difficult to obtain. Shared strategic outlooks fall somewhere in the middle. While not a substitute for having a long history of international solidarity, shared outlooks nonetheless help unions focus on their long-term interests, encouraging TLA members to consider campaigns in a broader context. Global unions, for their part, can foster shared strategic outlooks and help resolve differences among unions from different countries.

Intraunion Coordination: Associational Power in Action

Most studies of transnational campaigns recognize the need for actors to coordinate with each other across national borders but take for granted the internal cohesion of these actors within their own organizations. A TLA is a collective actor, but so too is each union (or other workers' group) in that TLA. Each union in a TLA therefore faces its own internal coordination challenges that must be resolved before it can meaningfully participate in a transnational campaign. In other words, TLAs need *intraunion coordination*.

All transnationalism is local. The concrete activities that constitute a transnational campaign do not occur in some abstract "international arena" but rather in specific cities, towns, neighborhoods, and other identifiable localities (Lillie and Martinez Lucio 2004, 176). Actual workers, union members, and labor activists have to walk off the job, maintain picket lines, march in rallies, meet with managers, attend shareholder meetings, communicate with consumers, or perform any number of other concrete actions related to the exercise of structural, institutional, or coalitional power. These actions cannot happen unless individual workers have mobilized themselves to act collectively.

Most labor scholars are familiar with the concept of associational power, defined by E. Wright (2000, 962) as "the various forms of power that result from the formation of collective organizations of workers." While the concept is widely used (McCallum 2013; Selwyn 2011; Anner 2011; Chun 2005; Silver 2003), rarely is it clear what associational power actually enables workers to do. Wright's definition explains only where associational power comes from, not what it is. Selwyn's definition, "*a product of* workers' collective organization" (Selwyn 2011, 216, emphasis added), likewise identifies only the source, not the substance, of associational power, while Chun's definition, "*the process whereby* a group of workers actively transform themselves from a state of invisibility and marginality to one of explicit recognition as a collective social group" (Chun 2005, 490, emphasis added) explains not what associational power is but rather only the process of attaining it.

The concept of associational power thus becomes more useful when one identifies it not through the mere existence of organized labor but through specific features of an organization that enable it to behave as a collective actor (Brookes 2015). This is because simply belonging to a union or other organization does not automatically translate into a worker's willingness to take action (Hyman 2010), as collective action can be precluded by a divided, apathetic, or unwilling membership or stifled by an unsupportive leadership. In contrast, some unions are capable of collective action because their leaders and members work together to take planned, purposive action. I therefore argue that at the core of associational power is really intraunion coordination, defined as the capacity of union leaders and members to act collectively.

As Hyman pointed out, "strategic capacity in trade unions is a product of *both* leadership *and* internal democracy," which exist in "a complex dialectic" (Hyman 2010, 23, 20, emphasis in original). Unions therefore need a balance between bottom-up and top-down approaches because collective action depends as much on membership-driven activity as it does on leadership guidance and support (Bieler and Lindberg 2010, 229; Milkman 2006, 152–53; Heery 2005). This balancing act is the essence of intraunion coordination, which unions achieve when strong leaders support a rank-and-file membership who is active and engaged and when the relationship between members and leaders is characterized by cooperation and mutual respect. None of this is automatic, of course. Within a union, individual workers face challenges similar to those that whole unions confront when trying to coordinate across countries. These include lack of resources, conflicting interests, and incentives to free ride. While rank-and-file workers might solve some of these problems on their own, overcoming these obstacles often hinges on support from the union leadership.

First, union leaders can help members secure the material and human resources necessary for on-the-ground mobilization. They do so by providing a strike fund, maintaining offices and other meeting spaces, and dedicating staff to strategic research (Lévesque and Murray 2010, 340; Piven 2008, 11). Union officials can also use their personal and professional ties to connect with global unions and other international organizations that provide funding, information, and research staff to support strikes, demonstrations, organizing, and other local-level activities.

The second major way union leaders can support the membership is by using their skills as campaign strategists to help the membership develop a proactive agenda (Tattersall 2010, 144; Lévesque and Murray 2010, 343). In doing so, effective union leaders often engage in the process of learning— that is, the ability to "reflect on . . . past and current change in contexts and organizational practices and routines in order to anticipate and act upon change" (Lévesque and Murray 2010, 344). Learning not only helps unions apply lessons from past experiences over the long run but also makes it possible to quickly rework short-term strategies during a transnational campaign (Anderson 2009, 959).

Third and most fundamentally, union leaders play a vital role in mediating contending interests and conflicting identities among union members (Lévesque and Murray 2010, 341; Piven and Cloward 2000, 415; Kelly 1998). They do so by encouraging democratic participation in union proceedings and conveying shared values, ideologies, and stories that establish cohesive class identities within the union (Lévesque and Murray 2010, 336–40). Over time, as union members participate in solidarity actions, they become more likely to engage in costly behavior for which there is no direct, personal benefit. This is because these individuals begin to perceive themselves as belonging to a "community of fate" (Levi and Olson 2000, 313) comprising fellow workers who are "engaged in similar struggles for similar goals" (Ahlquist and Levi 2013, 2).

If supportive union leadership facilitates intraunion coordination, it should not be surprising that unsupportive leadership has the opposite effect.

Conservatism on the part of union leadership—which can be a product of ideology, close ties to management, or entrenched officials' resistance to strategies that threaten their personal control (Durrenberger 2009, 133; Voss and Sherman 2003, 75)—can be particularly detrimental to intraunion co-ordination when members wish to proceed with a more risky or radical course of action, such as a transnational campaign. The result could be a leadership that obstructs union democracy, cuts members off from vital re-sources, or fails to forge a common identity among the membership.

CCAP: A Comprehensive Theoretical Framework

Combining the foregoing insights, in this book I assert that successful TLA campaigns fundamentally depend on workers solving the double coordina-tion problem and exercising a type of power that directly challenges the core interests of the specific employer targeted. That is, to succeed, a TLA must meet three necessary conditions: (1) intraunion coordination, (2) interunion coordination, and (3) context-appropriate power. Intra- and interunion co-ordination facilitate collective action, and context-appropriate power compels the employer in question to behave in ways it otherwise would not. I call this the coordination and context-appropriate power theory.

The CCAP theory maintains that these three variables are individually necessary and jointly sufficient for success. Hence, the absence of one or more of the three variables is sufficient for a TLA campaign to fail. We should therefore expect all failed campaigns to lack at least one necessary condition and all successful campaigns to feature all three. The CCAP theory cannot, however, predict the specific mix of material and capacity-related gains and losses a given group of workers attains or incurs. Moreover, it is possible for a TLA to make some gains despite lacking intraunion coordination, interunion coordination, or a context-appropriate power strategy, though in such cases the CCAP theory would predict those gains to be offset by significant losses.

Case Selection and Methods of Causal Analysis

To test the causal claims of the CCAP theory, in this book I analyze six TLA campaigns—three failures and three successes—matched into pairs of highly similar cases with different outcomes: the Liverpool dockers' dispute versus the Australian waterfront conflict; the Tesco Global Union Alliance versus the Alliance for Justice at G4S; and the Shangri-La Hotel campaign versus the Raffles Hotels campaign. This logic of case selection approximates John Stuart Mill's method of difference insofar as it allows one to control for otherwise confounding factors within each pair, including the type of conflict prompting the campaign, the institutional context of the country in which the conflict originated, the TLA's goals, the type of employer targeted, whether the campaign was proactive or reactive, and the time period in which the campaign took place. If the CCAP theory is correct, any campaign lacking intraunion coordination, interunion coordination, or context-appropriate power should be unsuccessful. Conversely, all three variables should be present in each successful campaign.

This basic identification of correlation between variables and outcomes across cases (also known as congruence testing) is limited, however, because it does not allow one to check for omitted variables or spurious correlations (George and Bennett 2005, 185). Therefore I also utilize process tracing, a within-case method of causal analysis that enables the researcher to "identify the intervening causal process—the causal chain and causal mechanisms—between an independent variable (or variables) and the outcome of the dependent variable" (George and Bennett 2005, 206). By obtaining detailed information on the sequence of events and the interplay of key actors in each case, as opposed to just identifying a simple correlation of variables, I am able to connect each relevant explanatory variable to the outcome of each case. Moreover, significant variations between cases in the same matched pair that are not captured in the CCAP theory suggest potentially important explanatory variables worth further examination. Process tracing thus allows me to identify and test for alternative explanations. In sum, across-case comparisons are important, but only within-case analyses can confirm or falsify the theoretical framework proposed in this book.

Data Sources

In an effort to develop case narratives that are as complete and balanced as possible, I collected data from a multitude of primary and secondary sources. Between March 2009 and March 2012, I conducted over eighty on-site, semistructured interviews with union officials, campaign participants, labor activists, global union staff, and others directly involved in or with close knowledge of these six TLA campaigns in Chicago, London, Manchester, Melbourne, San Francisco, and Sydney. Where time or funding did not permit personal interviews, email, telephone, and Skype communications with key actors in Jakarta, Phnom Penh, Siem Reap, and Washington, DC, contributed additional interview data. Between August 2014 and April 2016, I conducted additional in-person interviews, including some follow-up interviews, with union officials and global union staff in Geneva and Washington, DC. A wide range of print and online sources pertaining to the six campaigns also inform this book's analysis. These sources include archives of newspaper articles from the LexisNexis database, campaign updates and corporate information posted on union and company websites, articles published in academic journals, and official reports from the International Labour Organisation (ILO) and OECD. All of these sources provide crucial background information on the six cases, in addition to a diverse range of perspectives and interpretations of events for each case under analysis.

Overview of the Book

In chapter 2, two dockside labor disputes set the stage for the first pair of case studies: the 1995–98 Liverpool dockworkers' campaign in Britain and the 1998 Patrick Stevedores campaign in Australia. Both drew strong support from a global network of maritime unions, who used their *structural power* to physically disrupt the loading and unloading of cargo in ports around the world. In both cases TLAs with effective *interunion coordination* exploited vulnerabilities in the time-sensitive shipping industry, thus exercising a *context-appropriate power strategy*. The Liverpool campaign failed, however, leaving hundreds of British dockers unemployed and financially devastated. In contrast, the campaign in Australia compelled the Patrick Corporation to rehire seven hundred fired dockers with back pay and full collective bargaining rights. I argue that *intraunion coordination* explains these cases' divergent outcomes. The Liverpool dockers failed at intraunion coordination, as the leaders of their own union, the TGWU, worked against the campaign, denying the dockers the legitimacy of official recognition and withholding access to crucial organizational and financial resources. Consequently, the dockers could sustain neither their local protests nor the TLA, despite their international allies' active support. In contrast, leaders of the MUA coordinated effectively with union members, allowing them to solicit support from the International Transport Workers' Federation (ITF), which played an indispensable role in sustaining the transnational actions that directly impacted Patrick's profits. Strong leader-member ties also made it easier for the MUA to mobilize members of the local community, whose dockside demonstrations helped physically disrupt Patrick's operations. Intraunion coordination thus made the exercise of structural power possible on both the international and local levels in this successful case.

Chapter 3 features the second set of cases, which centers on two service-sector industries: supermarkets and private security. Launched respectively in 2008 and 2006, the Tesco Global Union Alliance and the Alliance for Justice at G4S both began as attempts by US-based unions to organize workers in the United States before expanding into full-scale TLA campaigns aided by the global union UNI. In both cases American unions (United Food and Commercial Workers [UFCW] and SEIU) with strong *intraunion coordination* attempted to exercise *institutional power* by leveraging the influence of unions in Britain, the home country of both companies. Nevertheless, the Tesco campaign fell apart, while the G4S campaign concluded successfully with a GFA committing G4S to the protection of union rights across all of its global operations. I argue that *interunion coordination* made the difference. UFCW failed to secure support from the British Union of Shop, Distributive and Allied Workers (USDAW), which refused to jeopardize its good relationship with Tesco by backing the TLA campaign. In contrast, SEIU convinced the General, Municipal, Boilermakers and Allied Trade Union (GMB), G4S's home union, to use its positive relationship with the company to help bring G4S to the bargaining table. GMB also backed a complaint to the OECD citing G4S for violating the OECD Guidelines for Multinational Enterprises. This *context-appropriate exercise* of institutional power—invoking formal rules internationally and leveraging the home union relationship on the national level—threatened the corporation's reputation and financial position and ultimately compelled G4S to concede. The G4S TLA could not have exercised institutional power, however, without interunion coordination.

Campaigns aimed at luxury hotels in Southeast Asia are the subject of chapter 4. The 2000–2002 Shangri-La Hotel campaign in Indonesia and the 2004 Raffles Hotels campaign in Cambodia both began when local protests erupted over the mass dismissal of hundreds of workers employed at foreign-owned, five-star hotel chains. Bolstered by strong *intraunion coordination*, unions in both Indonesia and Cambodia reached out to other labor organizations abroad, which took action alongside and on behalf of the fired hotel workers, signaling effective *interunion coordination*. The Shangri-La campaign failed to win back the Indonesian workers' jobs, while the Raffles campaign won the Cambodian workers reinstatement, back pay, and full union rights. I argue that a *context-appropriate power strategy* distinguished Raffles from Shangri-La. The Shangri-La TLA relied mainly on structural power, physically disrupting the hotel's operations through pickets and protests in Jakarta while union allies threatened industrial action abroad. Management easily endured these short-term disruptions, however, countering them with violent intimidation tactics and resource-draining court battles. In contrast, the Raffles TLA exercised *coalitional power* by calling on business travelers, foreign ambassadors, and members of the US Congress to boycott and cancel bookings at the Raffles hotels in Phnom Penh and Siem Reap. The result was real financial damage and a public relations disaster for Raffles' owners, who tried but failed to keep the conflict local. Coalitional power thus proved to be context appropriate, given luxury hotel chains' long-run interests in maintaining a positive image with potential customers worldwide.

The concluding chapter summarizes findings from the case studies and discusses their implications. One of this book's main messages is that TLAs are far more likely to succeed if they are conscious of strategy and precise in their tactics. While workers cannot control the structural conditions that make it possible to coordinate, exercise power, and ultimately succeed, the matched pairs make it clear that workers can consciously choose to take advantage of opportunities for coordination and strategic action that arise within the economic, political, and social environments in which they are embedded. In other words, agency matters. If union leaders had supported the Liverpool dockers, if UFCW had won USDAW's trust, and if the Shangri-La TLA had exercised coalitional power, then these three unsuccessful campaigns would have had different outcomes. Interestingly, the successful campaigns analyzed occurred just months after extremely similar campaigns had failed, indicating that TLAs may be relatively quick to learn from the past. Whether these gains can be sustained over time will depend, however, on the extent to which these and other successes continue to enhance workers' capacities to put pressure on employers and protect their rights.

Chapter 2

Dockers, Wharfies, Longshoremen Unite

Coordinating the Liverpool and Patrick Campaigns

> I think our struggle will be remembered as an important event in global trade unionism, not just unionism in the UK. The people who supported us were the longshoremen on the West Coast of America, the longshoremen on the East Coast, the Australian dockworkers, and the dockworkers in Europe. They showed what support meant, and physically they gave it.
>
> —MIKE CARDEN, FORMER LIVERPOOL DOCKWORKER[1]

> I was called an economic terrorist! . . . We are a threat to what they are doing to our own societies—and I'm proud of that!
>
> —PADDY CRUMLIN, NATIONAL SECRETARY, MUA[2]

It is not surprising that some of the earliest episodes of new labor transnationalism occurred at a time of dramatic workplace restructuring in the highly globalized shipping and stevedoring industries. Neoliberal reforms enacted in the 1990s privatized ports, deregulated labor markets, and altered industrial relations laws on key waterfronts around the world, igniting fears among dockworkers that conditions would rapidly worsen. These fears were well founded. Those who load and unload cargo for a living—known as dockers in the United Kingdom, wharfies in Australia, longshoremen in the United States and Canada, and stevedores in much of western Europe—have since suffered from lengthened working hours, unpredictable shift changes, an accelerated pace of work, diminished job security, and sharp legal limits on industrial action.

At the same time, however, late twentieth-century waterfront reforms gave dockers the impetus to unite to an extent previously precluded by Cold War divisions and inadequate communications technologies. Although the TLAs that developed in response to the neoliberal reforms of the 1990s did not fully prevent the rise of precarious employment on the docks, they later became the backbone of what is now one of the most formidable global labor networks ever known. Through their global union, the ITF, dockers and seafarers have made significant gains, including global collective bargaining between the ITF and the International Maritime Employers' Committee over pay scales in the shipping industry (Lillie 2006). Without the TLAs that first consolidated two decades ago, the ITF would not have become the force it is today.

In this chapter I do not examine the global network of dockers and seafarers as a whole. Rather, I analyze two transnational campaigns crucial to the eventual development of that network: the 1995–98 Liverpool dock dispute and the 1998 Australian waterfront conflict. Both are among the most well-known labor disputes in recent history. Both developed in national political contexts that had grown increasingly hostile to organized labor. Both also involved transnational cooperation among dockworkers who physically obstructed the handling of cargo from ships linked to intransigent employers as part of their coordinated campaigns.

For all their similarities, however, the Liverpool and Australian dock disputes ended very differently. At the conclusion of the twenty-eight-month-long Liverpool campaign, five hundred union dockers lost their jobs, over one hundred without any compensation. After living on income from the union hardship fund for over two years, most of the fired dockers remained unemployed for years due to blacklisting or an inability to compete with nonunion workers. Though the dispute did help dockers build a foundation for an improved transnational labor network over the long term, the Liverpool campaign itself is widely considered a failure.

The equally infamous Australian waterfront conflict left labor in a better place. Union officials and management agreed to keep the docks a closed shop, seven hundred workers won back their jobs, and the MUA maintained its powerful position vis-à-vis Patrick Stevedores, the second-largest shipping company in Australia. Nonetheless, significant material concessions, including approximately seven hundred (fully funded) redundancies, rendered the wharfies' victory only a partial success. Still, both in Australia and abroad, the dispute is widely viewed as a win for the union and a major loss for the employer.

Why was the Liverpool campaign such a resounding failure, while union rights prevailed in the Patrick campaign? In this chapter I solve this puzzle by arguing that a lack of intraunion coordination in the Liverpool case caused that campaign to fail. Specifically, the dockers' own union, the TGWU,[3] not only refused to endorse the rank-and-file's campaign but also worked against it, cutting off financial and logistical support from the ITF and undertaking closed-door negotiations with the employer without the consent of the rank-and-file dockers. TGWU officials feared legal repercussions due to union members' illegal picketing. TGWU leaders also sought to scuttle the dockers' construction of a rival organization to the ITF, the International Dockworkers Council (IDC), which developed partially out of the worldwide work stoppages coordinated in the transnational campaign.

Unlike the TGWU, the MUA had leaders who strongly supported the union's rank and file. MUA officials used their clout, resources, and connections with the ITF to steer the Patrick campaign toward effective tactics, notably nonviolent community pickets across Australia and transnational cargo boycotts similar to those that were central to the Liverpool campaign. Although both TLAs used similar tactics and exhibited impeccable displays of international solidarity, the MUA's much stronger intraunion coordination enabled wharfies in the Patrick campaign to more fully exercise structural power.

In this chapter I review some sweeping reforms on the British and Australian waterfronts that tie into the incidents that sparked the Liverpool and Patrick campaigns. I then show how both campaigns took a transnational turn and how strong interunion coordination in both cases helped dockers use structural power to physically disrupt their employers' operations. Equally important were the simultaneous local protest actions in Liverpool, Melbourne, Sydney, and other cities that kept these campaigns alive. Variations in employers' strategies are explored as a potential alternative explanation for these campaigns' divergent outcomes; however, I maintain that intraunion coordination is what truly accounts for the difference. The importance of intraunion coordination for the exercise of structural power by TLAs is explored in this chapter's conclusion.

Sea Change: Neoliberal Reform on the Docks

In 1989 Margaret Thatcher's Conservative government passed legislation abolishing the National Dock Labour Scheme, which had protected dock-workers against insecure employment since the late 1960s. Trade unions lost their influence over hiring and firing, wages, and working conditions, as casual labor came to dominate the British docks. Once-stable jobs transformed into part-time, highly flexible arrangements with the rise of "as-needed" employment, meaning dockers could be called to work on short notice at an employer's discretion (Costello and Levidow 2001, 9). "No one could make any social plans. People were on call for the company 24 hours a day, seven days a week," explained former Liverpool docker and TGWU general executive council member Mike Carden in an interview (Bacon 1998a).

Thatcher's reforms threw union docks into turmoil. Large numbers of dockers exited the industry outright (Castree 2000, 277). Those remaining competed with each other for work. Threatened with unemployment, they accepted longer shifts, weekend hours, and other flexible labor practices (Costello and Levidow 2001, 9). With the privatization and deregulation of British ports, labor costs dropped—as did unionization rates. By 1995, the port of Liverpool was one of only two fully unionized ports left in the United Kingdom.

A similar pattern soon unfolded in Australia after the Liberal-National Coalition rose to power in the 1996 federal election. Prime Minister John Howard led the drive to weaken unions across the country with the 1996 Workplace Relations Act, which imposed severe penalties for illegal industrial action (such as sympathy strikes), allowed for individual contracts to supplant collective agreements, and reduced the role of the Australian Industrial Relations Commission in resolving industrial disputes (McConville 2000, 400; Svensen 1998, 5). "No more black bans. No secondary boycotts. Or anyone can sue the union for damages, make us pay a fine," noted one MUA official (personal interview, March 10, 2010).

Waterfront reform was not an exclusively right-wing initiative. The Hawke and Keating Labor governments in the 1980s and early 1990s pushed through several productivity-enhancing workplace reforms, inducing thousands of dockworker redundancies. It was under the Howard government, however, that Australian unions came under explicit political attack. By 1996, according to one MUA official, "trade unionism was seen as an impediment to the new conditions. This coincided with the technological revolution, when the nature of trade changed to just-in-time, et cetera. But Howard also had a specific political agenda that was exclusive, not inclusive" (personal interview, May 5, 2010). That political agenda entailed the recruitment of nonunion workers, the proliferation of individual contracts, and the implementation of employer-led hiring practices. Pro-Howard Australians viewed the government's waterfront reform efforts as history in the making, "a defining moment comparable to the Falklands War or President Reagan's victory over air traffic controllers" (Svensen 1998, 4).

The political attack on unions in both Britain and Australia left labor leaders unable to protect their members' interests through traditional industrial action and standard collective bargaining procedures. At the same time, however, advances in information and communications technologies had begun to improve prospects for international networking. TLA campaigns thus became an increasingly attractive avenue for circumventing antiunion institutional contexts on the national scale. Moreover, the potential for TLAs to alter the industrial relations playing field was especially great in shipping and stevedoring, which are highly vulnerable to structural power. This logic led both the Liverpool dockers and the MUA to adopt the tactics they did.

Mass Dismissal on the Port of Liverpool

The port of Liverpool remained a bastion of union power well after the 1989 Tory legislation altered the nature of dock work across Britain. Nevertheless, despite working on what was regarded as "the most resilient unionised port" in the UK (Carter et al. 2003, 291), the dockers employed by the Mersey Docks and Harbour Company (MDHC) on the port of Liverpool suffered from declining wages, a demanding pace of work, and unpredictable layoffs. Additionally, MDHC subcontracted several jobs to Torside, an employment agency that effectively casualized dockers by employing them on inferior contracts and at lower wages than received by those directly employed by MDHC. "MDHC was heavily involved in Torside's affairs" (Castree 2000, 277), and Torside was "really a creation of the MDHC" (Costello and Levidow 2001, 9).

Torside dockers had grown accustomed to working compulsory overtime on short notice. Thus it was not especially shocking when, on September 25, 1995, twenty-two Torside dockers received orders to work overtime twenty minutes before their shift was supposed to end. What was distressing was that the usual overtime pay rates were not to apply. Seeking to discuss this situation with their shop stewards, five of the workers walked across the docks for a meeting at the canteen. The managing director met them there instead and promptly fired all five. When the other seventeen came to the canteen, managers told them to return to the ship they had been working on, or they would be sacked as well. The next morning, with no explanation, Torside's managing director fired the entire Torside workforce shortly after the dockers learned what had happened to their coworkers the night before. About eighty dockers suddenly found themselves unemployed.

MDHC refused to acknowledge any role in the Torside sackings. When TGWU shop stewards tried to discuss the issue with MDHC representatives on September 27, "the company disavowed any involvement with Torside and argued that the sackings were the internal affair of an independent company" (Castree 2000, 278). On September 28, the former Torside employees set up a picket at Liverpool's Seaforth dock. In solidarity, the MDHC dockers refused to cross the picket line. They were promptly fired. Hence, in a period of four days, with almost no warning whatsoever, five hundred Liverpool dockers lost their jobs.

Nonunion replacements took over, and MDHC stripped the union's shop stewards of official recognition, despite overwhelming support for the stewards from the union membership. The shop stewards nevertheless refused to disappear, and through the Merseyside Port Shop Stewards Committee, they helped the sacked dockers launch a campaign for reinstatement. The dockers expected a hard fight. They did not expect their struggle to grow into what is now considered "the most protracted industrial dispute in British history" (Castree 2000, 272).

The Australian Wharves Lockout

Around midnight on April 7–8, 1998, security guards burst into several wharves across Australia run by Patrick Stevedores. Clad in balaclavas, the guards used menacing Rottweilers and physical force to cease crane operations and escort wharfies off the docks via helicopter and motorboat. Patrick then delivered a message to 1,400 startled workers: you are all sacked.

Had the wharfies been directly employed by Patrick, legally binding contracts would have precluded mass dismissal. Seven months before the midnight lockout, however, Patrick had undergone a complex corporate restructuring that outsourced its wharfies to four separate labor-hire companies "whose services could be terminated immediately by Patrick if there was any interference or delay in providing the contracted services" (Svensen 1998, 6). Patrick claimed no financial responsibility for the labor-hire companies (Bramble 1998, 11), which themselves claimed financial insolvency. The sacked wharfies were thus technically "the victims of being employed by insolvent companies" (C. Smith 2010, 561).

The morning after the lockout, thousands of Australians picketed Patrick docks to protest the attack on the wharfies, all of whom were MUA members. Throughout the rest of April, warehouse, construction, metal, mining, and transport workers, alongside a variety of community members, showed their support through solidarity actions, including walk-offs in Melbourne, Sydney, and Fremantle. The conflict would last four months and serve as "a dramatic test of the ability of employers to dismiss an entire workforce under the Workplace Relations Act" (Sadler and Fagan 2004, 36).

Expanding Solidarity: Dockworkers' Interunion Coordination

While the Liverpool dockers and the Australian wharfies benefited from an outpouring of public support in their own countries (discussed later), both sets of workers also turned to TLAs to enhance the impact of their campaigns. Though they went about it in different ways, the Liverpool dockers and MUA members both attained interunion coordination[4] with relative ease. The century-long history of solidarity among stevedoring and seafaring unions worldwide provided a solid foundation on which to do so.

Among maritime unions, international solidarity is the stuff of legends, kept alive in oft-repeated anecdotes traded among unionists and echoed in songs, stories, slogans, and art. Their stories reflect a powerful imagined community. "Dockers imagine that they once knew who they were, what they were, where they were. They were workers, exploited but militant, supporters of the union and the party, breadwinners and men. They were a class, a band of brothers, and hard-working members of an occupational community, one with great traditions, songs, flags and rituals. They were almost a tribe. Class solidarity was their creed" (Carter et al. 2003, 296). Memories of shared struggle contribute not only to "an ideology that was compelling and an essential part of what it means to be in a trade union" but also to "this notion that our fates are all linked" (ILWU staff, personal interview, August 18, 2010). International solidarity among maritime unions stems from more than a shared identity; it also reflects a pragmatic understanding of the economic and political pressures that threaten dockers' and seafarers' working conditions, job security, and living standards in the present era of globalization.

Interunion Coordination in the Liverpool Campaign

In the Liverpool campaign, the fired dockers coordinated actions with unions in several countries despite lacking the backing of their own union, the TGWU. For reasons discussed later, the Liverpool dockers had to work around union leaders and network through informal channels. Technology provided one way to make these connections. Activist and LabourNet.org cofounder Chris Bailey was instrumental in helping the Liverpool dockers connect through the internet. Bailey set up a daily information service through a website frequently updated with photos and news of the dockers' struggle (Bailey 2006, 233; Castree 2000, 282)—a novel idea in the phone-and-fax world of the mid-1990s. LabourNet helped coordinate the campaign's first "international day of action" with a message posted in five languages imploring "dockers of the world" to "blockade Liverpool on January 20th."

Face-to-face communication also secured interunion coordination. In January 1996, a small delegation of Liverpool dockers visited Canada and the United States to inform longshoremen in Montreal and Newark that ships landing there had used the port of Liverpool. Delegations to Philadelphia and San Francisco delivered similar messages. Additional delegations traveled to Australia, Belgium, France, New Zealand, Spain, and Sweden. When the dockers arrived in Australia, "everyone they met seemed well informed about the dispute and were already producing leaflets they had printed from the internet" (Bailey 2006, 232).

According to shop stewards Jimmy Nolan and Terry Teague, the original intention of these delegations was to raise money and obtain solidarity statements. Although the Liverpool workers did receive substantial financial contributions—including 1 million yen from the All Japan Dockworkers Union and almost $100,000 from the ILWU in the United States—the delegations ultimately secured promises of industrial action from unions in different countries (Castree 2000, 280–82). Workers from various countries also voiced their commitment to take action on behalf of the Liverpool dockers in international conferences arranged by campaign activists, including a five-day conference at Liverpool City Hall in February 1996 and a second international conference in August 1996.

Technology, delegations, and conferences all helped the Liverpool dockers achieve what Castree (2000) refers to as "grass-roots internationalism," in which workers and union members self-organize transnational activities using direct, face-to-face interactions with fellow workers. As one ILWU official put it, "The Liverpool workers *themselves* were really the catalysts, taking the message to the world. That's how they got support internationally" (personal interview, August 18, 2010).

Interunion Coordination in the Patrick Campaign

The wharfies involved in the Patrick dispute achieved a level of international solidarity no less impressive than that obtained by their counterparts in Liverpool. Their methods of interunion coordination differed, however, as the Australian wharfies had the full, official support of their union, the MUA. Moreover, at the time of the Patrick campaign, a transnational network of dockworkers had already been reinvigorated by the then newly concluded Liverpool campaign, which made interunion coordination far less complicated for the Australians than it had been for the British dockers a mere two years earlier.

As in the Liverpool case, the MUA wharfies drew on the decades-long history of solidarity shared by dockers and seafarers worldwide. The MUA is the oldest continuously operating maritime union in the world, having formed in 1993 as an amalgamation of previously separate maritime unions, notably the Waterside Workers' Federation and the Seamen's Union of Australia, which themselves comprised older iterations of stevedore and shipping unions, including the Sydney Wharf Labourers' Union and the Seamen's Union of Melbourne, which was the first maritime union the world, established in 1872. Australian wharfies and seafarers have a long and rich history of reciprocity with labor movements in other countries, as well as a reputation for highly politicized transnational solidarity actions.

Some of the Australians' earliest solidarity actions include Sydney wharfies' donation of £500 to support striking dockers in London in 1889, wharfies' refusal to handle wool that had been black-banned by striking shearers in 1890, and the Waterside Workers' Federation–led national boycott of pig iron shipments to Japan in 1938 (Bramble 1998, 9). "We took political stands on international things," emphasized one MUA branch secretary in an interview, continuing, "After World War II, when Indonesia was seeking independence, we refused to load Dutch ships. That was the 1940s. During the Vietnam War, we were taking a stand. Some ships were going to Vietnam, carrying munitions. We refused to let them sail. That was 1967. Both unions (the WWF [Waterside Workers' Federation] and the Seamen's Union) had bans on the whole Vietnam war going on" (personal interview, March 10, 2010). Australian wharfies and seafarers also challenged apartheid in South Africa. In time, workers around the world grew to understand that "so long as the MUA remained strong, any other union facing drastic assault had a ready and powerful ally" (Bramble 1998, 3).

When the time came to call on their international allies in the Patrick dispute, the MUA leaned heavily on its US ties. Through the ITF, MUA officials contacted the International Longshoremen's Association (ILA) on the East Coast, which assured the Australians of its support. It was the ILWU on the West Coast, however, with whom the MUA had the strongest relationship. Direct links date back to the 1930s when Australian seafarer Harry Bridges docked in San Francisco, decided to stay there, became a longshoreman, and helped found the ILWU.

An ILWU staff member emphasized in an interview his union's strong ties with the MUA: "Other unions have made similar pledges to international solidarity with each other, but those are different. The ILWU has consistently followed a creed of international solidarity with [the MUA]. It's a straight, clear, consistent commitment to international solidarity. For the MUA, ILWU support is always a given" (personal interview, August 18, 2010). A branch secretary at the MUA echoed these sentiments: "With the ILWU, there's a strong relationship there" (personal interview, March 10, 2010). An ITF coordinator and former member of the Seamen's Union of Australia offered his own take on the ILWU-MUA relationship: "The situation we're in, it's very, very familiar to them. They're easy to talk to, so we know there's no bullshit. We can identify with Americans. They're not scared to tell the boss to get fucked" (personal interview, March 31, 2010).

No-Loads and Go-Slows: Structural Power at Home and Abroad

> A bunch of janitors can't alter the economy. But 100,000 ships going
> through ports worth trillions of dollars—that'll make everyone pay
> attention. That is a true sense of power.
> —ILWU OFFICIAL[5]

Strong interunion coordination in both the Liverpool and Patrick campaigns facilitated the exercise of structural power on the international scale. At the same time, the community pickets and protests that physically disrupted port operations within Britain and Australia helped the dockworkers exercise structural power locally and nationally as well. The Liverpool and Patrick campaigns were thus multiscalar (Brookes 2013; Ellem 2006; Castree 2000). Hence, in analyzing how campaign actions unfolded in both disputes, activities on the international, national, and local scales must be considered for their combined impact.

The main point, however, is that despite their different outcomes, both the Liverpool and Patrick alliances used highly similar campaign tactics, drawing on the same type of power, which had a material impact on both companies in question. Although the exercise of structural power by the Liverpool TLA fell short of actually altering MDHC's behavior, the power strategy itself cannot explain why the Liverpool campaign failed. Another factor—weak intraunion coordination (discussed later)—diminished the impact of an otherwise context-appropriate power strategy. Conversely, stronger intraunion coordination enhanced the TLA's structural power in the Patrick campaign, which concluded as a partial success.

Transnational Action in the Liverpool Campaign

From early 1996 through late 1997, the Liverpool dockers mobilized a TLA to take on the MDHC. Adopting the slogan The World Is Our Picket Line, the Liverpool TLA exercised structural power and caused millions of dollars of damage to various port and shipping companies. Transnational structural power took two forms. First, dockers took industrial action at individual ports. In Sydney, for example, MUA wharfies practiced go-slows (deliberate delays on cargo handling) on vessels owned by a company known to ship several hundred containers through Liverpool per trip. On the US East Coast, ILA members took short-term industrial action against the shipping company ACL, one of the Liverpool port's most prominent users. MUA official Paddy Crumlin "was proud of [ILA president John] Bowers for the solidarity the ILA had shown Liverpool workers. He said the ILA stopped ships when the Liverpool dockers set up their picket lines and faced a $3 million lawsuit because of it" (Erem and Durrenberger 2008, 120). MDHC suffered serious costs when ACL ceased using the port of Liverpool in June 1996.

The second form of transnational structural power entailed action on several ports at once. These simultaneous efforts culminated in an international day of action, a series of legal and illegal work stoppages at 105 ports and cities in twenty-seven countries on January 20, 1997. The All Japan Dockworkers Union shut down over fifty ports in Japan. Dockers in Denmark halted work for a day at the port of Copenhagen and three other ports. In Sweden stevedores boycotted all ACL ships and containers for the day. Go-slows continued on the Australian wharves. French dockers imposed a half-day no-load in the port of Le Havre on a Canadian CANMAR ship that used the Liverpool port. As a result, CANMAR stopped using the port of Liverpool, causing an almost 20 percent drop in MDHC's share price (Castree 2000, 282–83).

For its part, the ILWU enacted a twenty-four-hour stoppage along the US West Coast, circumventing no-strike rules by holding "stop work meetings" about legitimate grievances—after which the dockers simply went home (Bailey 2006, 233). According to the Los Angeles Times on January 21, 1997, "Pacific Rim trade sputtered to a halt and dozens of mammoth cargo ships sat idle in their ports Monday as union dockworkers from Los Angeles to Seattle stayed off the job in a one-day show of support for striking longshoremen in Liverpool, England. The work stoppage, which silenced the usually bustling San Pedro Bay harbors during the day but was expected to end in time for the night shift, will result in millions of dollars in extra fees for steamship lines. . . .

At the Los Angeles-Long Beach harbor complex, the nation's busiest, 33 ships were either stranded in berths with no one to handle their cargo or were anchored in the San Pedro Bay with nowhere to go." The news piece also notes that the longshoremen had "collectively sacrificed millions of dollars of their own pay to demonstrate unity with their European brothers" (Leeds 1997).

The TLA coordinated further actions at a May 1997 conference in Montreal, where dockworkers from seventeen countries met to discuss shared concerns over privatization, deregulation, and casualization. Workers also demonstrated at British embassies around the world. In August dockers in South Africa announced a block on ships carrying citrus fruits destined for the MDHC-owned port of Sheerness (Bailey 2006, 242). A group of Swiss anarchists even occupied the office of a shipping company, a noteworthy show of solidarity given Switzerland's unsurprising dearth of maritime activity (Carter et al. 2003, 299).

What really gained global attention, however, was the boycott of the *Neptune Jade*, a container ship sailing from England's Thamesport, whose port authority, Medway Ports Limited, was a wholly owned subsidiary of MDHC. According to Jack Heyman, who had visited Liverpool on behalf of the ILWU in early 1996, the *Neptune Jade* sailed into Oakland, California, on September 28, 1997. Community members and activists promptly set up a picket line. ILWU longshoremen refused to cross the picket line on "health and safety" grounds, defying a court injunction that ordered them to return to work.[6] For three and a half days, the ship sat docked in Oakland. Still full of cargo, it sailed on to Vancouver, Canada, only to meet another community picket, which ILWU longshoremen refused to cross. The *Neptune Jade* then sailed to Japan, where union dockers in Yokohama and Kobe, informed of the hot cargo, also refused to handle the ship (Heyman 2005). The *Neptune Jade* eventually sold off its cargo in Hong Kong in lieu of returning to the United Kingdom. According to labor activist Chris Bailey, "This action terrified the shipping companies even more than the days of action had. The losses to a shipping company through carrying containers around the world without being able to unload them can be horrific" (Bailey 2006, 237).

All of these events—the individual port stoppages, the synchronized day of action, and the *Neptune Jade* boycott—offered evidence that the TLA, ably led by the Liverpool shop stewards committee, had supplanted the authority of the TGWU (Bailey 2006, 235). At the same time, however, the Liverpool dockers still had to contend with TGWU leaders, who fought to suppress the transnational campaign from going further. The deal TGWU officials eventually negotiated with MDHC to end the dispute prevented structural power from having the impact on MDHC that it otherwise could have had. That is not to say, however, that the Liverpool dockers lacked local support. On the contrary, in Liverpool and throughout the United Kingdom, students, athletes, activists, and other community members came out in full support of the dockers, as I discuss next.

Local Protest in the Liverpool Campaign

Mass picketing on the Mersey docks was not an option. The TGWU leadership made no effort to prevent nonunion replacements from entering the port and refused to condone any illegal industrial action. The Liverpool dockers thus relied instead on daily mass pickets of the dock complex in which community members blocked or delayed entrance through the gates. Dockers also lobbied local members of Parliament and city council members and organized a community march and rally on October 21, 1995 (Castree 2000, 279).

Public support grew. Solidarity groups held public meetings throughout the United Kingdom to strategize ways of supporting the dockers. The London Support Group for the Liverpool Dockers published *Dockers' Charter*, a monthly newspaper with updates on the dispute, and organized national demonstrations in London in December 1996 and April 1997. Women of the Waterfront, an organization of dockers' wives and mothers, traveled around Britain giving speeches, performing satire, hanging banners, and hosting benefit evenings. Mass rallies in March and September 1996 attracted thousands of attendees. Activist organization Reclaim the Streets helped mobilize protesters to march and dance throughout central London and blockade London's Victoria Station. In May 1996 national support groups picketed the head office of Drake International, the company responsible for hiring nonunion replacement workers for the Seaforth dock, where most of the former MDHC dockers worked.

Socialists, anarchists, students, family members, and workers all demonstrated their support for the Liverpool dockers in visible, physical ways. Yet perhaps the most memorable show of support, at least for football fans, occurred when Liverpool footballer Robbie Fowler, upon scoring his second goal in the quarterfinal match of the European Cup Winners' Cup, pulled off his red Liverpool shirt to reveal a T-shirt that read, "500 Liverpool Dockers Sacked since September 1995" (Harris 1997). He was fined 2,000 Swiss francs for violating the regulations of the Union of European Football Associations. Nevertheless, the fine deterred neither Fowler nor his teammate Steve McManaman (who wore the same T-shirt) from making significant financial donations to the dockers' hardship fund. Shop steward Bobby Morton expressed thanks: "Robbie Fowler and Steve McManaman are both local lads, they both come from working class families, and we're glad of their support" (Harris 1997).

Transnational Action in the Patrick Campaign

Transnational labor solidarity in the Patrick campaign began months before the mass lockout. In December 1997 MUA national secretary John Coombs and Australian Council of Trade Unions (ACTU) assistant secretary Greg Combet uncovered evidence that Patrick and the federal government planned to fly thirty ex-military personnel to Dubai to train as replacement dockworkers on the port of Rashid. Coombs and Combet immediately contacted the ITF. London-based ITF officials then met with the ambassador for the United Arab Emirates and calmly threatened to call for mass industrial action affecting UAE ports and ships unless the covert training operation were called off. Shortly after that meeting, the UAE revoked the trainees' visas, forcing the men to return to Australia. "We used the ITF to stop the Dubai training," explained an ACTU organizer. "They said to the port authorities that there would be an international union campaign if they tried to do the training. The ITF really helped in exposing and stopping that plan" (personal interview, May 10, 2010).

The MUA has long been in good standing with the ITF as one of the global union's most active affiliates. The Dubai incident was not the first time the ITF had threatened international industrial action to support Australian union workers, even that year. Just two months earlier, in September 1997, the ITF intervened when International Purveyors attempted to employ non-union labor to operate its facilities in Cairns. The company's plans fell through after the ITF threatened industrial action on ports owned by Freeport-McMoRan, International Purveyors' parent company.

The ITF continued to play an important coordinating role in the Patrick campaign following the mass lockouts of April 1998. Along with MUA officials, the ITF helped organize international work stoppages, protests, strategy sharing, fund-raising drives, and messages of solidarity from its affiliates around the world. Although Australian law prohibits unions from calling for international boycotts, seemingly spontaneous, self-organized actions by workers and community activists are harder to trace back to any particular union or official. The ITF also used some clever tactics to avoid legal trouble in its call for transnational action, such as circulating the official list from the Australian Competition and Consumer Commission of ships that unions were "not supposed to boycott."

Pro-MUA demonstrations erupted outside Australian embassies in India, Indonesia, Japan, the Philippines, South Korea, and the United States. ILWU president Brian McWilliams and seven other ILWU officials were reportedly arrested within hours of the Patrick lockouts while picketing outside the Australian consulate in San Francisco (Bacon 1998b). In late April dockers in South Africa and Japan announced bans on Australian cargo. Dockworkers at Port Moresby in Papua New Guinea enforced a twenty-four-hour no-load on the *Queen Amelia*, which had been loaded in Australia by nonunion labor. Short-term industrial action also occurred in India, Indonesia, the Netherlands, and the Philippines.

The most significant action taken by the TLA was the boycott of an Australian container ship called the *Columbus Canada*. Labor-community pickets appeared almost instantly upon its arrival at the Matson Terminal in the port of Los Angeles on May 25, 1998. "The *Columbus Canada* had been loaded by scabs in Victoria," explained an ITF coordinator in an interview. "It came to LA, and there were rallies in the streets, over a thousand people. I was there, living in the mud and shit of the picket line. Everyone was shouting, 'MUA! Here to stay! No scab labor in LA!' in an American accent" (personal interview, March 31, 2010). Members of ILWU Locals 13 and 63 refused to cross the 1,500-strong picket line in front of the Matson Terminal, invoking the same "health and safety" considerations the ILWU had used during the Liverpool dispute. The ship sat idle for seventeen days. It then returned to Australia to be reloaded by union wharfies.

Local Protest in the Patrick Campaign

Daily demonstrations of solidarity on the local level were a crucial component of the multiscalar Patrick campaign. Community pickets in Melbourne, Sydney, and Fremantle drew diverse crowds comprising wharfies' families, representatives from different unions, Labor Party politicians, students, professors, pensioners, musicians, political activists, and media crews. Church leaders held Easter services on the picket line the weekend after the mass firings, and organizers set up children's play areas on the wharves, affording the community pickets a friendly and "festive" feel (McConville 2000, 398). These local assemblies not only demonstrated public opinion against Patrick's actions but also helped the wharfies exercise structural power by physically blocking the movement of trucks, containers, and cargo through the ports. "Within a week, more than $500 million of cargo was stranded on the wharves of Melbourne and Sydney, and by May more than ten thousand containers were stacked up on the wharves" (McConville 2000, 398).

One of the campaign's most dramatic confrontations occurred on the East Swanson Dock on the port of Melbourne on the night of April 17, 1998. Approximately four thousand workers and community members set up a picket to prevent the passage of trucks. Welded-together railway tracks, concrete blocks, old car bodies, containers, and an overturned trailer—dubbed a "community arts project" by protesters—reinforced the barrier to the dock's entrance road (Bramble 1998, 16). Around three o'clock in the morning, MUA officials received a tip that one thousand police officers were on their way to break up the picket. Police arrived to find picketers standing arm in arm in row after row in front of the dock's entrance. The tense standoff finally ended around eight o'clock in the morning, when two thousand union construction workers suddenly appeared on the picket site and encircled the police, compelling their retreat. No violence occurred. Containers remained frozen on the port of Melbourne, and at the start of the next week's trading, shares in Lang, Patrick's parent company, fell by 13 percent (Bramble 1998, 16).

Other significant local actions contributed to the Patrick campaign. On April 23 a day of action entailed union workers and students marching to Fisherman's Island in Brisbane. About a week later, Brisbane witnessed its largest May Day rally since 1985, with over ten thousand community members in attendance. The Victorian Trades Hall Council Day of Action rally in Melbourne on May 6 attracted over seventy-five thousand[7] people (Wilson

1998, 34). Generous financial contributions helped sustain the local pickets, marches, and rallies through late May. ACTU raised $1.2 million through a direct appeal, with thousands of individuals paying into the fund. Wharfies employed by Patrick's competitor, P&O, donated up to half of their own pay per shift to the sacked Patrick employees.

Reflecting on the Patrick campaign as a whole, an organizer at the ACTU summed up its multiscalar nature: "Our challenge was how to find the strategic levers, how to develop capacity and strategic thinking across unions. Patrick was really the first of our campaigns that strategically used the internet and community pickets and international solidarity" (personal interview, May 10, 2010). Local and transnational actions clearly complemented each other, offering evidence that deep, in-place coalitions of workers and local community members can anchor and enhance campaign actions on the international scale. Similar multiscalar dynamics characterized the Liverpool campaign, which featured the same set of power strategies.

Comparing the Employers' Strategies

As discussed earlier, there is no indication that either interunion coordination or power strategy differed significantly between the Liverpool and Patrick campaigns. Both sets of workers connected effectively with labor activists overseas, and both TLAs subsequently exercised structural power. Moreover, strong local support characterized both campaigns, indicating that the Liverpool dockers' eventual failure had nothing to do with antiunion sentiments on the part of the British public. Yet to be explored is another possible explanation for these campaigns' divergent outcomes: differing employer strategies. As I show in this section, however, MDHC and Patrick used similar strategies in attempting to deunionize the docks in Britain and Australia and in their responses to the TLAs. Hence, employer strategy cannot explain why workers failed in Liverpool and partially succeeded with Patrick.

First, neither MDHC nor Patrick Stevedores provided an adequate explanation for, respectively, sacking five hundred TGWU dockers in September 1995 and locking out 1,400 MUA members in April 1998. Instead, both companies carefully disassociated themselves from the "actual" perpetrators. MDHC claimed to have little to do with Torside, technically the employer of the twenty-two dockers originally involved in the Liverpool dispute.

MDHC later opted to cease direct employment of dockers altogether and become a port authority that simply contracted out cargo handling to private stevedoring companies in the United Kingdom. Patrick likewise dodged direct responsibility for its mass sackings by employing wharfies through four separate labor-hire companies, which became financially insolvent. Patrick chairman Chris Corrigan also publicly denied any knowledge of the covert training operation in Dubai (Svensen 1998, 7).

In reality, both MDHC and Patrick were actively involved in larger efforts to restructure the British and Australian waterfronts. Both companies also had the backing of their respective national governments in these efforts. In the Liverpool case, business-friendly industrial relations laws, including a prohibition on secondary strike action that allows unions to be sued for authorizing such activity, aided MDHC and other employers even after the rise of the Blair Labour government in 1997. For its part, the Blair government simply "would not be drawn into making any substantive statements of support for the dockers," despite the fact that the UK government had retained a 15–20 percent stake in MDHC since its privatization in 1970 (Castree 2000, 277).[8] Yet according to one of the Liverpool dockers, intervening in the Liverpool dispute "was one of the easiest things the government could have done. . . . It had every right to intervene and say, 'Look, what's happened here is clearly unfair. There are illegal labor practices being carried out in the port of Liverpool.' The Mersey Docks and Harbour Company was still nearly a nationalized industry. It had benefitted from taxpayers' money during numerous economic crises. The government had every right to intervene. It chose not to. And I think the actions of the government concerning the Liverpool dockers shows the direction it wants to move in" (Bacon 1998a). In other words, the government not only distanced itself from the dispute but also appeared to approve of the actions taken by MDHC to deunionize the docks and restructure the labor market.

Corporate-government ties were even stronger in the Patrick case. In July 1997, the Howard government voted to support Patrick financially in its decision to take radical action against the MUA. This decision followed from nine months of meetings between Minister for Workplace Relations Peter Reith, Transport Minister John Sharp, the ministers' departmental advisers, Patrick Stevedores' Chris Corrigan, business consultants, and Don Mc-Gauchie and Wendy Craik of the National Farmers' Federation (Bramble 1998, 10). Leaked documents later revealed detailed plans for wide-scale deunionization, recruitment of immigrants for nonunion replacement labor, and the use of public funds to facilitate the Patrick lockout. Both the federal government and the National Farmers' Federation also provided financial support to P&C Stevedores, one of the labor-hire companies to which Patrick had outsourced its workforce.

Neither MDHC nor Patrick wanted to appear as though union busting were its main objective. Both companies thus deliberately shifted the focus to productivity issues. Evidence suggests, however, that greater efficiency was neither company's main goal. Shortly before the Liverpool dispute began, "the respected shipping publication *Lloyds List* (15 September 1995) [had] described the Liverpool work force as 'the best in Europe' in reference to the good industrial relations and high productivity rates enjoyed in the port since 1989" (Castree 2000, 278). "They said we were the most productive dockers in Europe," remarked former Liverpool docker Mike Carden. The real issue, Carden continued, was that MDHC had grown concerned about "the young Torside dock workers becoming more aggressive in their demand for equal status, for permanency, and for the establishment of a proper pension scheme, including holiday pay and sick pay" (Bacon 1998a). There is also evidence that MDHC sought to speed up the retirement of older dockers whose seniority and union experience threatened the company's restructuring plan.

Patrick likewise pushed the productivity issue in its conflict with the MUA. According to an ITF coordinator, "Patrick said they were about increasing the box rate from 20 to 30 containers per hour because supposedly wharfies were capping the box rate" (personal interview, November 3, 2011). Yet contrary to Patrick's assertions, Australian wharves were more productive than Patrick made them appear. According to others involved in the campaign, the numbers used by Patrick to calculate container rates per hour failed to account for the fact that containers come in two sizes, twenty-foot and forty-foot. Different calculations using twenty-foot equivalent units showed a box rate of twenty-two twenty-foot equivalent units per hour in Australian ports, comparable to the twenty-four containers per hour average in Singapore, one of the most productive ports in the world.

Nevertheless, Patrick and the Australian government were aggressive in their attempt to portray dockworkers as unproductive. Working closely with the Howard government, television station Channel Nine aired an episode of its current affairs program that showed "waterfront workers allegedly leaving early on their shifts and questioned their pay, conditions, and productivity" in attempt to create "a perception of the MUA as a minority interest" and part of "the labour productivity 'problem' on the wharves" (Wilson 1998, 26). "They had all their cameras down here, tried to cast a negative light on us," recalled an MUA branch secretary (personal interview, March 10, 2010). There were also antiunion radio talk shows and antiunion opinion articles in national newspapers.

"It wasn't about the money for these companies. It was about power and control," argued an ILWU official. "Liverpool was definitely the blueprint for what Patrick tried to do in 1998" (personal interview, August 18, 2010). An MUA official concurred that "the Liverpool failure created the conditions for Patrick's lockout. In both cases, it was the employer taking militant and radical industrial action by lockout and replacement" (personal interview, May 5, 2010).

The similarities between MDHC's and Patrick's strategies are notable. Moreover, the few differences between the two employers' positions suggest that, if anything, it was Patrick, not MDHC, that had the stronger advantage over labor: Patrick not only benefited by learning from MDHC's success in the recently concluded Liverpool campaign but also drew on deeper collaborative ties with government officials. Nevertheless, union workers prevailed over the Australian stevedoring company despite the fact that Patrick had advantages that MDHC did not. The two cases' different outcomes cannot be explained by differences in employer strategy.

There Is Power in a Union: Why Intraunion Coordination Mattered Most

> Trade union officials are all full of ego.
> We all think we've got the very best ideas.
> —Construction, Forestry, Maritime, Mining and Energy
> Union official[9]

One variable yet to be explored is intraunion coordination, defined as the capacity of workers to mobilize themselves to act collectively. An essential indicator of intraunion coordination is a strong, positive relationship between union leaders and members (see chapter 1). Union leaders in both campaigns not only controlled access to material resources but also channeled their organizations' learning into strategic action. Union leaders thus had substantial control over the implementation of strategy in both campaigns, and their relationships with rank-and-file members greatly influenced these campaigns' final outcomes.

TGWU versus the Dockers: How Lack of Intraunion Coordination Led to Failure

In the January 29, 1998, issue of the *Guardian*, journalist John Pilger published a scathing critique of TGWU leaders' handling of the Liverpool dock dispute. According to Pilger, the Liverpool campaign "was lost because the Transport and General Workers' Union virtually guaranteed its failure. Had this rich and powerful organisation launched a national campaign challenging the sinister circumstances and the sheer injustice of the dockers' dismissal . . . the battle could have been won there and then. Instead, it was the craven silence of the union leadership that finally ended the imaginative and courageous efforts of men once described by Lloyds List as the most productive work force in Europe" (Pilger 1998). TGWU officials made several arguments in defense of their actions; however, even they did not deny that the dockers' rank-and-file campaign lacked the union leaders' full support.

To their credit, TGWU leaders did provide some financial assistance to the fired dockers. "For the record, the docks dispute on Merseyside has probably been the most expensive in the union's history," TGWU general secretary Bill Morris told the press. "The union has, at all levels, spent over £1million in relieving the hardship amongst the sacked dockers [*sic*] families and my senior colleagues and myself spent hundreds of hours in the search for a negotiated settlement" (Morris 1998a). Yet according to others involved in the campaign, official union support stopped there.

TGWU leaders stood by while MDHC continued to operate the port of Liverpool with nonunion replacements. Truck drivers in the same union even crossed the dockers' picket lines to get to work. The union's officials also refused to call for solidarity action from other British unions or even mention the dispute in its own newsletter, the *T&G Record*. At one point, the union's officials collaborated with MDHC in hiring financial consultants to plan for the reemployment of some of the dockers as "self-employed" workers (a plan the dockers naturally rejected) (Costello and Levidow 2001, 10). Even

TGWU's financial support was not enough to free the fired dockers from daily financial hardship and personal stress due to over two years of unemployment. By the end of the dispute, the average debt accumulated by each docker was £20,000 (Carter et al. 2003, 294).

Especially damaging to the TLA campaign was TGWU leaders' refusal to request help from their global union, the ITF. "The ITF should've played a stronger role," argued MUA national secretary Paddy Crumlin, who kept a close watch on the Liverpool campaign (quoted in Erem and Durrenberger 2008, 178). As discussed shortly, the ITF was hesitant to support the Liverpool dockers' campaign without TGWU leaders' full approval.

EXPLAINING TGWU LEADERS' LACK OF SUPPORT

In assessing the relationship between leaders and rank-and-file members of the TGWU, it is important to distinguish between the unions' top officials, who distanced themselves from the campaign, and the union's shop stewards, who sided with the rank and file and were in fact among those sacked by the company. The shop stewards had been "socialized as activists" during the 1970s and 1980s and remained militant in their approach to management over the years (Castree 2000, 286). In contrast, TGWU leaders were "full-time paid union officials [who] sought to 'modernise' union structures by tearing up the old union rulebooks and imposing much less democratic structures that were firmly under their own control" (Bailey 2006, 238). Given this difference in perspective between the TGWU leadership on one hand and the shop stewards and rank-and-file members on the other, it is not inconceivable that, in the words of activist Greg Dropkin, "utter lack of democracy within the union" was "one key factor in the defeat of the Liverpool dockers" (Dropkin n.d.b).

Still, one should not exaggerate the importance of differing ideological perspectives in explaining TGWU leaders' approach to the Liverpool campaign. The structure of the TGWU is important to consider as well. Unlike the MUA, whose membership consists almost entirely of wharfies, seafarers, and other port-related workers, the TGWU had a more complex membership that included a wider variety of workers in different parts of the transportation sector. The TGWU's structure reflects the fragmentation typical of the British labor movement, which itself "reflects a diverse history of organising efforts and internecine struggles" (Cumbers 2004, 838).

Consequently, dockers were a small (though by no means insignificant) proportion of the union's membership. TGWU leaders could thus argue that they had to consider the interests of tugboat operators, clerical workers, truck drivers, and others as well.

According to TGWU general secretary Bill Morris, "There was no support for solidarity action whatsoever within the T&G [TGWU]." As evidence, Morris pointed out that "over 800 T&G members employed by Mersey Docks, workmates of those dismissed, continued working normally throughout the dispute, which was called without their involvement. I have as much responsibility to them as to the dismissed [dockers]" (Morris, 1998b). Other TGWU members and labor activists disputed these claims, arguing that many of the union's members in fact offered the dockers their direct help. Nevertheless, the union's leaders had another reason to distance themselves from the campaign: picketing the Liverpool port was illegal. Direct support for campaign actions against MDHC from the TGWU leadership therefore would have risked serious legal repercussions. According to campaign participants, however, TGWU leaders could have provided several indirect forms of assistance as long as they steered clear of officially endorsing illegal secondary boycott action (Castree 2000, 281).

Moreover, even if UK law prevented TGWU leaders from calling for national industrial action, it is not clear that helping the dockers obtain transnational support through the ITF would have put the union in as precarious a position as its officials suggested. The only evidence of impending legal danger that Morris pointed to concerned an attempt by the shipping company ACL to take legal action against the Liverpool dockers in December 1995 and an attempt by MDHC to sue shop stewards in US courts in early 1996. In the ACL case, the target was the dockers themselves, not the TGWU, and the legal actions were dropped in favor of negotiations. The MDHC case "was thrown out by the National Labour Relations Board, which was astounded that a UK company would attempt to use the US courts against a UK organisation" (Dropkin n.d.b).

Finally, TGWU leaders believed that the shop stewards and rank-and-file dockers were attempting to undermine their authority through the creation of an organization outside official union structures. The IDC was formed during the dispute by the Liverpool dockers and their allies in Canada, Denmark, France, Germany, Italy, Spain, Sweden, and the United States in order to enhance international solidarity and help reinstate the fired workers "with dignity," according to an open letter from IDC founders to the TGWU general secretary. A fax leaked to Liverpool shop stewards from within the ITF confirmed that leaders of both the TGWU and the ITF were disturbed by the creation of the IDC and revealed plans for a meeting between Morris and ITF general secretary David Cockroft to discuss the "final offer" they were going to give the shop stewards.

CUTTING OFF THE ITF

The ITF's refusal to help the Liverpool dockers out of disdain for the IDC is ironic since "the ITF's inertia had caused the birth of the IDC" in the first place (Erem and Durrenberger 2008, 22). It was not just the threat of the IDC undermining its authority that kept the ITF from assisting the dockers, however. Lack of official recognition by TGWU's leadership made the campaign difficult to support in the eyes of the ITF leaders and many of its affiliates.

Like all global unions, the ITF relies on its affiliates for funding and legitimacy. The TGWU was the largest affiliate in the ITF at the time of the Liverpool dispute. According to campaign supporters, the British union used its clout within the ITF to reverse the global union's initial support for the Liverpool campaign. An ILWU official expressed this view: "The Liverpool dockers had a militant strategy, traveling the world and raising money and awareness. If they would have gotten help from their own union, they'd have gotten help from the ITF. Bill Morris was head of the T&G, and he did not help at all. I don't know what his thinking was" (personal interview, August 18, 2010).

The ITF did publicly support the first international day of action organized by the dockers' grassroots TLA. ITF general secretary David Cockroft even stressed the need to harness the TLA's power. As the January 20 actions unfolded across the continents, however, it became clear that the ITF had no control over the actions taken by the hundreds of stevedores and seafarers who participated. This lack of control generated anxiety among ITF officials since, according to campaign activist Chris Bailey, they "wanted to give the appearance of being in charge of events, but the information channels were bypassing them completely" (Bailey 2006, 234). Cockroft also sought to have the ITF support the second day of action, but "the TGWU vetoed this and insisted that the ITF should not support the action" (Bailey 2006, 235).

As the Liverpool campaign progressed, ITF officials grew increasingly contemptuous of the grassroots TLA. ITF communications director Richard Flint derided the TLA as "disorganized and foolish" and consisting of "trade union tourists in every sense of the word." He also suggested that transnationalism should be left to "people who know what they are doing." Flint added, "This does not mean that we do not 'really support' the Liverpool dockers. It just means that as trade unionists we are seeking a trade union response. . . . Uncoordinated, independent action can all too easily undermine real trade union work. Unfortunately, too many people are romantically attached to the concept of rank and file purity and they automatically assume that all trade union leaders and all trade union internationals are run by heartless right-wing bureaucrats intend [*sic*] on selling out the workers at every junction. The world just is not like that and all generalisations are false. There are bad bureaucrats and heroic rank and file workers and the opposite exists as well" (Flint, n.d.).

Not every ITF official was quite as dismissive or derisive. In interviews ITF representatives explained that the organization was split over whether and how to support the Liverpool dockers. As an assistant secretary for the ITF Dockers' Section explained, "Every GUF has to deal with its own internal politics as well as managing interunion relationships and strategizing versus the company. So something like Liverpool becomes very complicated" (personal interview, November 23, 2009). Complications deepened when officials from many of the ITF's affiliate unions declared their personal support for the Liverpool dockers and expressed disappointment at the ITF's lack of support.

Overall, the Liverpool dockers and their transnational allies felt "stonewalled by the ITF" (Erem and Durrenberger 2008, 83). Had TGWU leaders authorized the ITF to assist the Liverpool dockers, their campaign might have concluded with more positive results. Instead, TGWU officials actively discouraged the ITF from providing support, and there is evidence that the absence of ITF support contributed to the Liverpool campaign's failure.

DIMINISHED STRUCTURAL POWER

On January 23, 1996, ITF affiliates received a circular from the secretary of the ITF Dockers' Section, Kees Marges, with the following message: "ITF affiliates must await the signal of the ITF before organising any solidarity action. *Do not intervene* against a boat which has loaded or unloaded cargo in the Port of Liverpool without having previously contacted the ITF Secretariat."[10] The message was a clear attempt to break the solidarity of the Liverpool TLA.

Over the next several months, ITF officials continued to dissuade their affiliates from contributing to the campaign. In August 1996, for example, ITF general secretary David Cockroft sent faxes to specific stevedoring unions in Europe, insisting they refrain from participating in the Liverpool TLA's upcoming international conference. Consequently, dockers in Belgium and the Netherlands withdrew their delegations from the conference.

Jack Heyman, who worked for both the ILWU and the ITF, vented his frustrations with the ITF leadership in an open letter to Flint, dated October 23, 1996. In the letter Heyman explained how Marges had ordered him not to attend the International Dockers Conference in Liverpool in February:

> The day before I was to fly to Liverpool, Kees Marges, who'd not been able to reach me by fax, insisted in a telephone conversation that I not attend the International Dockers Conference in Liverpool. He stated that 1) the strike was illegal and unofficial, not having been endorsed by the TGWU 2) the TGWU, an ITF affiliate, was not requesting support and the ITF was adhering to that request 3) the dockers couldn't win. After I refused his orders, he stated the ITF couldn't stop me but that I shouldn't mention ITF at the Conference or to the media. In order that we wouldn't "mix our banners" since the ILWU was supporting the dockers and the ITF was not, it was decided to take me off the ITF payroll . . . [which] was a political not a financial decision. (Heyman 1996)

Heyman attended the conference in Liverpool as an ILWU representative. He also resigned from his position as an ITF inspector.

Even more damaging to the Liverpool campaign than the ITF's effort to dissuade its own members from participating in it was the ITF's refusal to provide any sort of logistical support. As Castree (2000) argued, one major disadvantage of a grassroots TLA, as opposed to one coordinated through a global union or other established organization, is that its actions tend to be sporadic and unsystematic. Although the Liverpool TLA appeared to cause financial damage to MDHC, closer examination reveals that the damage was only temporary and did not threaten MDHC's core, long-term interests.

Without the ITF's logistical support, the TLA could not sustain its campaign. Appearances can be deceiving. MDHC did suffer some short-term profit losses due to the TLA's campaign actions. Yet throughout the dispute, most companies using MDHC facilities, including the two largest, ACL and CAST, operated without disruption for months at a time (Nolan 1996). ACL, which cut ties with MDHC in June 1996, began using MDHC's Liverpool port again just one month later.

Part of the problem was that several different shipping companies use the port of Liverpool. Mapping out each shipping route and optimizing TLA responses at key pressure points would have required the tools, knowledge, and expertise of ITF officials and staff. Even if the Liverpool TLA had managed to fully coordinate its transnational campaign, actions on such a large scale could not have been sustained over time without a substantial increase in funding—something to which the ITF, the wealthiest global union in the world, could have contributed. Instead, the Liverpool dockers faced serious financial problems, which limited their exercise of structural power.

In sum, the Liverpool TLA struggled to exercise structural power consistently enough to threaten MDHC's core interests. The ITF gave the campaign neither its stamp of approval nor logistical or financial resources. As an ITF coordinator put it, "Liverpool was a failure nationally and institutionally. There was no international focus because there was no ITF backing" (personal interview, November 3, 2011). And there was no ITF backing, one might add, because there was no backing from the leadership of the TGWU.

BACKDOOR NEGOTIATIONS

As the Liverpool campaign lost steam, TGWU and MDHC set out to negotiate a "final deal" to offer to hundreds of the sacked dockers. In reality MDHC had already offered a few "final" deals during the dispute in hopes of restoring the port to picket-free normality. The rank-and-file workers consistently rejected those offers because the union-employer negotiations had involved none of the union's shop stewards. Jimmy Nolan, president of the shop stewards committee, explained that the stewards and the rank and file had "a feeling that MDHC [were] not honourable in their commitment to reach a settlement and [were] more intent on using the negotiations as a cosmetic exercise to appease the international employers' associations and the big shipping consortiums" (Nolan 1996). In an essay dated September 20, 1996, Dave Graham of the Dockers Support Group in Liverpool added his perspective: "The only 'negotiations' going on are those sponsored by Bill Morris and the T&G national and local officials, ably abetted by the ITF, who have made it quite plain that a 'compromise' must be found over the heads of the dockers. And obviously not in the interests of the dockers but because Morris and Co. have been visibly shaken by the dockers' international campaign and the open discussion on five continents of the idea of forming a new international dockers union" (Graham 1996).

In early 1998 TGWU's leadership, under increasing pressure from MDHC, adopted a more aggressive approach to ending the dispute. According to shop stewards involved in the final negotiations, TGWU officials blackmailed the stewards into accepting the company's final offer by threatening to cut off contributions to the dockers' hardship fund, withhold redundancy payments, and revoke older dockers' rights to their own pensions, earned after a lifetime of labor on the docks (Bailey 2006, 237; Carter et al. 2003, 293). Although TGWU officials deny this version of events, the results of those final, backdoor negotiations, which were never made public, indisputably led to the end of the Liverpool campaign.

On January 26, 1998, the union's shop stewards announced the official end of the dispute. To the dismay of rank-and-file campaigners, the stewards emphasized that continuing the campaign would be impossible but did not fully explain why that was (Bailey 2006, 237). Picketers dispersed, websites disappeared, and the dockers were left to face their fate.

THE OUTCOME: THE LIVERPOOL CAMPAIGN
CONCLUDES UNSUCCESSFULLY

The deal ultimately accepted by the Liverpool dockers did not differ substantially from MDHC's earlier offers and did little to ameliorate the financial pain the sacked dockers incurred over twenty-eight months of unemployment. Around 350 of the dockers received a redundancy payment of up to £28,000 per worker (Nolan 1996). Much of that money, however, went directly toward the repayment of debts, which averaged £20,000 per person (Carter et al. 2003, 294). Some older dockers simply retired and collected their pensions. Over 100 workers, including most of those who had been employed by Torside, received nothing at all.

Those unable to retire either accepted jobs with long hours at very low pay or suffered from severe, long-term unemployment, exacerbated by being blacklisted in a city that at the time had an unemployment rate of 25 to 30 percent (Bacon 1998a; ILWU official, personal interview, August 18, 2010). Other losses could hardly be quantified. "Tragically, four dockers died during the course of our struggle . . . as a direct result of the stress created by such a long and bitter struggle," explained Nolan in an open letter to the TLA (Nolan 1996).

Most agree that the Liverpool campaign was a failure. Many point out, however, that the TLA forged new ties among dockworkers worldwide, ultimately strengthening stevedores' and seafarers' international solidarity for years to come. Former Liverpool docker Terry Teague put it simply: "This is without a doubt the greatest legacy to come out of the Liverpool dockworkers—twenty-one countries, thirty-five unions, 60,000 members" (quoted in Erem and Durrenberger 2008, 177).

MUA, Here to Stay: How Intraunion Coordination Led to Partial Success

Mere months after the Liverpool campaign ended, the MUA led its rank-and-file members to victory against Patrick. "We all learned from Liverpool," remarked MUA general secretary Paddy Crumlin at an event commemorating the tenth anniversary of the Liverpool dockers' strike. "We need a multifaceted strategy. . . . You've got to have a legal strategy so that you don't get bankrupted; you got to have an industrial strategy so you're prepared to break laws; and you've got to have a community and media strategy so you don't separate yourself from your community" (quoted in Erem and Durrenberger 2008, 178). In a personal interview (May 5, 2010), an MUA official elaborated on additional lessons learned: "Now we know that we need an integrated and decentralized process and mechanisms that deliver communication and education, and a process to ensure the smooth delivery of trade union capacity. We know that funding is a constant challenge. We know the flaws in GUFs still remain. But we also know we need to change that."

When the Australian waterfront conflict broke out in 1998, MUA leaders translated their new knowledge into effective strategizing. A crucial part of that process involved maintaining a close and positive relationship with the union rank and file, particularly the 1,400 wharfies who had just lost their jobs. Strong intraunion coordination, in turn, enabled the MUA and its allies to exercise structural power far more effectively than the Liverpool dockers had.

The MUA's strong leadership-membership ties were not entirely the product of lessons learned from Liverpool. The size and structure of the MUA helped as well. Unlike the large and occupationally diverse TGWU, the MUA comprised mainly wharfies and seafarers and had at its founding in 1993 only ten thousand members. MUA members were also concentrated in five key ports and a handful of major coastal cities such as Melbourne, Sydney, and Fremantle, which helped generate solidarity within the union (McConville 2000, 395–96).

Another reason MUA leaders so strongly supported the sacked Patrick wharfies was the fact that Patrick's attack had implications beyond the waterfront. Were labor to lose the Australian waterfront conflict, it would mean the weakening of union rights across the country. "The MUA was smart enough to realize this. Clearly, [Patrick and the Howard government] were not just fighting the MUA," noted an ILWU official (personal interview, August 18, 2010). This realization also made it easy for MUA leaders to convince the ACTU that the MUA could be the first domino to fall in a series of antiunion actions that would ultimately undermine the Australian labor movement. Securing ACTU's assistance, along with that of the ITF, turned out to be an important step toward the MUA's successful exercise of power.

VITAL ASSISTANCE: MUA LEADERS, THE ACTU, AND THE ITF

In order to exercise structural power effectively—that is, compel Patrick to do something the company otherwise would not have done—the MUA had to mobilize local union members, community activists, and transnational allies willing to take direct action. At the same time, to avoid the mistakes made in the Liverpool campaign, the MUA had to steer clear of any industrial action deemed illegal under the draconian Workplace Relations Act. MUA officials thus had to convince the sacked wharfies and other campaign supporters to trust the union leadership's strategic vision.

It was a hard sell at first. Many rank-and-file wharfies continued to insist on traditional industrial action. ACTU officials, with whom MUA leaders worked closely, instead encouraged restraint. While some approved of the

ACTU's message of moderation, others viewed the peak association's rhetoric more cynically. Representing the latter view, activist Tom Bramble complained that, "in the first couple of weeks after the mass sackings, all the talk from ACTU president Jennie George was of the need for financial support for the wharfies and their families. On no account should there be hasty action, or the Government given an excuse to take legal action against the union federation, or there be 'inconvenience' to the Australian community (Bramble 1998, 11). Despite some rank-and-file resistance, ACTU and MUA leaders eventually persuaded the majority of the union's members that the most effective way to fight Patrick was with "a combination of international embargo, local community action and spatially perceptive union thinking" (Rainnie, Herod, and McGrath-Champ 2007, 113) rather than with a national strike or similar action.

With both the leadership and membership agreeing to the same strategic plan, the MUA as a whole was able to implement its tactics smoothly. Locally, this entailed the transformation of traditional picketing into peaceful, community-wide assemblies that boosted the wharfies' public approval ratings and the workers' morale. More importantly, the local protests helped channel campaign supporters' energy into physical disruptions of Patrick's operations. For its part, ACTU defied a court injunction in order to sanction the protests officially and join the thousands-strong picket line at East Swanson Dock in Melbourne (Bramble 1998, 17).

Strong intraunion coordination was equally essential for exercising structural power on the international scale. Because the MUA had a strategy that was not only backed by the majority of union members but also officially endorsed by union leaders, it was relatively easy for the MUA to secure support from the ITF. The ITF, in turn, provided essential assistance in the Patrick campaign both directly and indirectly. "Australia is small, but the ITF helps us punch above our weight internationally with employers," explained a Sydney-based ITF campaign coordinator (personal interview, March 31, 2010).

As detailed earlier, the ITF helped directly by halting Patrick's attempt to train nonunion replacement workers in Dubai. The ITF also supplied the MUA and its transnational allies with information about Patrick's operations and frequent updates on the campaign as a whole. Most importantly, however, the ITF gave logistical support to facilitate the global no-loads and go-slows. "When their ships came in, the ITF made sure everyone knew what the story was, what to do. They were effective with getting the word out," recalled an MUA branch secretary (personal interview, March 10, 2010). "The international component was huge, crucial," emphasized an ILWU official. "MUA was not going to fail because everybody was engaged and on point" (personal interview, August 18, 2010). An ITF coordinator elaborated on the global union's role in the Patrick campaign: "We told our [affiliates] to urgently contact shipping lines and tell them they are in solidarity with the MUA. The MUA used the ITF to connect the dots, to have coverage of the dispute. At one point union leaders were locked out because of a court injunction and not allowed to talk to their members, so instead they went through the ITF. The MUA consolidated the union and recognized that the ITF has a big role to play. Hooking in with the ITF, and with the ILWU and with Europe, helped the wharfies get attention. Otherwise, this is a small group in Australia, a small country way out of the way" (personal interview, March 31, 2010). In addition to the physical actions carried out on the international scale, the mere threat of further ITF interventions during the dispute helped move Patrick and the government toward settling the conflict. Had the dispute lasted longer, the ITF was prepared to organize an international boycott of Australian shipping. Patrick thus conceded in part because the balance of power and the TLA's potential became clear.

In short, just as the ACTU helped the wharfies exercise structural power on the local scale, the ITF helped them exercise structural power on the international scale. Crucially, the "strategic paralysing of the Patrick business—both internationally through the ITF and through the pickets in key states—circumvented the risky process of generalising the dispute through sympathy strikes" (Wilson 1998, 33). Had the MUA's leaders and rank and file clashed over campaign strategy, however, it is doubtful that the wharfies would have had either the ACTU's or the ITF's full support. Intraunion coordination thus helped the MUA secure assistance from other organizations, which in turn helped implement the TLA's power strategy.

SELECTIVE IMPLEMENTATION AND THE LIMITS OF THE MUA'S
ASSOCIATIONAL POWER

Years after its conclusion, union officials and members who were involved in the Patrick conflict overwhelmingly attribute the wharfies' victory to the combination of community pickets and transnational action. "We couldn't have survived without community engagement and international solidarity," asserted an MUA official (personal interview, May 5, 2010). An ILWU official echoed those sentiments: "The MUA won because they were militant enough and used everything at their disposal, especially the local and international labor community" (personal interview, August 18, 2010). An ACTU organizer agreed that "the Patrick dispute was mainly won by community mobilization, combined with internationalism" (personal interview, May 10, 2010).

Though few challenge the fact that local community members and the TLA contributed greatly to the implementation of the MUA's power strategy, some question whether the specific strategy MUA leaders used precluded a fuller exercise of structural power. Critics charge that MUA leaders did not truly see eye to eye with rank-and-file members, many of whom envisioned a more ambitious, proactive campaign despite their acceptance of MUA leaders' and ACTU officials' restraint-based approach. While far stronger than the relationship between TGWU leaders and the rank-and-file dockers in the Liverpool case, leadership-membership ties within the MUA were not without their complications.

The fundamental point of contention was over whether wharfies across Australia should engage in more direct, though possibly illegal, industrial action. Part of the problem with the Patrick campaign was that the local pickets often failed to prevent nonunion replacement workers from entering the wharves. According to activist Tom Bramble, "trucks moved freely in and out of the wharves in Brisbane," and "in all ports, even Melbourne, Fremantle and Sydney, the MUA decided to allow scabs to enter Patrick's premises to carry out their work" (Bramble 1998, 23, 25).

Bob Carnegie, an organizer for the MUA South Queensland branch, recalled how divided his union was over whether to call for a boycott of the *Australian Endeavour*, a container ship loaded by nonunion labor at one of Patrick's terminals in Sydney. MUA leaders decided against a boycott despite the fact that letting the ship sail would weaken the union's bargaining power. According to Carnegie, this decision

> created a great deal of confusion internationally and it also showed the limitations of the union strategy. The "Australian Endeavor" is a modern container ship on the Japan-Korea-Australia run. It has a full Australian crew with the MUA covering the ratings. After the vessel was discharged and

loaded by scabs it went to Japan's largest port, Yokohama, and after a small protest Japanese Dockers serviced it. The hoped-for supportive action did not occur. There is no doubt the sight of MUA members sailing on a ship loaded with scab cargo would have provided a convenient excuse to take only very limited protest action. By limiting such an enormous dispute such as this to just Patrick's, the union's national leadership was ensuring the dispute's limited outcome. (Carnegie 2000)

Had the MUA's leaders authorized a more aggressive approach, including the physical prevention of nonunion workers from entering local docks, as well as additional international boycotts of ships loaded by nonunion labor, Patrick might have settled on terms more favorable to the union. According to more militant members of the MUA, union leaders instead adopted a top-down approach to decision-making and authorized only a selective implementation of their power strategy out of fear that too much rank-and-file activism would undermine the disciplined tactics promoted by the ACTU. This does not mean that the Patrick campaign lacked intraunion coordination. MUA leaders and members coordinated with each other rather effectively in carrying out campaign tactics. The point, rather, is that decision-making was not always democratic, and John Coombs, then general secretary of the MUA, was accused at times of centralizing control of the campaign to himself and a small handful of national MUA leaders.

MUA leaders rationalized their top-down decision-making by arguing that any ill-conceived, illegal action on the part of the wharfies would have jeopardized their case in the courts. Union leaders also justified their limit on strikes and boycotts by pointing out that "the Howard government had been hoping for, and developing plans against, a general strike on the waterfront and beyond"; hence, more militant union action would have been "disastrous" for the campaign (Svensen 1998, 9). "We weren't about to walk into their bear traps," as one official put it (ITF coordinator, personal interview, November 3, 2011).

Rank-and-file dissidents contend that union leaders should have worried less about the legal system and more about the long-term implications of "playing it safe." Even after the High Court upheld the Federal Court's interim injunction against the mass sackings—effectively opening the door to the wharfies' return to work in early May—a seven-week period followed in which the wharfies worked without pay while MUA leaders negotiated a settlement with Patrick. With the wharfies back to work, community pickets dispersed, transnational allies backed down, and the MUA lost its "trump card" of "containers stacked high on the wharves" while still in the negotiation process. "Once the workers were reinstated pending a final settlement and the backlog of containers was shifted, this card was gone" (Bramble 1998, 27).[11]

THE OUTCOME: THE PATRICK CAMPAIGN CONCLUDES SUCCESSFULLY

In late June 1998, Patrick Stevedores and the national leadership of the MUA revealed the terms of their compromise in the form of a twelve-page memorandum of agreement. After eight hours of internal debate, the majority of MUA members voted in favor of the final deal, though more than a quarter of the union's Melbourne membership rejected it. With all outstanding issues resolved by August 1998, the Australian waterfront conflict was officially over.

The compromise resulted in a mix of material and capacity-related gains and losses for the MUA. The most important material gain was the reinstatement of 687 MUA wharfies who composed Patrick's core workforce. Those not reinstated had the option to apply for an additional two hundred unionized jobs in cleaning, maintenance, and security at Patrick's terminals. The wharfies also received full back pay, including all wages lost since the dispute began on April 7 (Svensen 1998, 9; Hannan and Mitchell 1998). Additionally, workers won a 12 percent higher base wage and the opportunity to earn productivity bonuses for achieving at least twenty crane lifts per hour (McConville 2000, 402; Svensen 1998, 11). Both parties also agreed to drop all legal action against each other, and Patrick paid for the MUA's legal costs, amounting to millions of dollars (Hannan and Mitchell 1998).

Even more significant than these material gains were the MUA's gains in capacity. Since Patrick agreed to remain a closed-shop operation, the MUA regained its control of the waterfront. "Patrick's was a major victory because, at the end of the dispute, the docks were still 100 percent unionized. To me, that's the real victory of the MUA dispute. They're still strongly unionized," remarked an ACTU organizer (personal interview, May 10, 2010). The four nonunion labor-hire companies disappeared, along with the 370 nonunion workers who had replaced the MUA wharfies during the dispute, thus reestablishing the direct relationship between Patrick and the union (Bramble 1998, 53).

Battling Patrick also enhanced the MUA's internal cohesion and learning capabilities. "In a way, we are fortunate to have had such a hard fight. It rehabilitated our union," remarked an MUA official (personal interview, May 5, 2010). Others agreed that "the thing that really consolidated the MUA was Patrick and John Howard. It helped us a hell of a lot. If we had lost, the union movement would have crumbled" (ITF coordinator, personal interview, March 31, 2010). Victory reinvigorated the rest of the Australian labor movement as well and "was thus historic in renewing a tradition of solidarity and communal support, one that could be opposed successfully to the ideology and practices of neoliberalism" (McConville 2000, 394). Although workplace restructuring would continue into the future, employers now knew that no major reforms would pass without the unions' approval.

On balance, the Patrick campaign was mainly a success for the workers involved. Yet the material and capacity gains just described came at a cost. Seven hundred wharfies lost their jobs. Though 217 of those redundancies had been conceded before the dispute, and most workers received monetary compensation for their loss, the settlement effectively halved the Patrick workforce. Workers suffered additional material losses with the reduction of overtime rates, an increased pace of work, and sweeping casualization measures. The new rules designated two-thirds of MUA members as casuals who could be called to work twenty-four hours a day, 365 days a year, for shifts as short as two hours. Overtime rates no longer applied to twelve-hour shifts, weekend work became compulsory, and it was not unusual for wharfies to work up to fifteen midnight shifts in a row. Management control over rostering (worker allocation) was another significant item conceded by the MUA.

When asked who won the Australian waterfront conflict, John Coombs, MUA national secretary during the dispute, stated that his union "probably finished up just in front" (quoted in Svensen 1998, 9). MUA leaders and members both acknowledge that the final deal hardly left the wharfies unscathed; nonetheless, union rights prevailed. Moreover, few view the outcome for the Howard government as anything but a decisive defeat. The government failed in its goals to deunionize the waterfront, intimidate the broader labor movement, and win over public opinion. In the end the MUA's campaign forced Patrick and Howard into an embarrassing retreat and bolstered the position of trade unions throughout Australia. The MUA secured its position at the bargaining table for the long term, and its capacity remains intact.

Conclusion: All Transnationalism Is Local

In examining the Liverpool dockers' dispute and the Australian waterfront conflict—both multiscalar campaigns characterized by similar levels of interunion coordination and the exercise of structural power on the local and international scale—I sought to uncover the reasons for the former's failure and the latter's partial success. I argue that different levels of intraunion coordination explain the campaigns' different outcomes. A major disjuncture between the Liverpool dockers and the leadership of the TGWU harmed the dockers' ability to carry out campaign tactics, despite their best efforts to cope without assistance from either TGWU officials or the ITF. In contrast, MUA officials maintained relatively strong ties with the rank-and-file wharfies. Despite criticism of MUA leaders' tendency to centralize decision-making, evidence suggests that strong intraunion coordination overall facilitated the exercise of structural power in the Patrick case.

There is therefore evidence that intraunion coordination is a necessary condition for a TLA campaign to succeed. In other words, workers can only exercise power on the international scale if they have cohesion within their own organizations at individual sites of action—that is, on or near specific streets, city blocks, docks, ships, and so on. Intraunion coordination is especially indispensable in the locality in which a campaign originates because power strategy tends to be determined by the union closest to the conflict. An enduring divide between a union's leaders and members at the original site of conflict can disrupt the planning and implementation of campaign strategy. Conversely, internal cohesion helps union members and leaders effectively exercise power. All transnational campaigns thus depend crucially on local-level union capacity.

Chapter 3

SERVICE-SECTOR SOLIDARITY

Coordinating the Tesco and G4S Campaigns

Service industries are being globalized so that a few transnational corporations determine standards around the world both for service quality and for
treatment of employees. We have to make sure that globalization benefits
working people and the public interest, and not just global corporations.

—PHILIP JENNINGS, GENERAL SECRETARY, UNI GLOBAL UNION[1]

While the right to form unions and bargain collectively exists throughout all of the economically advanced democracies, the United States remains
an outlier for the enormity of obstacles facing American workers attempting to exercise this right. Political opposition to union-friendly legislation,
broad cultural antipathy toward unions, and employers' widespread use of
threats, dismissals, and antiunion consulting firms to dissuade workers from
voting pro-union in secret-ballot elections have made unionization far more
difficult in the United States than in other OECD countries (Godard 2009;
Bronfenbrenner 2009; Logan 2006; Bronfenbrenner and Hickey 2004). Union
organizing is particularly problematic in the low-wage private service sector, characterized by part-time employment, temporary contracts, erratic
hours, and irregular shifts. Hence, although strategies for "union revitalization" dominated the agenda of American labor leaders in the early and mid-
2000s (Turner 2005; Hurd, Milkman, and Turner 2003; Voss and Sherman
2000), US unionization rates continue to decline.

Despite these difficulties, two US unions, UFCW and SEIU, attempted in the mid-2000s to organize workers employed at US-based subsidiaries of two transnational service-sector corporations. Starting in 2007, UFCW sought to organize employees at Fresh & Easy, a grocery store chain owned by Tesco, the third-largest retailer of groceries and general merchandise in the world. Meanwhile, since 2003, SEIU had been attempting to organize security guards employed by Wackenhut, a subsidiary of G4S, the world's largest private security services provider. In neither case did the union achieve its goal—at least initially.

Lacking traction on the national level, UFCW and SEIU both transformed their local organizing efforts into broader transnational campaigns aimed at bringing Tesco and G4S to the bargaining table. In 2008, with the help of global union UNI Commerce,[2] UFCW spearheaded a TLA that came to encompass workers in South Korea, Thailand, Turkey, Poland, Hungary, and Malaysia. In 2006, SEIU, likewise launched a TLA, aided by UNI Property Services.[3] The TLA involved workers in Indonesia, India, Malawi, Mozambique, South Africa, and Uganda.

The Tesco Global Union Alliance failed to engage corporate leaders. From the time Tesco first announced its plans to enter the US market in 2006 through the sell-off of its Fresh & Easy stores in 2013, Tesco repeatedly rejected—and then outright ignored—UFCW's request for a meeting with high-level managers to discuss union recognition and social partnership. By early 2010 UFCW had withdrawn from the TLA it had created, and the campaign failed. In contrast, the Alliance for Justice at G4S was a success: SEIU achieved its original goal of unionizing Wackenhut security guards. More significantly, the company and the TLA signed a GFA, which sets out provisions for dispute resolution, regular meetings between top management and union officials, and explicit recognition by G4S of workers' rights to freedom of association and collective bargaining. Since its signing in December 2008, the GFA has helped G4S workers in several countries in Africa and Asia achieve union recognition, overtime pay, holiday bonuses, and other measurable gains (McCallum 2013, 2011).

Outcomes aside, the Tesco and G4S TLAs shared several similarities: Both entailed cooperative efforts led by American trade unions representing service-sector employees of UK-based transnational corporations, each with a large, well-established, and expanding global presence. Both alliances also formed initially as reactions to these employers' opposition to unionization in their US operations before expanding into full-scale TLA campaigns for labor rights in various developing countries. These cases' divergent outcomes, despite such strong similarities, suggest a puzzle worth greater attention.

In this chapter I explain why the UFCW-led Tesco alliance faltered while the SEIU-led G4S alliance achieved its goals. A lack of interunion coordination between UFCW in the United States and USDAW, Tesco's home union in the United Kingdom, prevented the Tesco Global Union Alliance from effectively exercising institutional power, leading to the breakdown of the campaign. In contrast, the G4S campaign succeeded precisely because SEIU and G4S's home union, GMB, overcame the seemingly intractable conflict between them. This interunion coordination enhanced the legitimacy of the Alliance for Justice at G4S in the eyes of developing-country unions, which would not have otherwise supported SEIU's efforts. Moreover, interunion coordination was crucial for leveraging GMB's good relationship with G4S to get the company to sign the GFA.

Lost in the Supermarket: Origins of the Tesco Dispute

In November 2007 Tesco launched a new chain of small-format supermarkets called Fresh & Easy Neighborhood Markets in the western United States, specifically Southern California, Nevada, and Arizona. Although Tesco earned over half of its revenues in its home country, the United Kingdom, the company had been developing a track record of success in foreign markets, notably Malaysia, South Korea, and Thailand. Fresh & Easy marked Tesco's first attempt to break into the US market, with plans to open three hundred Fresh & Easy stores by 2012. In its first year, Fresh & Easy created 2,500 jobs.

Well before the first Fresh & Easy opened its doors, UFCW sought to organize the stores' employees. Between early 2006 and mid-2007, UFCW president Joe Hansen and vice president Rick Icaza made five formal attempts to speak with Tesco corporate leaders about cooperating with managers to unionize the soon-to-be-formed Fresh & Easy workforce. Their letters to Tesco CEO Terry Leahy and Fresh & Easy CEO Tim Mason were all but ignored, however, as the company dismissed the union's request for a meeting as premature. Yet even after Fresh & Easy stores began to operate, Tesco still refused to meet with UFCW. In a letter dated December 2006, UFCW warned Leahy that if the company continued to ignore their request for a meeting, "we will start a drive [to] let the public know they are not going union, and we will do what we can to stop them from developing stores here" (*Supermarket News* 2007a.)

True to their word, UFCW representatives set up informational pickets outside Fresh & Easy stores, leafleted neighborhoods, mass-mailed flyers, distributed brochures at store grand openings, and held rallies outside hotels where Tesco investors were meeting throughout 2007 and early 2008. Protesting the "British invasion" of Tesco, UFCW disseminated its message through local media in Southern California and the Phoenix and Las Vegas metropolitan areas. UFCW Local 135 president Mickey Kasparian called Tesco "the Wal-Mart of the United Kingdom" and warned that the company intended "to saturate the marketplace and use their monopoly power to drive small- and medium-sized stores out of business, much like Wal-Mart does. All their profits will go to the U.K., while all losses will be experienced by local business owners and workers" (*Supermarket News* 2007b). Using glossy, full-color brochures and a website, freshandeasyfacts.com,[4] UFCW publicly attacked everything from Tesco's alleged selling of liquor to minors (Zwiebach 2007b) to the freshness of meat and produce sold in Tesco stores (*Fresh & Easy Buzz* 2008b) to the negative environmental impact of Fresh & Easy's 820,000-square-foot distribution center in Riverside, California. Tesco refuted all accusations, stating that Fresh & Easy follows all US laws.

UFCW continued to apply pressure. As part of a coalition of twenty-five labor, community, environmental, and faith-based organizations called the Alliance for Healthy and Responsible Grocery Stores, the union convinced Senators John Edwards and Barack Obama to write Tesco's corporate heads. Obama's letter, dated November 5, 2007, insists that "only by working with communities can Tesco's Fresh & Easy Markets be the 'good neighbors' they pledge to be" (Zwiebach 2007a). Tesco remained unfazed. In a second letter, dated June 23, 2008, Obama scolded Leahy for his silence. "Eight months after my first letter, Fresh & Easy has still not engaged positively with its stakeholders and refuses to meet the UFCW to discuss the principles of partnership," Obama wrote. "I strongly request you to revisit that decision . . . and advise your executives at Fresh & Easy to meet with the UFCW" (Finch 2008). Tesco responded briefly: "We strongly believe union membership is a matter of individual choice, and if our people want to join a union, then they can and will. All the signs so far are that there is little interest in doing so" (Zwiebach 2008).

Enter the Tesco Global Union Alliance

UFCW's local tactics were not working. As one UFCW organizer admitted, these early attacks on Fresh & Easy were "the wrong strategy, telling customers to not patronize the store because of personal concern to health and things like that. If you do that, then the employer will say to the workers, this union is driving away customers. . . . But really, neutrality of the employer is our first priority" (personal interview, January 23, 2009). What UFCW needed was noninterference; tarnishing Tesco's reputation would only anger and alienate managers at home and corporate leaders abroad. The other problem with UFCW's early tactics was the small size of Fresh & Easy relative to Tesco's other operations. "Even if we harm [Tesco's] US business, it's insufficient to get their attention financially," explained a UFCW official, "because half of their revenues are coming out of the UK. US operations are tiny. So we need to bring the fight to the company in a bigger way" (personal interview, December 11, 2008). Another UFCW official concurred: "Tesco has 107 stores. It's a global company worth $108 billion. It's not a massive impact if we just hit Tesco in the US. . . . Tesco is just a blip here. So instead, we have an international strategy for UFCW because it is a necessity. Without the transnational dimension, we would have no power [with respect to Tesco]" (personal interview, January 13, 2009).

In June 2008, under the aegis of the commerce division of the global union UNI, the Tesco Global Union Alliance made its official debut. Comprising a dozen unions representing Tesco employees in the Czech Republic, Hungary, Ireland, Japan, Malaysia, Poland, Slovakia, South Korea, Turkey, Thailand, the United Kingdom, and the United States, the alliance aimed "to develop constructive labour relations with the company and to become a recognised and constructive social partner with Tesco to promote the wellbeing of the company's workforce" (UNI 2008c).

"We created a Tesco Global Union Alliance in response to a rapidly globalising Tesco, which is now present in many countries," explained UNI deputy general secretary Philip Bowyer. "We think the way forward is a global dialogue. . . . We are seeking local consistency with Tesco's global standards" (Tesco Union Alliance n.d.). Philip Jennings, UNI's general secretary, explained the alliance simply: "Tesco can pretend not to be a global company but we will not pretend that we are not a global union. We will press on with our efforts to build a global dialogue with Tesco" (UNI 2008a).

Caught Off Guard: Origins of the G4S Dispute

Five years before UFCW began battling Fresh & Easy, the 1.5 million member SEIU was in the midst of a struggle to organize workers in another service industry: security. Wackenhut, a provider of contract guards and other security services to corporations and government agencies, became the focus of an SEIU organizing drive not long after the Danish firm Group 4 Falck acquired Wackenhut as a wholly owned subsidiary in 2002. In 2004 Group 4 Falck merged with a British company, Securicor, to become a new UK-based corporation called Group 4 Securicor PLC, the largest private security services company in the world, with Wackenhut[5] now a wholly owned subsidiary of G4S (Parfomak 2004, 6).

As the second-largest private security provider in the United States, Wackenhut was an ideal target for SEIU. Organizing its thirty-five thousand workers would not only boost the union's membership substantially; it would also propel SEIU's national campaign to improve working conditions across the entire security services industry. Nevertheless, the obstacles associated with the industry's high turnover, the National Labor Relations Board election process, and employer opposition prevented SEIU from relying on a straightforward strategy of workplace organizing at Wackenhut. Instead, the union attempted to highlight the benefits of joining SEIU while attacking the company's current practices as shoddy and even harmful to the public. Among other charges, SEIU publicly claimed that poorly trained Wackenhut workers had cut corners on antiterrorism drills, violated weapons inventory and handling policies, and provided lax security at nuclear power plants (Horowitz 2006; *Business Wire* 2006).

The union also attempted to leverage its political connections. In the midst of the Group 4 Falck–Securicor merger, senator and presidential candidate John Kerry wrote a letter to the two companies' chief executives expressing his "great respect and admiration for SEIU, their efforts to improve conditions for workers and their leadership on the issue of private security." In the same letter, dated July 2004, Kerry urged the corporate heads to work "towards the goals of improving private security standards and elevating the working conditions of American security officers" and insisted that G4S will have "responsibility to maintain high standards and respect the rights of its workers" (Townsend 2004). Neither of the two executives made much of the letter.

SEIU persisted. In May 2005, before G4S's annual general meeting (AGM) in London, SEIU published an "alternative annual report" to distribute to leading institutional shareholders.[6] The report continued with the theme of Wackenhut's poor performance, low pay, and inadequate training and suggested that Wackenhut could lose valuable government contracts as a consequence of the way it treats its employees. Wackenhut fought back, issuing a legal proceeding against the union that accused SEIU of circulating unfounded claims about the company. Marc Shapiro, a senior vice president at Wackenhut, refuted claims that the company is antiunion by pointing out that almost 10 percent of Wackenhut's employees already belong to a union, just not SEIU. Nick Buckles, who became G4S's chief executive after the merger, argued that "SEIU is trying to force Wackenhut into a recognition agreement with them. They are trying to put pressure on" (Macalister 2005).

Although SEIU continued its local campaign—conveying additional concerns about the company on a website, eyeonwackenhut.org,[7] and describing Wackenhut as "a vicious anti-union security company" in its 2007 annual report (SEIU 2007, 18)—these public relations tactics were not working. SEIU officials thus sought to switch their campaign's strategic focus.

Enter the Alliance for Justice at G4S

"SEIU could never win in America alone," explained SEIU organizing director Michael Crosby in an organizing workshop.[8] "We had a top-down campaign, attacking the company on infringement of laws, lax security. . . . But it was water off a duck's back. Wackenhut is a tiny part of G4S. Even they were to lose 100% market share, it'd be no big deal. . . . We had to go all over the world." SEIU's Stephen Lerner and Jill Hurst, along with Glenn Adler from the American Federation of Labor and Congress of Industrial Organizations (AFL-CIO), expressed similar sentiments: "We understood that as companies globalized, we could not win better standards for guards through a national campaign alone. Our bargaining power had declined as we became just one market—albeit a large one—in the new parent companies' worldwide operations" (Lerner, Hurst, and Adler 2008, 261).

Comprising unions from twenty countries in Asia, Africa, Europe, North America, and South America, the Alliance for Justice at G4S transformed SEIU's local campaign into a global one. In November 2006 UNI Property Services formally convened the first meeting of the alliance, whose goal was "to ensure that workers in this industry have the opportunity to join strong unions and receive decent treatment, including a living wage and social protection" (Hoffman 2008, 4). The TLA further sought to have UNI sign a GFA with G4S that would formalize the company's commitment to upholding union rights. Still, the original goal of organizing workers at Wackenhut in the United States remained a priority for SEIU.

Case Comparisons: Similarities between the Tesco and G4S Campaigns

The events leading up to the formation of both the Tesco Global Union Alliance and the Alliance for Justice at G4S look remarkably similar: UFCW's early troubles with Fresh & Easy led it to launch a local campaign publicly attacking the retailer's reputation. When those efforts fell flat, the union organized a TLA comprising affiliates of the global union UNI. Likewise, SEIU's lack of traction with Wackenhut prompted the union's corporate blaming and shaming campaign and subsequent refocusing on G4S as a whole through a UNI-backed TLA. In both cases the US-based union wove its original goals into a new, international agenda.

A few differences are immediately apparent. SEIU's initial ambitions were larger, as it sought not only unionization at Wackenhut but also an industry-wide agreement covering pay, conditions, and training. In contrast, UFCW sought simply to unionize Fresh & Easy. Moreover, SEIU's initial campaign was national in scope, while UFCW's early efforts spanned only the US Southwest. Third, SEIU's overall commitment to and experience with transnational campaigning was more fully developed than that of the UFCW. Nevertheless, these differences do not explain why the G4S TLA ultimately prevailed and the Tesco TLA did not. In fact, SEIU's grander goals stacked the odds against it, while UFCW's more modest aims should have been easier to achieve. Additionally, SEIU's extensive experience with transnationalism actually hurt the G4S campaign early on, as GMB and other potential labor allies distrusted SEIU's leadership and perceived the push for transnationalism as one-sided and self-serving. As I show later, it was only after SEIU shifted toward more genuine inclusivity in the G4S campaign that the TLA attained true interunion coordination, without which the workers could never have convinced G4S to come to the bargaining table.[9] Furthermore, UFCW could have attained interunion coordination in the Tesco campaign by continuing to reach out to developing-country unions, a strategy it began to use but later abandoned. In this section I explore other factors that theoretically could have accounted for these two cases' divergent outcomes but are rendered less relevant upon closer examination: intraunion coordination, the TLAs' power strategies, and the interests and strategic responses of each employer.

Intraunion Coordination: Similar Strengths

As I argued in chapter 1, intraunion coordination is a prerequisite for the effective exercise of power in a transnational labor campaign. Weak intraunion coordination caused by unsupportive union officials can cripple an otherwise well-functioning TLA, as the failed Liverpool campaign revealed (see chapter 2). There is no evidence, however, that the Tesco and G4S campaigns' divergent outcomes were due to differences in the lead unions' capacities for collective action. The strength and quality of the leadership-membership relationship did not differ significantly between UFCW and SEIU. In both the Tesco and G4S campaigns, union leaders not only supported but actively promoted transnationalism. UFCW president Joe Hansen is well known for his global union activism and his conviction that "only global solidarity can confront global corporations" (UFCW, n.d.). Between 2003 and 2010, Hansen even served as president of UNI.[10] Andy Stern, SEIU's president from 1996 to 2010, was also renowned for his global union activism. As the force behind SEIU's global organizing program, Stern invested millions of dollars in international organizing activities after centralizing and consolidating SEIU.

Moreover, neither UFCW nor SEIU lacked material resources, another indicator of intraunion coordination. With well over one million members each, both unions had a steady stream of financial resources from membership dues, allowing each to fund organizers who strategized campaign actions, researchers who analyzed corporate vulnerabilities, international flights for officials' face-to-face meetings, and a range of other campaign activities. There is little to suggest that what hindered the Tesco TLA was a lack of intraunion coordination. This variable thus cannot explain why the G4S campaign succeeded and the Tesco campaign did not.

Exercising Power: Similar Strategies

Both labor alliances exercised the same two power types in their transnational campaigns: coalitional power and institutional power. Coalitional power came in the form of protesting at the corporations' AGMs, publishing research reports on the employers' poor labor practices in developing countries, and maintaining a constant media presence. In terms of institutional power, both TLAs attempted to invoke the authority of bodies responsible for promoting workers' rights: the Joint Committee on Human Rights and the Tesco EWC in the Tesco campaign and the ILO and OECD in the G4S campaign.

COALITIONAL POWER IN THE TESCO CAMPAIGN

The Tesco TLA's exercise of coalitional power was informed by UFCW's goal of establishing a partnership with Fresh & Easy similar to the one Tesco shared with its home union in the United Kingdom, USDAW. Signed in 1998, the Tesco-USDAW partnership was the largest private-sector collective bargaining agreement in the United Kingdom and covered 360,000 employees in 2008. In addition to serving "as recognition among senior management that employee involvement and participation in decision-making can contribute to the achievement of strategic goals" (Wilton 2010, 41), the partnership provided for regular, formal meetings between Tesco managers and USDAW officials and gave USDAW direct input on issues ranging from working hours and employee transfers to store temperatures, cashiers' seating options, and the prevention of underage liquor sales (USDAW 2009; UFCW 2008a, 7). The success of this cooperative relationship led one member of Parliament to call Tesco a "hallmark of employee involvement" (Braithwaite

2008). Most significantly, the Tesco-USDAW partnership made union organizing in the United Kingdom virtually effortless. USDAW was involved in all new employee inductions and had the right to hold union meetings on company time for two paid hours per month. New hires received tear-off membership forms in their orientation packets, which greatly simplified the process.

UFCW was in awe of this arrangement. If partnership worked so well in the United Kingdom, why not try it in the United States? This was the logic behind the UFCW-sponsored report released in June 2008 under the title *The Two Faces of Tesco.* Unveiled at a press launch in the United Kingdom, the forty-five-page document expressed UFCW's desire "to build the same constructive partnership that Tesco enjoys in the UK with the shop workers' union Usdaw" (UFCW 2008b). Its main function, however, was to highlight the disparity between conditions at Fresh & Easy in the United States and Tesco stores in the United Kingdom. As an attempt at coalitional power, *Two Faces* aimed at the right targets—namely, British consumers, investors, and politicians who could theoretically use their financial and institutional resources to pressure the company. Whether *Two Faces* actually stirred these groups into action is another question. One problem was that the report did not distinguish clearly between disparities due to differences in Tesco's own policies and those due to differences between the two countries' industrial relations institutions and legal systems. That Tesco's British workforce had written contracts, more annual holidays, and free universal health care— while US workers had no contracts, few days off, and no guaranteed health insurance—had less to do with corporate policy than it did with differences in national institutional contexts. It was therefore easy for Tesco executives to emphasize, quite simply, that Fresh & Easy's labor practices in no way violated US law. Tesco further justified disparities between its home and host country practices by implying that partnership made more sense in the UK context, given that country's stronger legislation in support of union recognition and government advocacy for a partnership approach to employment relations. Conversely, institutional and political support for unions in the United States is weak, and competitiveness considerations often justify a TNC's "lowering itself to US standards" (Wilton 2010, 42).

Undeterred, the Tesco TLA attempted another exercise of coalitional power, focusing on investors. While leveraging the influence of consumers might have been a more direct way to alter the company's behavior, "in retail, the power of the consumer is extremely hard to harness," especially since, in the midst of the global financial crisis, consumers had become more price conscious than ever (UFCW official, personal interview, January 13, 2009). Investors, on the other hand, might be moved by accounts of Tesco's poor labor practices. A UFCW official elaborated: "Tesco espouses to be a good corporate actor, holds itself up to a particular standard. This is how we're going to hold them accountable. We say to the investors that we actually want the company to succeed, but they need to pay attention to the corporate social responsibility they have to their workers" (personal interview, January 13, 2009).

To this end, the TLA dispatched top researchers to conduct on-site assessments of labor practices at Tesco supermarkets and distribution centers in Thailand, South Korea, and the United States. UNI then released three separate country reports on June 30, 2009, at a press conference in London. The South Korea report documented instances of unpaid overtime, forced resignation of union leaders, and serious breaches of health and safety laws, such as blocked fire exits, pallets stacked too high, and warehouse conditions inducing nasal pain, coughs, colds, and eye irritation (UNI 2009w). Similarly, the Thailand report revealed management manipulation of safety audit procedures, a lack of accident investigations, and rampant health and safety violations in Tesco warehouses. Describing the rat, cat, and pigeon infestations in his workplace, one Thai employee commented, "It's like a zoo. We are tired all the time—and worried about catching diseases and having other respiratory problems. . . . There is no air filtration or screening system to take the dust out of the air" (UNI 2009x, 13). Others spoke about working eighteen- and twenty-four-hour shifts with no overtime pay while earning only marginally more than minimum wage. Workers also reported anti-union activities, with managers firing workers for union organizing, photographing union leaders "as criminals," demoting or relocating labor activists, and visiting workers' families at home to intimidate union members into resigning (UNI 2009x, 19).

The third report focused on the United States and covered some of the same ground as *Two Faces*, including the lack of a living wage, strict conditions on pensions, prohibitively expensive health insurance, and union avoidance activities at Fresh & Easy. What differed was a conscious effort in this newer report to situate the US case in a broader global context. A foreword by UNI general secretary Philip Jennings suggested that this report was the product of the whole TLA and not purely UFCW driven. At the same time, the emphasis on UFCW's original goal remained clear, as the report made numerous mentions of Tesco heads' refusal "to respond positively and even to meet the USA's retail union," implying that management had been unreasonable, given that "the UFCW's only request to the company was to have a meeting" (UNI 2009y, 3, 12).

If the goal of the country reports was to capture public attention, they succeeded. Following the reports' release, press coverage flowed in from the *Financial Times*, the *Wall Street Journal*, the *Guardian*, the *Independent*, the *Malaysian Insider*, the *Thailander*, the *Bangkok Post*, Bloomberg, the *Gulf Times*, CNBC, Yahoo, and the BBC. In late July 2009 the TLA convened a press event for the US report at Los Angeles City Hall, generating more media attention. Los Angeles council member Richard Alarcon repeated the TLA's main message: "By refusing to treat all of its workers fairly, Tesco is letting its shareholders down, letting its workers down, and failing to rise to its own standards" (UNI 2009f).

Nevertheless, the three country reports could not compel a change in corporate behavior. This became clear when, on behalf of the labor alliance, UNI asked Tesco's Terry Leahy to meet "to discuss the findings of the reports and to start a dialogue which enables the company, workers, and their union representatives to jointly resolve the issues" (UNI 2009f). Yet from Tesco's perspective, there were no issues. Tesco stood by its official statement:

> This is a politically motivated report paid for by a union which is trying to recruit more members. The reports are a travesty and misrepresent the truth. UNI are using a standard tack of going to far off places, producing reports which are very difficult for people in the UK to check. We do check these matters and can tell you that the allegations are untrue. Wherever we operate in the world, all staff are free to join trade unions and can voice their opinions in a number of ways, including our anonymous annual staff survey. We have productive relationships with unions in a number of countries including USDAW in the UK and Solidarity in Poland. If a member of staff wants to join a union, they can. There are clear rules [in the United States] on how businesses have to recognise unions if they get to a certain level of support, and we would abide by this. At the moment, the level of support is not there. (Felsted 2009)

Pointing to its partnership with USDAW became a recurring theme in Tesco's strategic responses to the transnational campaign (discussed later). Of course, from the TLA's perspective, the USDAW-Tesco partnership was exactly the point. As a UNI representative put it, "It is the company's refusal to engage with us on partnership issues that causes the UNI Tesco Global Union Alliance to criticise the company" (UNI 2008f).

Unfortunately for the TLA, USDAW also criticized the reports. In a statement, the British union remarked that it has a good working relationship with Tesco and refused to back the findings of the country reports. "The allegations made in this report are not something Usdaw would recognise in relation to Tesco," their statement read (UNI 2009c).

Tesco's obstinacy and USDAW's cold shoulder did not deter the TLA from attempting to reach out to shareholders at the company's 2009 AGM in Glasgow. Yet no progress came from this effort. When a UFCW representative accused Tesco of refusing to engage with labor leaders, CEO Leahy responded curtly: "Your union has accused us of bad labour practices and tried to destroy our business before we'd even opened a shop or taken a dollar [in the United States]. We do work with unions." Interactions between Tesco executives and unionists were reportedly "fiery," and the three hundred shareholders in attendance "seemed bemused by the tenor of the debate, with many clapping the board's responses" (*Guardian* 2009).

In June 2010 the alliance tried again. Through the CtW Investment Group,[11] the TLA sent a letter to Tesco senior independent director Patrick Cescau, asking him to address several issues at the upcoming AGM, including the excessive pay awarded to US chief executive Tim Mason, whose £4.2 million remuneration made him the second-highest-paid director in the Financial Times Stock Exchange 100 consumer services sector (CtW Investment Group 2010). Representatives from several US unions also attended the 2010 AGM, where over 37 percent of shareholders voted against Tesco's remuneration report (*Guardian* 2010). Still, the executive pay plan passed, and the TLA made no gains on the issue of union recognition.

In its attempt to exercise coalitional power, the Tesco Global Union Alliance gained some support from investors, consumers, and politicians in the United States, the United Kingdom, and beyond. Support is not action, however, and only when the stakeholders mobilized by labor take direct action to influence the company can one say that a TLA has effectively exercised coalitional power. Nevertheless, the country reports and the new tenor of the transnational campaign signaled a broadening of the TLA's goals, which still included, but did not focus solely on, resolution of UFCW's Fresh & Easy troubles. It is significant that requests for dialogue and partnership with Tesco had been reframed as an initiative of UNI Global Union and the TLA as a whole.

INSTITUTIONAL POWER IN THE TESCO CAMPAIGN

The Tesco Global Union Alliance also attempted to exercise institutional power. One institutional channel the TLA pursued was the Joint Committee on Human Rights, a select committee of the British Parliament comprising twelve members of the House of Commons and the House of Lords who can examine witnesses, require the submission of written evidence, and make reports to both houses. In a letter to the joint committee signed by UFCW and dated April 24, 2009, the union explained that the TLA's complaints were "prompted by our experience of Tesco's operation in the USA, which in our opinion is in breach both of key conventions on human rights and of Tesco's own stated policies on human rights." To support these claims, the letter cited ILO Conventions 87 (Freedom of Association) and 98 (Right to Collective Bargaining), as well as the 1998 ILO Declaration on Fundamental Principles and Rights at Work. The joint committee then called on Tesco representatives to respond in person on June 30, 2009.

At the hearing, Tesco's executive director of corporate and legal affairs, Lucy Neville-Rolfe, refuted the TLA's claims that Tesco is antiunion by directing attention to USDAW: "If we talk about the UK example, we have had a business for nearly 80 years in the UK, and we have been unionized for about half of that. We work with the unions in the stores, when we put our induction packs out, they recruit, and they work with us on training, they work on health and safety, have consultation machinery[, and so on]."[12] When joint committee member Lord Dubs asked Neville-Rolfe why Tesco's approach to unions differed in the United States, Neville-Rolfe gave the stock answer: "Our policy is to support free association. The trade unions in the United States have not come along in a collaborative and constructive way in quite the way I describe for USDAW." After several more minutes of questioning and defensive responses from Tesco, the joint committee chair stated simply, "We are not going to get any further now." On December 16, 2009, the Joint Committee on Human Rights published a report expressing its concerns about Tesco being "associated with allegations of human rights abuse overseas" (UK Parliament, Joint Committee on Human Rights 2009a, 16). This report indicates that there was some potential for the joint committee's members to use their institutional position to influence Tesco's behavior. Nevertheless, the committee's recommendations did not compel Tesco to take any specific action or otherwise alter its policies.

The TLA also pursued another potential avenue for institutional power, Tesco's EWC. An EWC comprises employee representatives from every European country in which a company operates in order to facilitate communication and consultation between employees and senior managers at the European Union level. Since EWC members communicate about items such as the company's annual results, market position, and future plans, EWCs are a potentially invaluable source of institutional power for workers who seek to influence a TNC's operations through a transnational campaign. Unfortunately for UFCW, the Tesco EWC afforded influence only to USDAW and its European counterparts, with no openings for the TLA's non-European members. Although UNI applauded the EWC's establishment and "the important role that USDAW will play . . . to ensure the introduction of a well-functioning EWC," it soon became clear that the TLA would remain a parallel structure alongside, and not invited to be part of, the EWC (UNI 2008c).

The Tesco Global Union Alliance was not successful in its attempt to exercise either coalitional or institutional power. Nonetheless, the Tesco TLA's lack of success must be seen as analytically separate from the logic underlying the labor alliance's power strategy. The fact that both the Tesco and G4S TLAs turned to coalitional and institutional power in their transnational campaigns is evidence that the two labor alliances used the same power strategies. Hence, differences in power strategy cannot explain why one campaign succeeded and the other one did not. As illustrated next, the G4S TLA exercised both coalitional and institutional power, which turned out to be context appropriate.

COALITIONAL POWER IN THE G4S CAMPAIGN

Even before the first official meeting of the Alliance for Justice at G4S, SEIU had been devising a strategy to influence investors. As noted earlier, SEIU issued an "alternative annual report" on Wackenhut in 2005. Members of the still-forming TLA also attended G4S's 2005 AGM to protest pay cuts and poor conditions resulting from the merger of Group 4 Falck and Securicor. In 2006 TLA members again attended G4S's shareholder meeting. That year the alliance also updated its report to highlight labor rights abuses by G4S subsidiaries not only in the United States but also in India, Indonesia, and Uganda. The report documents managers in these countries firing workers for forming unions, paying so little that workers could not afford food, mandating unpaid overtime, and denying compensation for families of guards killed on the job (Abrahamsen and Williams 2011, 228). Though SEIU still led the alliance, the campaign had been broadened well beyond Wackenhut and the United States. UNI Property Services organizing director Christy Hoffman explained the logic of this wider focus: "Investors are normally reluctant to insert themselves into what they perceive as 'routine' labor disputes or 'garden variety' labor rights cases. However, confronted with a detailed record of what looks like a systematic problem representing potential shareholder risk in such a major global corporation, some key investors and advisory agencies have become involved" (Hoffman 2008, 5).

Operating on that logic, the TLA intensified its efforts to unearth more evidence. In April 2007 TLA members funded a delegation of researchers to Johannesburg for a UNI-sponsored meeting of unions representing security guards in eight African countries. Along with the human rights NGO War on Want, the researchers then traveled to Malawi and Mozambique on "fact-finding trips" involving interviews with union leaders, G4S employees, and government officials (Lerner, Hurst, and Adler 2008, 262).[13] The result was another research report.

Released on May 31, 2007, on the eve of G4S's 2007 AGM, *Who Protects the Guards? The Facts behind G4S in Southern Africa* detailed yet more abuses of labor and human rights. According to this report, security guards in Malawi could not afford adequate housing, food, running water, electricity, or school fees on their meager salaries. One guard reported working 364 days a year, receiving just one day off to attend a funeral. In Mozambique G4S guards earned only one-quarter of a living wage on eighteen- to twenty-four-hour shifts with no overtime pay. G4S supervisors called workers "kaffirs" and "monkeys" and only let white guards use the company toilet (Lerner, Hurst, and Adler 2008, 262). The TLA also produced a report on India. Titled *The Inequality beneath India's Economic Boom: G4S Security Workers Fight for Their Rightful Place in a Growing Economy*, it illustrated that thousands of security guards have no union rights and no job security, work unreasonable hours, and remain trapped in poverty.

All of the TLA's country reports made it clear that G4S should not treat these issues as isolated incidents. Instead, the TLA argued, the "best way for Group 4 Securicor to demonstrate it is worthy of trust is to sign a global agreement with UNI Global Union in which it commits to pay a living wage, provide social protections, and recognize workers' freedom to form unions" (UNI Property Services 2007, 5). By no means, however, did the TLA expect G4S to sign such an agreement out of moral obligation or any commitment to values or norms. Rather, the labor alliance threatened real material consequences in the form of declining profits, loss of market share, and divestment.

Specifically, the Alliance for Justice at G4S zeroed in on the 2010 World Cup in South Africa and the 2012 Summer Olympics in London. In the country reports and other materials, the TLA told campaign supporters to "urge FIFA [Fédération Internationale de Football Association] officials to withhold any consideration of G4S as a contractor until it respects its workers in Southern Africa and around the world" and to "urge London Olympic organisers to withhold favourable consideration of the company as a contractor until it commits to change its practices" (UNI Property Services 2007, 17). As Hoffman explained, the 2012 Olympics not only was "an important high profile event" but also involved "millions of pounds in security services" (Hoffman 2008, 5). The TLA could thus threaten the loss of potentially enormous profits regardless of whether G4S cared about human rights.

Hence, like the Tesco Global Union Alliance, the Alliance for Justice at G4S attempted to exercise coalitional power by mobilizing nonlabor stakeholders with the capacity to influence corporate behavior. Among these actors were investors, politicians, the World Cup and Olympics organizing committees, and other potential clients of G4S. Throughout all of these activities, the TLA received a great deal of press coverage in print and online media, just as the Tesco TLA had. "Every meeting of G4S unions needed some local press or media angle to it. Our union even paid for independent PR capacity," one SEIU official noted (personal interview, April 28, 2010). And just as the Tesco TLA shifted from an emphasis on issues in the United States to a more global focus, so too did the G4S TLA reframe its campaign in terms of international labor rights.

INSTITUTIONAL POWER IN THE G4S CAMPAIGN

In an attempt to exercise institutional power, the Alliance for Justice at G4S approached both the ILO and the OECD. In 2007 UNI assisted in filing two complaints with the ILO Committee on Freedom of Association regarding the illegal dismissal of striking workers in Indonesia and Panama. Although little came of the latter, the ILO found in Indonesia that G4S used discrimination and harassment to intimidate union members (Hoffman 2008, 4). Still, the ILO finding was a symbolic victory that did little to deliver concrete gains.

It was the OECD that provided the G4S TLA with the most ammunition. In particular, the TLA drew on the OECD Guidelines for Multinational Enterprises, a set of legally nonbinding recommendations for TNCs endorsed and upheld by national governments. The guidelines cover corporations' actions related to employment, industrial relations, the environment, corruption, consumer interests, competition, taxation, and the responsible use of science and technology and are "the only comprehensive, multilaterally-endorsed code of conduct for transnational enterprises" (Vanden Eyde, Sutherland, and Dio 2008, 31).

Among the OECD's recommendations is that TNCs "respect the right of workers employed by the multinational enterprise to establish or join trade unions and representative organisations of their own choosing" and "promote consultation and co-operation between employers and workers and their representatives on matters of mutual concern" (OECD 2011, 35–36). The TLA referenced these and other provisions in its two submissions to the OECD's National Contact Point (NCP) in the United Kingdom in late 2006 and early 2007. Authored by UNI, the complaints point to violations of the guidelines by G4S subsidiaries in eleven countries,[14] covering much of the same information the TLA had in its country reports (Hoffman 2008, 4).

Months passed. Not until January 2008 did the NCP decide to reexamine parts of the TLA's case, accepting for initial assessment only those points concerning the Democratic Republic of the Congo (DRC), Malawi, Mozambique, and Nepal (Vanden Eyde, Sutherland, and Dio 2008). Issues that caught the NCP's attention included the blacklisting of workers for union activity, lack of employee access to water, lack of allowances for medical visits and leave, and nonpayment of overtime, severance, and back pay (Vanden Eyde, Sutherland, and Dio 2008). The UK NCP published its initial assessment of G4S in March 2008. Three months later a Norwegian fund, KLP (Kommunal Landspensjonskasse), divested from G4S, citing concerns over the company's unethical labor practices revealed in UNI's complaint to the OECD (Abrahamsen and Williams 2011, 229). According to one SEIU official, "Investors were impressed with the complaint to the OECD in the UK, and that affected the share price" (personal interview, April 28, 2010). This meant that institutional power was working.

The UK NCP soon appointed an external mediator, John Mulholland, who convened a series of discussions between UNI and G4S. According to the final statement by the UK NCP, dated December 12, 2008, UNI and G4S agreed on specific resolutions for issues affecting Nepal and the DRC and "agreed to a process to allow them to work more closely together on a number of specific issues at the national level" in Malawi and Mozambique. G4S also "reaffirmed its ongoing commitment to honour and respect national law and to respect the ILO core labour Conventions" (Vanden Eyde, Sutherland, and Dio 2008, 3).

Even more significantly, the end of mediation marked the beginning of the end of the G4S campaign. Although "the mediation faced many challenges, the process not only resulted in the resolution of the complaint, but also laid the foundations for more far-reaching negotiations between UNI and G4S" (Trade Union Advisory Committee [TUAC] 2008). UNI's Christy Hoffman elaborated on these sentiments: "Initially, the OECD process legitimized our complaints about the G4S global operations, and this was a very important element. Subsequently, the mediation meant that both sides in the dispute had to sit down face to face, peel away the rhetoric and try to grapple with some difficult problems which affected thousands of workers. Once some good will was established, the step towards a global relationship for handling similar issues in the future was a natural one" (quoted in Blackburn and Ewing 2009). An SEIU organizer put it more directly: "The OECD Guidelines were the killer blow" (personal interview, April 28, 2010).

Nonetheless, SEIU tells only one side of the story. The OECD mediation addressed only the DRC, Malawi, Mozambique, and Nepal, and Hoffman's claim that "the step towards a global relationship for handling similar issues in the future was a natural one" is only partially true. The British union GMB in fact played an indispensable role in facilitating direct dialogue between G4S and the TLA separate from the OECD proceedings. Only after these GMB-led negotiations took place did the TLA accomplish its ultimate goal of signing a GFA covering G4S employees globally. GMB's role in helping the transnational labor alliance exercise institutional power will be explained more fully later.

For now, one need only note that, as with its use of coalitional power, the exercise of institutional power by the G4S TLA mirrored that of the Tesco TLA. Despite the fact that only the G4S TLA exercised institutional power successfully, the logic of the unions' power strategies was the same: by invoking the authority of international institutions, both alliances intended to compel their target TNCs to alter their behaviors. The fact that the two TLAs' power strategies were the same suggests that this variable alone cannot explain the Tesco and G4S campaigns' different outcomes.

It is important to reiterate that the logic of a TLA's power strategy is analytically separate from its execution. It is therefore possible that the two cases' divergent outcomes were due to the labor alliances' differing *abilities* to exercise power, holding constant the logic and context appropriateness of their power strategies. I argue that the Tesco TLA's inability to exercise context-appropriate power on the international scale caused that campaign to fail. Yet this is only a proximate cause. Moving down the causal chain reveals that the true cause of trouble in the Tesco TLA was the inability of key alliance partners to coordinate well enough across national borders to exercise institutional power fully and effectively. In other words, the Tesco TLA lacked interunion coordination. Conversely, strong interunion coordination in the G4S campaign led to its success.

The Employers' Strategies: Similar Interests and Actions

Before examining the role of interunion coordination in these two cases, I turn to one last factor that could have accounted for the cases' different outcomes but does not: the interests and strategies of the TNCs in question, Tesco and G4S. One might hypothesize that the main reason the G4S TLA prevailed while the Tesco TLA did not rested on employers' strategic reactions to the transnational campaigns. If employer strategy were truly the cause of these cases' differences, one would see that Tesco handled transnational activists more astutely than G4S had. Yet evidence does not suggest this to be the case. Both TNCs in fact reacted to the TLA campaigns using similar tactics, defenses, and rhetoric.

One common strategy was silence. Early in both campaigns, corporate leaders in Britain frequently declined to comment on unions' actions in order to avoid giving the TLAs the attention they sought. UFCW referred to Tesco's refusal to engage the union in dialogue as a "deliberate tactic" of "delay and avoidance" on the issue of unionizing Fresh & Easy (UFCW 2008a, 7). Likewise, rather than involving senior management in SEIU's conflict with Wackenhut, G4S left its subsidiary to speak for itself. This strategy of employers outright ignoring transnational activists reflects an effort to restrict the scale of conflict, a common response to TLAs (see chapter 4).

Keeping conflict local at Fresh & Easy and Wackenhut helped Tesco and G4S evade responsibility for their subsidiaries' antiunion actions, at least for some time. Restricting the scale of conflict also allowed these companies to take advantage of the US institutional context, which privileges management prerogative over union rights. The TNCs thus framed this approach to their US subsidiaries as a mere matter of legal compliance. "There are different laws in this country," one Fresh & Easy human resource manager said, referring to the United States. "It's unfair of us to apply British law here" (UNI 2009y, 15). Similarly, G4S emphasized repeatedly that union rights are foremost a matter for national institutions. Upon the release of the UNI-sponsored country reports, G4S's response "was consistently that these were individual cases requiring attention at the country level" (Abrahamsen and Williams 2011, 229). TLA members "have their right to come along and make their point," a G4S spokesperson stated. "We would say, however, that they should raise their issues with local management or with their unions locally" (Glanville and Roberts 2005).

Even when authorities began to catch on to this strategy as a convenient excuse for union avoidance, corporate executives remained evasive. Asked by the Joint Committee on Human Rights whether UFCW was allowed to recruit inside Fresh & Easy stores, Tesco executive director of corporate and legal affairs Lucy Neville-Rolfe avoided a direct answer, spurring the following exchange with one committee member:

Earl of Onslow: With the greatest respect, you were asked a very, very, very simple question. Are they allowed to recruit inside your stores or not? I have noticed that you have been dodging. You may think it slightly odd for an hereditary peer on the right of

	the Conservative Party to suddenly be taking a pro-trade unions attitude but this is because I would quite like an answer.
Ms Neville-Rolfe:	Individuals are allowed to join the union.
Earl of Onslow:	That was not the question.
Ms Neville-Rolfe:	What we have said again and again is that there is a right of association but that the approach the unions have taken has been different in the United States to the one we have been used to in other places, including the UK.

(UK Parliament, Joint Committee on Human Rights 2009a, 44).

Another strategy used by both Tesco and G4S was to point to their positive home union relationships. Constantly referencing USDAW and GMB helped these TNCs deflect criticism from TLA members and other "outsiders." For example, Human Resources Director Jenni Myles emphasized that "G4S has a long history of building positive relationships with employees and their representatives. Our relationship with GMB in the UK has been in place for more than 40 years" (Telljohann 2009). Moreover, G4S "absolutely rejected claims that it violated human rights in the developing world," pointing out that "globally the company has agreements with more than 60 trade unions, that half its workforce is covered by them and that the firm supports international agreements on labour standards" (Chamberlain 2006).

Discrediting the TLAs while simultaneously emphasizing the legality of their own actions was another strategy the TNCs shared. Tesco often accused labor alliance members of attempting to damage its business, as when CEO Terry Leahy stated that UFCW "has never welcomed Tesco to the US," "opposed Tesco from day one," and "tried to destroy our business" (*Guardian* 2010). Likewise, G4S claimed that the TLA intended only to tarnish its corporate image. In an official statement, G4S spokesperson Innocentia Mangena suggested that the TLA was using "the manipulation of public perception in order to gain concessions to union demands" and to "force" Wackenhut into unionization, "which would be damaging to the business and employees of Wackenhut" (Hawker 2007). Another G4S spokesperson told the *Guardian*, "This [campaign] is all about recognition in the US, nothing else. . . . At a time when unions and employers are getting closer together in many countries, I think that [the unions'] approach is retrogressive" (Chamberlain 2006).

Finally, to further discredit the transnational campaigns, both Tesco and G4S suggested that the unions involved were not legitimate representatives of stakeholders' interests. Tesco referred to the CtW Investment Group, which assisted the TLA in protesting Tesco's 2010 AGM, as "a US union-sponsored body that is not a shareholder, does not speak for shareholders, and has tried to undermine the success of Fresh & Easy from the outset" (*Supermarket News* 2011). Referencing the labor dispute in Indonesia, a G4S spokesperson tried to discredit the Indonesian union ASPEK (Association of Indonesia Labor Unions), a member of the G4S TLA, by claiming that its members had unethically attempted to resign from their jobs, collect severance pay, then immediately become reemployed by G4S (*Observer*, April 30, 2006), when in fact this was not true.

Employing rhetorical evasiveness, restricting the scale of conflict, praising the home union, and calling into question the legitimacy of the TLA all helped the two companies to respond strategically to the transnational campaigns. The fact that both employers adopted such similar strategies suggests that differences in the campaigns' outcomes were not due to any difference between the actions of Tesco and G4S. In sum, neither intraunion coordination, nor the TLAs' power strategies, nor the employers' strategies explain why the Tesco campaign did not succeed and the G4S campaign did. Instead, as the remainder of the case studies show, the main cause of difference between the two campaigns centered on interunion coordination—defined as the capacity of unions to collaborate with each other across national borders.

Contrasting the Campaigns: Why Interunion Coordination Mattered Most

Throughout both campaigns, the American unions, UFCW and SEIU, faced a "home union problem" in which their respective British counterparts, USDAW and GMB, did not want to jeopardize their positive relationships with the employers in question by actively supporting a transnational campaign. Resolving this conflict of interest between SEIU and GMB proved essential for winning the campaign against G4S, while failure to achieve interunion coordination between UFCW and USDAW harmed the Tesco campaign considerably.

UFCW versus USDAW: The Home Union Problem in the Tesco Campaign

> Industrial relations, laws, regulations—they're all still very
> national. So there's limited pressure a national union can put on a
> company on another union's behalf.
> —USDAW member[15]

> You know what USDAW stands for? Useless Seven Days a Week.
> —UFCW member[16]

At the time of the Tesco campaign, USDAW had 150,000 members in Tesco stores across the United Kingdom. Even before USDAW and Tesco signed their partnership agreement, the union had a long-standing, positive relationship with the company (USDAW official, personal interview, November 18, 2009). A former staff member in USDAW's Education and Training Department described the Tesco-USDAW partnership as "fairly kind of mutual. . . . Our representatives have team meetings on company time, and we've managed to get better facilities in Tesco and paid leave to attend training courses" as a result of the partnership (personal interview, October 22, 2009). USDAW's close ties to Tesco's top management contrasted sharply with the silence UFCW faced from Fresh & Easy. Had USDAW used its strong relationship with Tesco to convince corporate leaders to meet with the American union, the Tesco Global Union Alliance could have made better inroads with their campaign. "USDAW has privileged access to Tesco," explained a UNI official in an interview, "so USDAW should really be the international coordinator. The home union has a role to rally the troops" (personal interview, January 23, 2009).

The potential for USDAW to play a more prominent role in the TLA was certainly there. Although the union at the time did not have its own international department, USDAW was affiliated with UNI and connected to several different international liaison organizations (USDAW member, personal interview, October 22, 2009). USDAW also led the Tesco EWC, which enhanced workers' access to senior management. "USDAW has a good relationship with other unions in Europe," an USDAW official emphasized, "especially in Ireland, Hungary, Poland, Czech Republic, Slovakia, France. . . . The EWC was a long time coming" (personal interview, November 18, 2009).

Nevertheless, USDAW kept the labor alliance at arm's length. While technically a member of the Tesco Global Union Alliance (USDAW is listed among its twelve founding members), the British union vacillated between lukewarm support, quiet neutrality, and overt distancing. Early in the campaign, USDAW showed some support. Its officials attended UFCW's August 2008 convention in Montreal, during which UNI general secretary Philip Jennings made a point of referencing USDAW in a speech: "I would like to acknowledge the support of the UK's shop workers' union, USDAW. They are here today. I would like to recognize John Hannett, General Secretary of USDAW" (UNI 2008b).

Yet as the transnational campaign against Tesco progressed, USDAW began to distance itself from the TLA. USDAW refused to back the findings of the Thailand, South Korea, and US country reports and issued its own statement emphasizing its good relationship with Tesco and denying that the reports' allegations in any way reflected USDAW's experience with the company (Felsted 2009). For the rest of the campaign, USDAW remained quiet and made no effort to get Tesco to talk with UFCW, UNI, or any other TLA members. "They won't take on their boss," one UFCW official complained of USDAW during the campaign. "They say, oh, it's a good company. Don't rock the boat" (personal interview, December 11, 2008).

Why did USDAW refuse to put its weight behind the Tesco TLA? Three interrelated issues explain the British union's lack of support. First, USDAW was unwilling to jeopardize its positive relationship with Tesco for fear of losing its comfortable position and easy membership supply. Second, USDAW felt put off by UFCW's early aggression toward Tesco, which it viewed as counterproductive. Third, UFCW appeared to be focused primarily, if not exclusively, on its own interests in the United States. Had UFCW invested more resources in other countries and demonstrated more genuine concern for alliance partners in Asia, Europe, and beyond, USDAW would have been more likely to support the transnational campaign.

THE HOME UNION'S HIDDEN WEAKNESSES: WHY USDAW WAS RISK AVERSE

In an interview, an USDAW official defended his union's lack of international solidarity by pointing to differences in national institutional contexts: "Industrial relations, laws, regulations—they're all still very national. So there's limited pressure a national union can put on a company on another union's behalf" (personal interview, November 18, 2009). While this is technically true, additional interviews with USDAW, UFCW, and UNI representatives revealed that USDAW's reluctance to support the TLA had less to do with national institutional differences than with the particular nature of its partnership with Tesco.

According to an official from the UFCW, despite the empowering aspects of the USDAW-Tesco partnership, any rift in USDAW's relationship with Tesco could lead to a steep decline in the union's membership. "USDAW is extremely fearful of what may happen to it. About 150,000 of their members are in Tesco out of 310,000 total in USDAW. People fill out the form that management gives them. Management basically recruits the employees to sign up for the union as they're being hired. If Tesco pulled the plug on this individual union, they would lose fifty percent of their membership in two years" (UFCW organizer, personal interview, January 13, 2009). "Global solidarity is a challenge because of the UK union's tenuous position," another UFCW official concurred. "So we can't leverage the UK union relationship directly. We have to go around them" (personal interview, December 11, 2008).

A UNI representative explained the situation further: "From a UNI perspective, I see two unions at loggerheads. UFCW is looking to gain about 3,000 members [by organizing Fresh & Easy], but it's very one-sided. We have to err on the side of caution because of the huge risk [to USDAW]" (personal interview, January 20, 2009). In other words, UNI felt it necessary to avoid implicating USDAW, a UNI affiliate, in any overtly anti-Tesco activities. The solution, according to the UNI official, was to "just say we want Tesco to treat US workers 'no less favorably' than its other workers. Language is very important here. We articulate a middle ground, allow USDAW to sit on the sidelines and say nothing. But in turn, they should allow UNI to go ahead with releasing our country reports in the UK. . . . There's the possibility Tesco will pressure USDAW and force USDAW into a public debate. It can become an USDAW versus UFCW dispute. But it helps to couch [the campaign] in UNI." If the TLA had remained as careful and compromising as UNI apparently intended it to be, USDAW might have been more supportive. Nevertheless, despite its sensitivity to USDAW's vulnerabilities, UFCW did not sufficiently promote inclusiveness in the transnational campaign.

PERCEIVED AGGRESSION: WHY USDAW DID NOT TRUST UFCW

UFCW and USDAW give two different stories regarding the actions UFCW took in targeting Tesco. According to UFCW, "It was only after our friendly overtures were rejected that we realised that Tesco had no intention of meeting us as potential partners. . . . Only then, having tried both direct and indirect friendly approaches, did we finally take the decision to raise public awareness of Tesco's approach in the USA" (UK Parliament, Joint Committee on Human Rights. 2009b). Yet USDAW maintains that UFCW took an aggressive approach from the start, which neither Tesco nor USDAW found appropriate. In a sense both unions are correct. In terms of the transnational campaign, UFCW remained fairly cautious of USDAW's position and deferred to UNI's diplomatic approach. It was the union's local actions in the United States that tended to lack tact.

UFCW's letter to Tesco's CEO in December 2006, in which the union threatened to "do what we can to stop [Tesco] from developing stores here" (*Supermarket News* 2007a), set the tone for the union's early tactics. As noted earlier, these included the "British invasion" rhetoric and protest actions outside Fresh & Easy stores, picketing at Fresh & Easy grand openings, mass leafleting, and the muckraking website freshandeasyfacts.com. All of these actions portrayed Tesco in a negative light and contributed to views of UFCW as divisive and confrontational. "If a union starts having a go at the company before they're even established somewhere, it doesn't help," remarked one USDAW official in reference to UFCW's actions in the United States (personal interview, November 18, 2009). Tesco CEO Terry Leahy, Fresh & Easy head Tim Mason, and other senior corporate executives were also reportedly surprised by UFCW's aggressiveness (*Fresh & Easy Buzz* 2008a).

The combination of USDAW's precarious membership structure and UFCW's confrontational local tactics was enough to make the former uneasy about the latter's intentions. Still, UFCW had several opportunities to remedy this situation by adopting a more inclusive agenda and even appeared for a while to be moving in that direction. With the help of UNI, UFCW began steering the TLA toward broader goals, including labor rights for Tesco workers in Thailand, South Korea, and Turkey. These efforts to enhance the inclusiveness of the transnational campaign fell short, however, and well into 2010 the TLA still appeared to be driven by the US union's local interests.

Early campaign materials focus on UFCW's problems more than any other issue. Shortly after the TLA formed, UNI made a point of stating, "The UNI Tesco Global Union Alliance is concerned at the company's unwillingness to enter into a dialogue with the UNI Commerce affiliate UFCW, in the United States" (UNI 2008c). UNI's June 2008 bulletin likewise stressed that the TLA was concerned "particularly over the company's unwillingness to meet UNI US Commerce affiliate UFCW." Though UNI did mention other goals, such as growing unions wherever Tesco operates and promoting the general well-being of Tesco's global workforce, it is clear that UFCW set the TLA's agenda. Notably, *The Two Faces of Tesco* makes some perfunctory references to union recognition issues in Turkey and Thailand (UFCW 2008a, 5) but otherwise focuses largely on Tesco's refusal to engage with UFCW in the United States.

Too much focus on the United States made it difficult for UFCW to generate active support from others in the TLA, especially USDAW. "Ten dollars an hour in the US is not a sweatshop," admitted one UFCW official, adding, "Workers in Malaysia make a few cents a day. Companies are much more horrible in other countries" (personal interview, December 11, 2008). Another UFCW official recognized the same problem. "If you go to the UK, it's hard to explain, but they think [US workers] are not suffering, especially when you juxtapose them with workers in Thailand or South Korea" (UFCW organizer, personal interview, January 13, 2009). Therefore, to gain USDAW's sympathy and support, the solution seemed to lie in expanding the transnational campaign to more directly address issues of concern to Tesco workers in other countries.

Genuinely incorporating countries other than the United States into the transnational campaign would have made it easier for USDAW to side with the TLA. This is because bringing Tesco to the bargaining table with international union representatives would have appeared more justifiable to both Tesco managers and USDAW members if the issues to be discussed concerned urgent matters of health and safety, blatant human rights violations, threats to the sustainability of new markets in the developing world, and other serious risks to Tesco's future profitability. USDAW could get behind a TLA campaign for better working conditions in developing countries without risking its relationship with Tesco executives, especially if Tesco workers worldwide supported the same broad agenda. USDAW could not, however, back a campaign designed to gain organizing rights for a single union in the wealthiest country in the world.

UFCW thus relied on UNI to help reframe the transnational campaign as one that could garner more active support. Under the UNI umbrella, UFCW's campaign actions could look less opportunistic and more motivated by genuine concern for workers in other countries. "UNI has very good relationships with other unions. So you've got to go through UNI to get these guys to play ball," a UFCW organizer explained (personal interview, January 13, 2009). For example, UFCW sent a letter to the CEO of Tesco Kipa as part of a UNI-coordinated effort to help workers in Turkey win union recognition. Reaching out to the Tesco EWC through UNI was also an attempt to render the campaign more genuinely transnational, though little came of that effort.

The country reports on Thailand and South Korea were another step in the direction of inclusiveness. Interestingly, upon the release of these reports, UNI noted on its website that these were to be "the first of a series of research reports" (UNI 2009e), and plans for a Turkey report appear on one of the TLA's meeting agendas. Nonetheless, additional reports never materialized, and the anticorporate undertones of the South Korea and Thailand reports led USDAW to refute their findings rather than warm to the transnational campaign. Arguably, however, a series of well-researched country reports that emphasized UFCW's and USDAW's shared, long-term strategic interests, such as improving health and safety standards across all Tesco stores or ensuring decent working hours for all Tesco employees, could have convinced

USDAW officials to act in support of the TLA, thereby turning the tide in terms of interunion coordination.

THE OUTCOME: THE TESCO CAMPAIGN CONCLUDES UNSUCCESSFULLY

Ultimately, UFCW's attempts to expand the inclusiveness of the TLA campaign through UNI were not sufficient to bring USDAW on board. UFCW was reluctant to pour resources into additional country reports, on-the-ground organizing in developing countries, and other potentially fruitful avenues of campaign expansion. One of the main reasons for this was UFCW's rational interest in developments on the national scale, specifically attempts to pass the Employee Free Choice Act (EFCA) in the United States. Also known as the "card check" bill, the EFCA, had it become law, would have drastically improved US unions' abilities to organize workers by allowing employees to obtain union membership by checking a box on a card in lieu of a National Labor Relations Board election, with a majority of employees in a workplace checking "yes" being sufficient for union recognition. When the Tesco campaign began, the EFCA looked unlikely to pass. Although the House of Representatives voted in favor of it (241 to 185) in 2007, with the Senate just barely voting against it (51 to 49), President George W. Bush would have undoubtedly vetoed the bill. With President Obama taking office in 2009, however, hope for the EFCA resurfaced, and UFCW began to turn its attention back to national politics. In the end UFCW's efforts to improve interunion coordination through UNI proved to be too little too late, and the campaign never became as inclusive and supportive of mutual long-term interests as it could have been.

UFCW's involvement in the Tesco TLA eventually fizzled out, and the original campaign to organize Fresh & Easy concluded unsuccessfully. Campaign web pages, the *Fresh & Easy Facts* blog, and most other online material from the Tesco Global Union Alliance are now dead links. The last official words on UFCW's fight to organize Fresh & Easy came from UNI's recounting of the TLA's March 2010 meeting in Liverpool: "The Alliance expressed its frustration at the continuing difficulties faced in the USA by the UFCW. There is continuing evidence of obstacles to union organisation and no dialogue with the company" (UNI 2010a).

SEIU versus GMB: Overcoming the Home Union Problem in the G4S Campaign

> GMB was a thorn in the side of the G4S campaign.
> —SEIU OFFICIAL[17]

> We have always been very reluctant to criticize SEIU. Unfortunately,
> SEIU's actions are not helping.
> —GMB OFFICIAL[18]

Like most success stories, the transnational campaign carried out by the Alliance for Justice at G4S was not without complications. Led by SEIU, the TLA effectively exercised institutional power and compelled the company to sign a GFA outlining specific terms for a new global partnership between UNI and G4S. Without the help of the home union in Britain, however, the TLA could not have accomplished what it did.

It is not merely a coincidence that GMB is, along with UNI and G4S, one of three signatories to the GFA that is the embodiment of the TLA's success. The fact that GMB signed the GFA separately from other alliance members reflects the unique role that the British union played in opening up communications between the TLA and G4S's top executives. "GMB was instrumental in negotiating the international agreement with G4S," noted a GMB organizer. "SEIU wanted to intervene but had no clout with the company," he added. "There were lots of politics behind the international agreement with G4S" (personal interview, October 15, 2009).

Shortly after Group 4 Falck and Securicor merged into G4S in 2004, GMB secured a national recognition agreement designating itself as the union to represent all 15,500 security guards employed by the company in the United Kingdom. Although it took fifteen months to negotiate the deal, it was soon hailed as a great benefit to the industry and praised by Prime Minister Tony Blair as "groundbreaking" (Chamberlain 2006). Even before the national recognition deal, GMB had maintained a positive working relationship with Securicor, the British half of the later merged company. Paul Kenny, general secretary of GMB, explained, "Our experience of working with G4S has always been constructive" (quoted in IFSEC Global 2008).

Like USDAW's relationship with Tesco, GMB's close ties to G4S made the British union an ideal source of leverage for the TLA campaign. As far as the alliance was concerned, GMB was not only indispensable for obtaining direct dialogue with upper management but also crucial for infusing any global agreement eventually signed with a certain degree of legitimacy. In trying to win GMB's support, however, the TLA confronted a "home union problem" exacerbated by three complications: clashing visions of how the TLA campaign should proceed, a history of conflict between GMB and SEIU, and GMB's aim to act only in its members' best interests.

CLASHING VISIONS: HOW GMB'S OUTLOOK DIFFERED

"GMB hated this campaign," remarked an SEIU organizer in an interview (April 28, 2010). He was not exaggerating. GMB viewed the Alliance for Justice at G4S first and foremost as a project of the SEIU and felt it was too top-down and controlling in its approach to transnational campaigns. GMB was particularly concerned about SEIU transforming global unions such as UNI into hierarchical structures commanded by Americans out of touch with the needs of most of the world's workers. In an interview, a GMB official offered his perspective: "SEIU has a 'Kevin Costner' problem with respect to global union organization. They think, 'if you build it (a global union), they (workers) will come.' But the truth is, we're not there yet. The day will come when GMB members in Cambridge go on strike with workers in California. We will get there one day. But we're not there yet. The working class will not just spontaneously form a queue" (personal interview, November 30, 2009).

According to the same union official, GMB also feared that such an undemocratic, top-down global union would be "captured" by the transnational corporations it had been created to combat. "If you build a global structure, companies will capture it," he continued. "It will become hijacked by corporate interests" (personal interview, November 30, 2009). Another GMB organizer echoed these concerns: "SEIU would make secret agreements with a corporation with a 'no-strike' clause and with the company determining where a union can organize and where it can't" (personal interview, October 15, 2009). In turn, SEIU defended its top-down approach to transnational campaigns: "We are criticized for these partnership agreements, but we can't afford to fight every boss. Workers don't want to be in a state of permanent revolution, despite how the radical left would have it" (SEIU organizer, personal interview, November 24, 2009). Yet GMB remained steadfast: "For GMB, power in the workplace is key. We really have different perspectives on organizing" (GMB official, personal interview, October 15, 2009).

PAST CONFLICT: WHY GMB DID NOT TRUST SEIU

Clashing visions of transnational campaigning and union organizing drove a wedge between SEIU and GMB well before the G4S TLA even formed. For some years, GMB had faced financial trouble and a shrinking membership. SEIU, whose membership had grown in the 1990s and early 2000s in spite of the United States' inhospitable institutional environment, visited GMB in the United Kingdom to offer money and advice. When GMB declined the Americans' help, SEIU appeared insulted. As a GMB organizer explained, "Initially, [GMB and SEIU] had a different dynamic. We reached out, asked for its expertise on its model of organizing. . . . GMB was offered funding by SEIU while we were in steep membership decline, but the terms were onerous. We said, 'thanks, but no thanks.' It wasn't taken too well. There was a chilling in our relationship due to this rebuff. The GMB-SEIU relationship fell off" (personal interview, October 15, 2009).

GMB's major concern was that SEIU intended to compel the British union to take part in its own brand of transnational organizing, despite GMB's distaste for SEIU's top-down style. A US-based union official close to both parties offered an insider's view of the two unions' officials: "Martin Smith and head of GMB Paul Kenny talked about what it was like to partner with SEIU. They talked about how [SEIU president] Andy Stern saw himself as the 'emperor of global labor,' but SEIU really had to buy themselves into these unions . . . so the emperor has no clothes" (personal interview, August 13, 2010).

MEMBERS FIRST: WHY GMB WAS RISK AVERSE

GMB's suspicion of SEIU was exacerbated by the British union's sensitivity to the needs of its own membership. GMB members had nothing to gain from a transnational campaign against G4S, nor did the union have anything to gain from risking harm to its positive relationship with the company. GMB's view was that "there's no logic in going international if there are no benefits locally. Our opinion on GUFs (global unions) is that they're not really effective. GMB always stresses accountability to our members. If we devote resources somewhere, are we accountable? Does it pay off? What outcomes do we achieve?" (GMB organizer, personal interview, October 15, 2009).

There was also a clear conflict of interest between G4S workers in the United Kingdom and the TLA, which was threatening G4S with the loss of valuable contracts at high-profile events. Telling the Olympics organizing committee to decline G4S's bid to provide security for the 2012 London Olympics risked thousands of potential jobs for GMB members. Additionally, "SEIU wrote to all the [members of Parliament] with a whole range of sins and crimes of G4S and asked them to end contracts they had with the company. But GMB had 20,000 members' jobs at stake!" a GMB official remarked (personal interview, November 30, 2009).

Arguably, SEIU and GMB had more bad blood between them than UFCW had with USDAW. Yet unlike UFCW, SEIU managed to get GMB to join the TLA by rendering the campaign more globally inclusive and genuinely supportive of non-US workers' needs. Although SEIU used similar tactics to the ones UFCW had tried in the Tesco campaign, the former invested more money and energy in developing strong interunion coordination.

INCLUSIVE INTERNATIONALISM: WHY GMB CAME TO SEE
THE TLA AS LEGITIMATE

Despite their disagreements with GMB, SEIU and UNI expressed keen awareness of the TLA's need for coordination with the home union. "The home union relationship is critical in these campaigns," argued an SEIU organizer (personal interview, November 24, 2009). SEIU therefore could not ignore the role GMB would play in either promoting or detracting from the TLA's goals. TLA members also seemed fairly aware of how difficult interunion coordination is to obtain. As Christy Hoffman, organizing director for UNI Property Services, noted, "The biggest challenge facing any global labor union is to maintain solidarity in the face of different national interests. Unions in Western Europe, generally speaking, have a relationship of social dialogue and mutual respect with G4S. At times [the G4S campaign] has put these interests in tension" (Hoffman 2008, 5).

In order to understand how SEIU and GMB resolved their differences, it is helpful to return to an earlier discussion from chapter 1, which outlined the three ways in which TLAs can secure interunion coordination. These are (1) emphasizing TLA members' shared material interests, (2) emphasizing the long-term strategic outlook shared by TLA members, and (3) drawing on TLA members' well-established history of reciprocity. The first and third methods would not have worked for the G4S TLA since SEIU and GMB shared few material interests and had a history of conflict, not cooperation. Hence, SEIU relied on the second means of attaining interunion coordination: emphasizing TLA members' shared, long-term strategic interests—namely, the development of high industry standards and strong unions in developing countries.

Refocusing a campaign to highlight unions' shared strategic interests often requires the coordination of campaign actions through an ostensibly neutral umbrella body such as a global union. In this case, it was UNI Global Union that helped alter perceptions of the G4S campaign as a mere cover for SEIU's own interests. Key to this strategy was gaining genuine grassroots support from workers outside the United States. An SEIU organizer explained the strategy: "When SEIU gets developing countries involved in international campaigns, we get more support, more legitimacy. . . . We went to UNI and invested in UNI's capacity. GUFs have no money and no expertise. Many [global union leaders] have never been union officials. So we put [former SEIU official] Christy Hoffman at the head of UNI Property Services with one million dollars. We then seeded organizing campaigns in India, Malawi, other African countries, Poland, and Indonesia" (personal interview, April 28, 2010).

With Hoffman at the helm, UNI Property Services began to provide training and other resources to G4S workers around the world. UNI funded organizing campaigns in the DRC, India, Malawi, Mozambique, Poland, and South Africa (Hoffman 2008, 5). Not all of this support came from scratch, however; workers in many of these countries "were already pursuing their own separate fights" when UNI stepped in (Lerner, Hurst, and Adler 2008, 262).[19]

The result was a series of small victories for G4S workers in several developing countries and a boost in legitimacy for the TLA. The most important early victory occurred in Indonesia, where 250 G4S employees represented by the union SP Securicor Indonesia[20] were fired following a fifteen-month strike. Despite a series of court rulings culminating in the Supreme Court's ordering the company to reinstate and compensate the workers, G4S resisted. Workers then occupied the company's local headquarters, demanding their jobs back (Chamberlain 2006). "So UNI stepped in. They paid to keep workers on strike and do sit-ins and fund their defense in the highest court" (SEIU organizer, personal interview, April 28, 2010). On July 28, 2006, G4S finally agreed to pay 159 of the workers double the legal minimum severance pay and eleven months of back pay, in addition to dropping criminal charges against the union's president (Champagne 2006).[21]

SEIU's and UNI's involvement in the Indonesian conflict is evidence that the Alliance for Justice at G4S went further than the Tesco Global Union Alliance did in actively supporting non-US unions. Support was not merely a matter of money. Rather, it meant having dedicated organizers on the ground in Indonesia. Along with UNI officials, SEIU global organizing co-ordinator Jessica Champagne traveled to Indonesia to support the workers directly. Champagne spoke the language and offered expert advice to the union while nonetheless maintaining a realistic view of the situation and the limits of her and UNI's role as outsiders. "Despite shared enthusiasm and complementary strengths, the partnership was not always easy," Champagne reported. "The campaign was a learning process for both unions. . . . SP Securicor Indonesia had the ultimate responsibility, and burden, of deciding which tactics would be most effective in an Indonesian context, and which could backfire" (Champagne 2006).

SEIU and UNI continued this approach in other countries. In Uganda, the TLA helped G4S security guards win a two-year struggle for union recognition in April 2007, resulting in a nationwide collective agreement covering four hundred guards (Lerner, Hurst, and Adler 2008, 262–63). Three months later, the TLA helped 13,000 G4S workers win union recognition in Malawi (PR Newswire Europe 2007). In June of that year, UNI also coordinated affiliates in Argentina, Australia, Hong Kong, Sweden, the United States, and elsewhere to demonstrate in support of hundreds of thousands of security guards seeking unionization in India (Lerner 2007, 129). These victories generated growing support for the TLA campaign from unions in advanced and developing countries alike. "Workers are heartened when they know there is a network of others facing similar issues with the same employer," Hoffman noted (Hoffman 2008, 5). The role UNI played in calling attention to G4S workers' shared, long-term interests should not be underestimated. "What really made the whole campaign so powerful is that other unions saw things as part of UNI. UNI provided a network and a space to build these relationships. . . . It was definitely a lot easier with UNI" (SEIU organizer, personal interview, July 14, 2009).

After two years of distancing itself from the G4S campaign, GMB stood in proud recognition of its own role in helping the Alliance for Justice at G4S achieve its ultimate goal: a working relationship with G4S executives at the global level. In December 2008 GMB's general secretary Paul Kenny announced, on behalf on his union, "We are pleased that we have been able to assist in facilitating a meaningful dialogue between G4S and UNI, which is good for G4S employees all over the world" (G4S 2008).

GMB could have approached G4S executives about a global agreement much earlier than it did. According to G4S human resources director Jenni Myles, "We [had] been considering whether an agreement with UNI is appropriate for a number of years and began serious discussions with the assistance of the GMB union back in 2007" (Telljohann 2009). Yet it was not until GMB became impressed by the demonstrated potential of the transnational campaign to genuinely serve workers' interests that the British union acted to secure the TLA's aims. SEIU's efforts to expand the inclusiveness of the transnational campaign through UNI and the resulting series of victories in various countries therefore helped secure GMB's support by demonstrating SEIU's commitment to the shared, long-term goals of building union power and elevating labor standards in the security services industry globally.

Although the breadth of the TLA campaign made it easier for GMB to approach upper management about engaging with UNI, GMB was not naïve about SEIU's intentions. GMB believed that the American union expanded the TLA campaign because "SEIU needed extra leverage outside the US. They had the dollars but not the members. So they bought the influence in the GUF" (GMB official, personal interview, November 30, 2009). GMB was thus wary of SEIU's leadership and sought to ensure that SEIU's self-interested strategy did not devolve into crass opportunism. If G4S were to lose valuable security contracts or suffer irreparable reputational damage as a result of the transnational campaign, the cost of GMB members' jobs would be too high for the British union to bear. GMB therefore chose to steer the campaign in a direction more beneficial to its own members.

"GMB decided to develop the global agreement with G4S because we have better relations with the company. We intervened because it was clear that the UNI campaign wasn't going to deliver in our favor. UNI just said they want an agreement. We had to make sure this wasn't really just about a few Wackenhut workers" (GMB official, personal interview, November 30, 2009). According to GMB, SEIU's original proposal for a global union partnership with G4S was too US-centric. "The actual draft of the global agreement with G4S was literally written by lawyers in Washington" (GMB official, personal interview, November 30, 2009). With its emphasis on card-check organizing, employer neutrality, and other access provisions, SEIU seemed to be imposing "the same rigid elements irrespective of the legal and social conditions workers face in different parts of the world," according to GMB national organizer Martin Smith (Smith 2008, 8). As another GMB organizer argued, "We see fundamentally different industrial relations environments even among English speaking countries. So the import of a model won't always work" (personal interview, October 15, 2009).

GMB finally approached G4S executives with a compromise compatible with corporate interests as well as the interests of the TLA. GMB also convinced SEIU to drop its most self-serving demands from the soon-to-be-signed GFA. "GMB said to SEIU, we will use our leverage to get you access [to G4S managers], but you need to tell your people to get rid of all the other junk [in the draft agreement]. The GUFs were resistant to that," a GMB official explained, adding, "We won the argument. And [SEIU president] Andy [Stern] agreed. Yes, G4S is a success" (personal interview, November 30, 2009).

THE OUTCOME: THE G4S CAMPAIGN CONCLUDES SUCCESSFULLY

On December 11, 2008, G4S, UNI Property Services, and GMB signed the Ethical Employment Partnership, a GFA covering all of G4S's 570,000 employees in more than 110 countries (Telljohann 2009). According to the document, the parties "agree to work together to raise employment standards throughout G4S and the wider market" (G4S and UNI 2008). UNI and GMB, for their part, agreed to support the commercial success of G4S, maintain a constructive dialogue with the company, settle disputes peacefully, and "promote G4S as an employer which offers job security and stability" (G4S and UNI 2008). G4S, in turn, "recognises UNI as its global partner as well as the unique position of GMB as the largest union in the home market of G4S" (G4S and UNI 2008). G4S also agreed to respect the ILO core conventions, work constructively with unions, support a living wage and work-life balance, and grant local unions access to employees without managers present "to freely explain the benefits of joining the union," a major win for SEIU (G4S and UNI 2008).

Perhaps the most interesting aspect of the GFA is its clear acknowledgment of the highly competitive environment G4S faces as one of several firms in the private security industry and the need for UNI affiliates to help G4S stay financially viable. As the document states, "The parties recognise that G4S operates in a highly competitive environment in which many local competitors do not respect laws on working hours and pay. If any improvements to terms and conditions of employment appear likely to result in a loss of market share or margin to G4S, the local union and management team will develop a joint strategy and action plan to monitor and raise standards among all of the companies in the market and create an environment in which G4S will be able to raise standards without compromising its competitive position" (G4S and UNI 2008). GMB's influence on the GFA negotiation process is evident here. Without such provisions, it is unlikely that G4S would have accepted any global agreement at all. SEIU has GMB to thank for those results.

While the ultimate impact of the G4S GFA is not yet known, early assessments suggested that its impact has so far been mixed (McCallum 2013). That said, since its signing in late 2008, the GFA has produced many positive, measurable results. In Malawi, Nepal, Poland, Uganda, and even the United Kingdom, the GFA helped G4S workers gain union recognition and improve relations with management (Hoffman 2008, 5). In the Congo, G4S agreed to conduct elections for union representation, clarify workers' rights, and guarantee overtime pay (TUAC 2008). In Malawi, the GFA helped G4S workers increase their overtime pay and clarify provisions for leave time, holidays, medical visits, and retirement (TUAC 2008). G4S workers in Ghana signed a collective agreement in August 2009 that increased their wages by 27 percent and provided for employer-paid registration in the National Health Insurance Scheme (UNI 2009a). Various other unions in Africa are now "able to talk to workers about the union directly, on the job" (UNI 2009d).[22] Moreover, the GFA helped the TLA campaign come full circle when SEIU and G4S finally agreed that the latter would honor a neutrality pledge allowing the former the right to run card-check elections in the nine largest US cities in which Wackenhut operates (Meyerson 2009).

Even G4S perceived the GFA in win-win terms. In a letter to Human Rights Watch dated February 20, 2009, G4S expressed positive sentiments regarding its relationship with UNI and the over two hundred unions representing more than a quarter of all G4S employees globally. "Our success as a business is based on the engagement and capability of our employees," G4S wrote, "and we remain committed to building constructive relationships with them, and their representatives, wherever we operate" (UNI 2010b). In its 2009 corporate social responsibility report, G4S pointed to labor peace in South Africa, where an industry-wide negotiation over pay "was settled without any industrial action," in contrast to the contention of years past. Already the GFA has helped G4S stabilize its labor relations and maintain its profitability. G4S's Jenni Myles summarized the company's sentiments in stating that the GFA "was great for the brand, and it turned a bitter relationship into something helpful" (Stevens 2010).

Conclusion: The Importance of Interunion Coordination

Launched respectively in 2008 and 2006, the Tesco Global Union Alliance and the Alliance for Justice at G4S both began as attempts by US-based unions to organize workers in the United States before expanding into full-scale TLA campaigns aided by UNI Global Union. In both cases American unions with strong *intraunion coordination* attempted to exercise *coalitional* and *institutional power* with the help of the home union in Britain. Coalitional power played an important role in both the Tesco and G4S campaigns, but in neither case did this power type compel the company in question to alter its behavior, at least not directly. Both TLAs also exercised institutional power, which played a central role in the G4S campaign and had potential to help the Tesco campaign gain momentum. Nevertheless, the Tesco TLA fell apart, as UFCW failed to secure support from USDAW, which refused to jeopardize its good relationship with Tesco by backing the TLA. In contrast, SEIU convinced GMB to bring G4S to the bargaining table, and the G4S campaign concluded successfully. Evidence thus suggests that *interunion coordination* made the difference.

Chapter 4

STRUGGLE IN PARADISE

Context-Appropriate Power in the Shangri-La and Raffles Campaigns

When you invest in a hotel, it is not for five to 10 years. It is for 100 years.

—JENNIE CHUA, RAFFLES INTERNATIONAL EXECUTIVE VICE PRESIDENT[1]

The key thing in Indonesia was the starting point there for the workers and the union. I mean, nobody had ever challenged a company like that in Indonesia. Nobody had ever told a company that it would cost them considerable amounts of money if they wanted to, basically, get rid of some workers.

—IUF OFFICIAL[2]

This is a struggle over power. . . . It's a struggle not just to get a little more service charge money but to stake out some space in the Cambodian economy.

—SOLIDARITY CENTER ORGANIZER[3]

The opulent Shangri-La Hotel towers thirty-two stories above Jakarta's teeming central business district, a glistening pillar of lavishness and escape. Its 668 deluxe guest rooms and executive suites feature plush bedding, immaculate washrooms, enormous open spaces, and captivating city views, while the hotel's majestic ballrooms, sleek conference rooms, and world-class banquet hall compete for admiration with the exterior's lush gardens and massive lagoon pool. Opened in March 1994, the Shangri-La Hotel, Jakarta, is today one of seventy-two luxury hotels and resorts scattered across Asia-Pacific, Europe, the Middle East, and North America under the names Shangri-La, Kerry, and Traders. By the early 2000s, the Shangri-La in Indonesia had built a strong reputation for providing customers with indulgent accommodations at an equally indulgent price. Unfortunately, those high prices barely benefited the workers supplying these five-star services, as their poor working conditions and low pay clashed sharply with the luxury they helped create.

For nearly three months in late 2000, the Shangri-La Independent Workers' Union (SPMS [Serikat Pekerja Mandiri Shangri-La]) and managers of the Jakarta Shangri-La remained locked in a stalemate over the union's demands for better wages, a pension fund, equitable distribution of the gratuity charge, and an Idul Fitri holiday bonus. SPMS argued that Shangri-La was the only five-star hotel in Jakarta without a pension plan and that the average monthly wage—less than half the cost of a single night's stay in the hotel—was inadequate. Management rejected this position, arguing that the transportation allowance of Rp 100,000 per month agreed to in the last collective bargaining round boosted workers' incomes substantially. Negotiations broke down completely on December 22, 2000, when managers fired SPMS president Halilintar Nurdin, sparking a spontaneous gathering of 420 employees in the hotel lobby. According to hotel managers and major media sources, the workers' gathering constituted an "all out strike" (*Jakarta Post* 2000) that left the hotel with no choice but to shut down and evacuate guests. According to supporters of the union, "The workers didn't go on strike. When they found out their secretary [*sic*] got sacked, they gathered in the lobby. They never declared a strike. They were just trying to figure out what was going on" (IUF researcher, personal interview, November 1, 2011).

The gathering grew into a sit-in, and for four days, workers occupied the hotel lobby. Then the police came. On the morning of December 26, hundreds of police officers violently dragged out scores of protesting workers and held thirty unionists without charge for twenty-four hours (*Jakarta Post* 2001i). The rest were locked out of the hotel. Management would later claim that a handful of agitators instigated the "strike" as a means of intimidating them into conceding to the union's demands. The workers would claim that they sought only further peaceful negotiations but were met with bad faith and pressure to quit the union as a condition for returning to work.

One week after the lockout, two hundred workers received notices immediately terminating their employment. More firings followed. In response, hundreds of former Shangri-La employees continued to protest outside the hotel and, in early January, marched to the House of Representatives and rallied outside the United Nations building in central Jakarta in an effort to gain political support. The Federation of Independent Unions (FSPM [Federasi Serikat Pekerja Mandiri]), the federation with which SPMS was affiliated, even considered calling a national strike. Meanwhile, hotel operations remained halted, with police guarding the building night and day.

Scores of hotel workers wore white headbands and carried colorful placards as they protested outside the hotel several times a week. At one point SPMS threatened to occupy the building with 1,200 workers and their families to highlight the hunger and suffering caused by the dispute. As the number of fired workers grew—eventually amounting to over 560 dismissals—the union's demands shifted emphasis from wages and pensions to, simply, re-employment. According to FSPM advocacy chairman Hamonangan Saragih, "as many as 570 employees of the Shangri-La [had] not been paid" since the dispute began in December (*Jakarta Post* 2001c). With starvation looming, the fight became, for many, "a matter of life and death" (AMWU organizer, personal interview, November 8, 2011).

In April 2004, a similar situation unfolded at the Raffles Hotel Le Royal in Phnom Penh and the Raffles Grand Hotel d'Angkor in Siem Reap, Cambodia. Like all Raffles-branded luxury hotels, the Royal and Grand featured lavishly furnished suites, elegant cocktail lounges, flourishing tropical gardens, cool poolside terraces, posh dining facilities, and indulgent spas, as they aimed to cater to "affluent leisure and business travelers who require something beyond five star accommodations" (PR Newswire 2001). In April 2004, Raffles guests experienced "something beyond five star accommodations" that unfortunately did not enhance the customer experience. More than one thousand hotel workers—including Royal and Grand employees—went on strike at seven luxury hotels across Cambodia.[4] Claiming that these high-end hotels owed employees roughly US$3 million in three years of back pay, the Cambodian Tourism and Service Workers Federation (CTSWF) coordinated a weeklong work stoppage, prompting five of the hotels to quickly resume negotiations with their employees (Burton and Kazmin 2004).

The other two hotels—the Raffles Le Royal and Raffles Grand d'Angkor—stood their ground. Taking the issue to municipal courts in Phnom Penh and Siem Reap, Raffles obtained emergency court injunctions from judges who declared the strikes illegal and ordered Raffles employees to return to work within forty-eight hours of the decision. Those who attempted to comply with the court order were surprised to learn, however, that they were required to sign statements promising not to participate in further strikes. Others attempting to report to work at the Royal and the Grand were simply refused entry. Raffles Le Royal then fired 97 workers. Raffles Grand d'Angkor sacked another 190. "In other words, Raffles refused to let the workers return to their jobs and then fired them for . . . not reporting to work," an IUF report notes, concluding that the dispute "at that point, became a conflict over fundamental rights" (IUF 2004a).

Scores of workers began to assemble daily in front of the two hotel buildings, along the street, and in a nearby park, while others held signs and distributed leaflets near high-traffic tourist attractions (Raffles Le Royal union official, personal communication, May 14, 2011). At one point over three hundred workers rallied outside the Grand in Siem Reap to demand reinstatement for those dismissed. Nonetheless, constant picketing took a toll. In Siem Reap workers sustained their families by fishing in the river by the hotel. "There was no strike fund, so it was essentially people figuring out how to survive during the months they were locked out," explained a Solidarity Center field director (personal interview, December 15, 2011). Raffles Le Royal union president Sao Vanthein put it bluntly: "Poor workers and their families will die if this dispute lasts any longer" (*Cambodia Daily* 2004d).

The Shangri-La and Raffles disputes both culminated in transnational campaigns aimed at restoring workers' jobs and rights. Their similarities are striking: Both were launched in response to mass dismissals of hundreds of employees of five-star hotels in major tourist and business destination cities in Southeast Asia. Both focused on employers with strong interests in maintaining a global brand. And in both cases local workers formed TLAs that staged rallies in various cities around the world and bombarded hotel owners with thousands of protest messages. Unlike their Indonesian counterparts, however, the Cambodian workers won: in less than six months, Raffles rehired the majority of the workers, recognized their union exclusively, negotiated a new collective bargaining agreement, and guaranteed their full pay. In contrast, despite dozens of international rallies, countless protest letters, and the threat of industrial action at one of the company's overseas properties, the

Shangri-La campaign concluded after nearly two and a half years with the destruction of the local union and the majority of the Indonesian workers suffering from prolonged unemployment.

Why did these two campaigns turn out so differently? In this chapter I argue that a difference in TLAs' power strategies is what set these two cases apart. Specifically, the Shangri-La TLA relied mainly on *structural power*, which failed to faze local hotel managers, whose court-based strategy meanwhile forced workers to focus on the local scale. In contrast, the use of *coalitional power* on the international scale by the Raffles TLA successfully threatened the core, long-term interests of Raffles Hotels and Resorts, which, for its part, failed to restrict conflict to domestic-level institutions. Evidence therefore points to the importance of context-appropriate power in TLA campaigns.

As explained in chapter 1, what determines context-appropriate power is the extent to which workers' actions directly threaten the economic structures, institutions, or stakeholders on which the target employer depends for its present and future profitability. One can therefore predict whether a particular power type will be effective in changing an employer's behavior by analyzing that employer's core interests and interdependencies. Such an analysis requires neither blanket assumptions about entire industries nor the assumption that individual employers' interests are so idiosyncratic that they can only be understood on a case-by-case basis. Hotels illustrate this well: Not all hotels share the same interests, as budget motels differ from five-star resorts when it comes to customer expectations and standards of service. Nonetheless, one can consider certain subsets of hotel types to share some set of core interests based on basic priorities, business strategies, and long-term goals.

One such subset is luxury hotels, an industry in which brand matters immensely. While short-term financial losses are relatively sustainable for most large corporations, lasting damage to a five-star hotel chain's global reputation can be devastating and irreversible. As an IUF official explained in an interview, for these hotels, image is everything: "Even if, before the dispute, the company spent tons of money to build up a good name, if the dispute is big and goes on for a long time, that money and investment go to waste. It's not the same as in a mining company. Hotels are more sensitive about their good name" (personal interview, September 16, 2011). The statement quoted in one of this chapter's epigraphs from Raffles International executive vice president Jennie Chua bears repeating here: an investment in a hotel "is not for five to 10 years. It is for 100 years." Hence, one should expect owners of five-star, luxury hotel chains to place high value on how potential hotel patrons perceive their company's reputation and brand since negative public perceptions can undermine profits permanently.

Because brand matters so much for luxury hotels, the CCAP theory would predict that a TLA campaign aimed at such an employer would be most effective if it leverages the pressure of influential media sources and high-profile hotel guests, a form of coalitional power. If the TLA can convince high-profile customers not to patronize that particular hotel chain, the employer in question would then give in to this pressure, not out of concern for short-term profit losses or fear of intervention by a powerful state but to secure its brand and the longevity of its business. Given the specific contexts of the two cases to be discussed, the CCAP theory would also predict less success with other possible power strategies, including strikes and demonstrations at the hotels in question (structural power), which would be rendered ineffective by an easily replaceable workforce, and appeals to legal authorities (institutional power), given workers' many disadvantages in the Indonesian and Cambodian court systems (discussed later).

This chapter begins with a story of shifting context. At the time of these two disputes, both Indonesia and Cambodia were experiencing not only an expansion in the tourism industry but also a changing landscape of labor laws, which in turn shaped interactions among overseas hotel owners, local hotel managers, local workers, and transnational labor allies. I then examine the events of the Shangri-La and Raffles campaigns through a close focus on actors' strategic interactions on the local, national, and international scales. Both TLAs featured strong intra- and interunion coordination, ruling out these factors as explanations for the campaigns' different outcomes. Both also faced employers who pursued similar strategies to restrict the scale of conflict. Evidence suggests that what made the crucial difference was context-appropriate power.

Labor and Capital in Context: Similar Institutional Environments

The 1990s ushered into Southeast Asia an era of political transformation and economic restructuring, including updates to industrial relations laws and labor rights across several countries in the region. Indonesia and Cambodia are among the most dynamic with respect to changes in labor relations. By the early 2000s, both countries featured newly established or revived rights to freedom of association, collective bargaining, and processes of dispute resolution. At the same time, however, employers in both countries remained resistant to implementing these new rules, a fact reflected in the hotel disputes under examination. While one might suggest that the Shangri-La and Raffles campaigns' divergent outcomes were due to differences in domestic institutions, evidence suggests otherwise. Cambodia's institutional context was no more favorable to upholding workers' rights than institutions in Indonesia. Local and national institutions in both countries offered, at best, minimal protection of labor rights and, at worst, a means through which employers could continue to pursue repressive practices.

Industrial Relations Institutions in Indonesia

In many ways, the turmoil at Shangri-La should not have been such a shock. Following Suharto's fall in May 1998, *reformasi* politics and persistent international pressure swept in a wave of reforms that expanded opportunities for organized labor throughout the country. These reforms restored workers' rights to freedom of association, collective bargaining, and redress in the face of employer obstruction or discrimination (Caraway 2004). Registration requirements were relaxed, enabling groups of ten or more workers to unionize not only at the enterprise level but also in whole sectors (Rupidara and McGraw 2010). This removal of New Order–era repressions thus unleashed "a pent-up explosion of long-supported workers' consciousness and militancy" (IUF researcher, personal interview, April 19, 2011), along with a considerable broadening of the occupations and industries unions covered (Ford 2000).

Nevertheless, remnants of New Order politics still permeated employment relations. Despite the Habibie administration's ratification of ILO Convention 87 on Freedom of Association and Protection of the Right to Organize in June 1998, and the Wahid government's passing of the relatively progressive Trade Union Act in August 2000, serious violations of labor rights still occurred—a fact foreign governments, investors, and international organizations found worrisome (Caraway 2004). In early 2001, ILO executive director Kari Tapiola publicly criticized Indonesia for failing to implement fundamental ILO principles (*Jakarta Post* 2001e). The country thus featured a de facto persistence of earlier labor practices despite de jure changes in institutions of industrial relations.

Employers were therefore still learning how to operate in the post-Suharto period. As Caraway pointed out, "Under Suharto there was no need to think much about labor law. If there was a problem with workers, it could be solved by calling the police or the military, or by paying a bribe to the relevant officials" (Caraway 2004, 40). Moreover, employers had grown accustomed to dealing with the predictably compliant All-Indonesia Workers' Union (Serikat Pekerja Seluruh Indonesia), the only state-sanctioned union under the New Order. In contrast, the proliferation of trade unions and the renewal of labor laws in this era changed the rules of the game.

The 900-strong SPMS represented this new generation of Indonesian unions. By December 2000, SPMS represented roughly 78 percent of the Shangri-La Hotel's 1,150 employees and strove to be a model of democratic, independent unionism. Still, like most new unions in Indonesia at this time, SPMS had yet to prove its power. "The challenge wasn't, do you have money? The challenge was, you had to have a 'win'" (Solidarity Center official, personal interview, April 19, 2011).

Industrial Relations Institutions in Cambodia

Labor rights in Cambodia are still new on paper and even more so in practice. Neither the 1993 Constitution—which includes articles on freedom of association and rights to strike and hold nonviolent demonstrations—nor the 1997 Labor Law—covering working hours, health and safety, dismissal procedures, and other rights—has been well enforced. Likewise, despite Cambodia's ratification of ILO Conventions 87 and 98 on freedom of association and collective bargaining, Cambodian workers still face substantial hardship, poverty, and exploitation. In the late 1990s the Cambodian Ministry of Labor came under pressure from the ILO and the US government to remedy this disjuncture between paper and practice (Hiatt and Greenfield 2004, 56–57). Labor unrest in the growing garment industry was especially troubling, as wildcat strikes occurred frequently and sometimes turned violent (Arnold 2002). A bilateral agreement between the United States and Cambodia in 1999 helped improve garment factory conditions by tying increased access to US markets for Cambodian companies to tangible improvements in health, safety, unionization, and other international labor standards. Between 1999 and 2004, Cambodia's annual exports tripled, and garment exports, 66 percent of which flowed to the United States, represented one-third of the country's gross domestic product (*New Republic* 2004). Nevertheless, it was not clear that these enhanced labor rights would spill over into other industries. Moreover, the expiration of the US-Cambodia agreement in 2005 threatened to reduce employers' incentives for improving the country's labor conditions. Yet with the rise of the tourism industry, a crucial driver of economic development, alongside garment manufacturing and agriculture, workers saw another opportunity to fight for better rights.

The notion of a luxury, five-star hotel thriving in Cambodia seemed far-fetched when the Raffles Le Royal and Grand d'Angkor reopened in the late 1990s. The horrors of the Khmer Rouge and turmoil of civil war had induced such a lasting trauma that the UN-led restoration of democracy in the early 1990s could only begin to restore normality to a country still rife with poverty and corruption. Nevertheless, in 1997, the Singapore-based Raffles Hotels and Resorts boldly chose to reopen two neglected remnants of Cambodia's more peaceful past. Built respectively in the 1920s and 1930s, the Royal and the Grand had drawn droves of well-heeled guests in the pre- and post–World War II years and endured the tumultuous 1970s and 1980s before emerging from refurbishment in the late 1990s as majestic structures comprising "a subtle blend of Khmer, Art Deco and French Colonial architecture" (Raffles Hotels and Resorts, n.d.). Raffles' launch of its luxury line sparked something of a revolution in the Cambodian tourism industry. By the mid-2000s, hundreds of hotels cropped up in Phnom Penh and Siem Reap (gateway to the ancient temple ruins of Angkor), aiming to attract tourists with more expensive tastes than those of the typical backpacker. Tourism soared. In 2004 the number of international visitors to Cambodia exceeded one million for the first time in the country's history (*New York Times* 2006).

A tourism boom meant expanding employment. Like the garment factories, Cambodia's hotels created thousands of highly coveted formal-sector jobs. Yet even in five-star hotels like the Royal and the Grand, workers still struggle to earn enough to live. For instance, a signed pay sheet from the Raffles Grand Hotel d'Angkor dated December 2003 shows temporary contract workers receiving between US$1 and US$1.57 a day to perform tasks such as gardening, valet services, room attendance, laundry services, cooking, and river cleaning. Records also show workers receiving no paid public holidays, no annual leave, and no medical insurance. "Our basic salary is as little as US$30 per month," reads an open letter to hotel guests from employees of the Raffles and other luxury hotels. "Cambodia is a poor country . . . [and we] struggle to feed ourselves and our families" (Cambodian Tourism and Service Workers Federation 2004).

In September 2003 ten unions came together to form the CTSWF. Closely tied to the Solidarity Center, a US-government-funded NGO affiliated with the AFL-CIO, the CTSWF set out to tackle long-standing labor issues in the hospitality industry.[5] Local news sources soon identified the CTSWF as "the strongest labor bargaining agent in the country" (*Cambodia Daily* 2003). Despite this, the CTSWF, like other unions across Cambodia, remained disadvantaged by domestic institutions. Workers complained that both the Ministry of Labor and the courts were rife with corruption and inefficiencies. Low wages encouraged civil servants to accept bribes, patronage networks stayed entrenched, and rent seeking was prevalent (Adler and Woolcock 2009, 178, 167; Chheang 2008, 284). "The court is corrupt. Whoever has the money will win the case," insisted CTSWF president Ly Korm (*Cambodia Daily* 2004e).

That same year, 2003, also saw the creation of the Cambodian Arbitration Council (AC), an independent, nonjudicial body that issues decisions on workplace disputes unresolved through regular industrial relations procedures. Its decision-making process is straightforward: a panel of three hears each case, and then determines a solution based on prior panel decisions, Cambodian law, and ILO standards. Nevertheless, either party can render a decision nonbinding by filing an opposition within eight days of receiving notification of the decision; hence, over 90 percent of AC cases are without legal effect (Adler and Woolcock 2009, 180). Moreover, since the AC cannot enforce laws, even binding decisions must be enforced in the courts. Despite (or perhaps because of) this flexibility, as well as the fact that unions, employers' associations, and the government have equal say in nominating AC members, both employers and workers hold the AC in relatively high regard.

Nevertheless, when it comes to labor law overall, "enforcement is patchy," and issues such as forced overtime, violence against union leaders, and long working hours remain a long way from resolved (Adler and Woolcock 2009,

168; Hiatt and Greenfield 2004, 59). As in Indonesia, employers are still learning how to handle unions. "Unions are relatively young in Cambodia," reflected one IUF official, and at the time of the Raffles dispute, "Cambodia was just opening up. Industrial relations were relatively new, and labor law came just a few years before that" (personal interview, September 16, 2011). The Raffles conflict thus developed during a high-stakes stage of institutional transition. Onlookers were therefore correct when they predicted that the "outcome of this struggle will have a major impact on unions' ability to win new members and influence conditions in Cambodia's growing tourism industry" (IUF 2004b).

Comparable Intraunion Coordination Levels

As the foregoing discussion shows, the similar institutional settings in Indonesia and Cambodia offer little to suggest that national context favored labor more in the latter than the former. Hence, institutional context cannot explain why one campaign succeeded but the other one did not. Another potential explanation for the cases' different outcomes rests on intraunion coordination. Since successful TLA campaigns require strong internal coordination on the part of the individual unions spearheading them, weak intraunion coordination can destroy an otherwise well-organized campaign, as the Liverpool case demonstrated (see chapter 2).

Yet for neither TLA in question was this the case: both the Shangri-La and Raffles hotel workers were members of activist, democratic unions characterized by strong, positive relationships between union leaders and rank-and-file members. The two main unions involved, SPMS in Indonesia and CTSWF in Cambodia, possessed comparable levels of intraunion coordination. This fact is reflected in the ease with which workers attained local mobilization at the beginning of both campaigns. That both the Indonesian and the Cambodian workers maintained almost daily protest activity for the duration of these disputes is evidence of both unions' internal unity and strength. Both campaigns also benefited from an influx of material resources, which sustained campaigners otherwise unable to support themselves and their families. Variation in intraunion coordination thus cannot explain the two campaigns' dissimilar outcomes.

Comparable Interunion Coordination Levels

Differences in *inter*union coordination also do not explain these cases. I show in this section how both sets of hotel workers attained interunion coordination with ease, thanks to existing links between SPMS and the IUF, on one hand, and between CTSWF and the Solidarity Center, on the other hand. In contrast to the Tesco campaign (see chapter 3), neither TLA had a home union problem since their strategies did not depend on gaining the support of unions from Hong Kong and Singapore, Shangri-La's and Raffles' respective headquarter countries. Instead, these campaigns were characterized by strong cross-border solidarity, especially between the Indonesian workers and Australian unions in the Shangri-La case and between the Cambodian workers and American labor activists in the Raffles case.

Australians' Special Solidarity in the Shangri-La TLA

Though clearly capable of mobilizing local protests, SPMS knew it could not sustain its campaign without additional support. Through its affiliation with FSPM, SPMS contacted the IUF, a global union with a history of assisting then-illegal independent unions in Indonesia during the Suharto years. The IUF immediately set out to support SPMS by donating Rp 20 million, communicating with the ILO, sending a letter to President Abdurrahman Wahid and the Ministry of Manpower and Transmigration, and bringing the dispute to the attention of its hundreds of trade union affiliates around the world. In response to the IUF's call to action, the Hong Kong Confederation of Trade Unions quickly organized a rally outside their local Shangri-La hotel. Over the coming months, dozens more rallies outside Shangri-La hotels and Indonesian embassies would follow in Bangkok, Brussels, Geneva, The Hague, Los Angeles, Melbourne, Seoul, Stockholm, Sydney, Toronto, and Washington, DC. Labor allies showed support in other ways as well, as when unions and NGOs intending to hold a conference at the Shangri-La Hotel in Shenzhen intentionally switched venues in solidarity with the workers in Indonesia.

Australian unions were especially well positioned to play a significant role in the Shangri-La campaign not only because the IUF's Asia-Pacific branch is headquartered in Sydney but also because Australian workers already had a history of supporting their Indonesian counterparts. This history spans far back into the 1940s, when Australian dockers and seafarers refused to service Dutch ships en route to deliver arms intended to be used to suppress Indonesia's national independence movement (Ivens 1946). Australians' strong interunion coordination with Indonesian workers is also motivated by practicality. As one unionist explained, "So far as Australia is concerned, Indonesia is close by, and they have been quite concerned for many years about the abuse of workers' rights in Indonesia. When called upon, [Australian unions] do whatever they can so workers are treated better and have decent working conditions. It's good for them to defend other workers' rights. A victory anywhere is a victory for them" (IUF official personal interview, September 16, 2011).

Australians' involvement in the Shangri-La campaign began with Sharan Burrow, then president of ACTU, who sent a media alert to unions across the country. Burrow also spoke at a rally outside Sydney's World Bank Offices in hopes of drawing attention to the fact that the Shangri-La Hotel in Jakarta had been funded by a US$86 million joint World Bank–private-sector loan. Although pursuing that institutional connection later proved ineffective (the loan had already been paid off), "it did put pressure on Shangri-La, and it raised their profile in Australia, which [the owners] didn't like" (IUF official, personal interview, September 17, 2011).

Members of the Liquor, Hospitality, and Miscellaneous Workers' Union (LHMU) coordinated mass letter writings and rallies. One LHMU member also visited Jakarta to deliver a donation to SPMS on behalf of ACTU, toured other Indonesian hotels to build support for the campaign, and personally participated in the workers' local protests (Australian Manufacturing Workers' Union [AMWU] organizer, personal interview, November 8, 2011). The head of the New South Wales Labour Council, who would later go on to become a shadow minister in the federal government, gave the campaign his explicit support. Every Australian union affiliated with the IUF donated funds to support the campaign, and, through organizations such as Unions New South Wales, even unions not affiliated with the IUF became involved by participating in demonstrations outside the Shangri-La offices in Sydney (IUF researcher, personal interview, November 1, 2011).

Several months into the dispute, it still remained to be seen how effective these tactics would be. The boldest show of solidarity from SPMS's Australian allies would come later in the form of a direct attack on the Kuok Group's development ambitions. This act of structural power (discussed later) would be further proof that the Australian labor movement fully supported the workers at Shangri-La.

Americans' Special Solidarity in the Raffles TLA

Like their counterparts in Jakarta, the hotel workers in Phnom Penh and Siem Reap had no problem achieving strong interunion coordination. Transnational ties, particularly to the AFL-CIO-affiliated Solidarity Center, were woven into the creation of the Cambodian hotel unions well before the Raffles campaign arose. "The development of trade unions in the hotel industry was really a project of the Solidarity Center. We had government money," explained a Solidarity Center field director in an interview (December 15, 2011). The Americans began to help Cambodian workers organize unions in the early 2000s, first in the garment industry, then in tourism. When the Raffles conflict broke out in mid-2004, Solidarity Center staff were still present in Cambodia yet careful not to overstep their bounds. "It's not that the Solidarity Center was endorsing the strike or supporting the strike," the field director clarified. "The role of the Solidarity Center could be called more of a mentorship between unions so that they would be able to learn how to settle their disputes" (personal interview, December 15, 2011). By focusing on training and advice, the Americans sought to empower the Cambodian unionists at the grassroots level without necessarily directing workers toward any specific course of action.

When the Raffles conflict erupted, however, Solidarity Center staff decided to assist the hotel workers in additional ways. Financial support was seen as particularly essential. Back in the United States, Solidarity Center staff helped arrange for SEIU to provide $25,000 to the CTSWF (Raffles Le Royal union official, personal communication, May 14, 2011). The IUF also contributed funds. According to a Solidarity Center field director, it was important "that we had some financial assistance because the management tactic was basically to wait it out. Workers were running out of money" (personal interview, December 15, 2011). More important than money, however, was the Solidarity Center's assistance in strategy. As will be shown, CTSWF's American allies provided guidance that shifted the TLA toward different tactics. The result would be a crucial change in the direction of the campaign.

Contrasting Campaign Strategies: An Analysis of Workers' and Employers' Actions

Neither intraunion coordination nor interunion coordination can explain the different outcomes of the Shangri-La and Raffles campaigns, as these did not vary across the two cases. Another potential explanation lies in an analysis of employers' strategies. In both Indonesia and Cambodia, domestic institutional context generally favored employers over labor, as de facto practices had not yet caught up with de jure institutional change. Hence, it made sense that local hotel managers in both Indonesia and Cambodia strove to restrict the scale of conflict to the level of local and national institutions that advantaged employers. Conversely, workers in both cases sought to do the exact opposite: expand conflict to the international scale.

Evidence suggests, however, that control over scale is only part of the story. What mattered most of all was whether workers were able to exercise context-appropriate power once they expanded the conflict to the international scale. At several points in both campaigns, workers had the opportunity to exercise context-appropriate power, yet only the Raffles TLA did so. These dynamics are explored in this section.

Labor's Lost Horizon: Scale and Strategy in the Shangri-La Campaign

As indicated earlier, the Shangri-La campaign entailed several local protests, daily on-site demonstrations, and numerous displays of transnational solidarity coordinated by the IUF. Although the Shangri-La TLA had the capacity to exercise coalitional power, it relied instead on various forms of structural power throughout the campaign. Meanwhile, local hotel managers made a great effort to refocus the workers' attention and energy back onto the local scale.

EMPLOYER ACTIONS IN INDONESIA, PART ONE

It was clear from the start of the dispute that management sought to channel it through formal conflict resolution bodies—specifically, the courts and the Central Committee for Settlement of Labor Disputes, a nonjudicial, government entity referred to as P4P (Panitia Penyelesaian Perselisihan Perburuhan Pusat).[6] Pointing to the workers' "illegal occupation" of the hotel in late December, Shangri-La Indonesia-Fiji general manager Peter J. Carmichael characterized the dispute as "a legal matter" (*Jakarta Post* 2001l), while the dismissal letter sent to workers in early January made reference to "acts ... which could be classified as criminal" and therefore best dealt with by legal authorities. Managers then attempted to secure termination permits through P4P and file a lawsuit in court. As justification for these actions, Shangri-La Asia chief operating officer John Segreti stated simply, "We regret that we cannot sacrifice our principles and our legal rights" (*Jakarta Post* 2001a).

Less clear was how much of a legal case management truly had. Certainly, business was hurting. According to the hotel's lawyer, Maqdir Ismail, by mid-January, the emergency closing and damages to facilities had cost over Rp 18 billion (US$1.8 million) in revenue losses (*Jakarta Post* 2001h). Nonetheless, SPMS maintained that its protests were peaceful and lawful. Moreover, SPMS deputy chairman Denny Suprihadi believed the firings were in fact "an effort to suppress the union" since the dismissals targeted union members, some of whom were not even present at the December sit-in (*Jakarta Post* 2001i). Written testimony from hotel bartender Heri Hartoyo, for instance, states that he had been on holiday at the time of the walkout and visiting his wife in the hospital in Bandung during the sit-in. When he later attempted to report for work as scheduled, he was confronted with the following response: "I was ordered to wait at home until I received a letter of summons. . . . I never received a letter of any kind from the hotel. Then my name was listed [among the dismissed]." SPMS further accused management of intimidation, failure to pay workers' salaries, and the unjust firing of union president Halilintar Nurdin.

In addition to legal proceedings, Shangri-La's managers relied on police and private security forces to disperse the protesters. In February 2001, during an otherwise peaceful demonstration, guards assaulted SPMS treasurer Muhammad Zulrahman, causing "severe bruising to the head, cuts, torn lips requiring stitching, and missing teeth" (Goss 2001). According to a report submitted to the ILO, witnesses identified one of the assailants as Kaleb Ehanusa, personal bodyguard to Osbert Lyman, local owner of the Shangri-La Hotel, Jakarta.[7] On March 17, 2001, police broke up another protest following a reopening of the hotel with replacement staff and security officers provided by the city. That afternoon, over three hundred headband-clad workers arrived and began chanting, waving banners, and hoisting up decorated coffins bearing the names of the hotel's owners and human resources manager. As the protest spilled off the sidewalk and onto the road, police intervened with rattan sticks. According to a statement from one of the workers present, SPMS members "were assaulted by police. Multiple injuries were inflicted, including a woman worker who suffered a miscarriage." Senior manager Wastu Widanto expressed regret about the "unfortunate and disappointing action taken by the striking workers," which, he claimed, "highlights the lack of respect for the legal processes and laws of Indonesia" (*Jakarta Post* 2001j).

Management's third tactic was to offer compensation packages worth up to three months' salary to workers willing to resign from their jobs immediately. By early April, 303 workers had resigned, accepted compensation, and left the picket line.[8] Widanto told the press that those resigning "told us that they were happy to put the matter behind them and that the campaign, raised by a few union leaders against the management, was wrong." He added that accepting the money was "better for them than awaiting dismissal" from P4P (*Jakarta Post* 2001k).[9]

In mid-April the Shangri-La campaign suffered another blow when four SPMS officials resigned from the hotel. According to Nurdin, the four officials—Denny Setiadi, Frits Risakota, Budi Susanto, and Wawan Rusmana—had received special "commissions" from management for each worker they compelled to resign. On these grounds, Nurdin kicked them out of the union. Others close to the situation suggested that the four had not been bought off but rather pressured and intimidated. "Some of the union board were terrorized at home. They were sent dead cats, dead rats, things like that" (SPMS union official, personal interview, March 5, 2012). The four claim that they quit of their own volition.

Shortly after the four officials quit, P4P finally handed down its decision authorizing the workers' mass dismissal. At this point over four hundred workers had already resigned and accepted compensation, leaving fewer than one hundred to either accept the ruling or pursue an appeal. Most of those remaining chose to press on by filing a suit against P4P through the state administrative high court. With less local leverage than ever, however, SPMS also looked to transnational solidarity as an ever more crucial part of their campaign.

STRUCTURAL POWER IN THE SHANGRI-LA CAMPAIGN

Shangri-La's labor relations were complicated by the fact that 55 percent of the hotel was owned not locally but by the Kuok Group, the business conglomerate that, through its major equity holding in Shangri-La Asia, managed all but eighteen of the seventy-two Shangri-La, Traders, and Kerry hotels worldwide, most of which were also wholly owned by either Shangri-La Asia or another company in the Kuok Group. The group's founder, Malaysian-born, Hong Kong–based billionaire Robert Kuok, established Shangri-La Hotels and Resorts in 1982 and is frequently cited by *Forbes* as one of the wealthiest men in the world. Although Shangri-La represented just a portion of the Kuok Group's numerous investments, Kuok expressed his personal commitment to upholding Shangri-La's reputation, even eschewing the moniker Sugar King of Asia in favor of Hotel King in an interview with China Central Television. Kuok therefore had considerable stake in the longevity and integrity of the Shangri-La brand.

The hotel's ties to Kuok inspired the Shangri-La TLA to counter managers' local tactics with actions on the international scale. In April 2001 SPMS's allies in Australia took a bold action when a builders' union threatened industrial action at a construction site tipped to be bid on by a company from the Kuok Group, which had tendered the government of the state of Victoria to build a hotel, a residential facility, and several shops and restaurants in the Docklands area of Melbourne over a span of fifteen years. Worth AU$1.8 billion, the contract was so important that Kuok himself visited Melbourne to view the proposed site in mid-February 2001.

Aware of the development bid, and despite the serious potential consequences of violating secondary boycott laws, the Victorian Building Workers Union publicly threatened a construction ban in the event that the Kuok Group won the Docklands contract without first ensuring the reinstatement of the workers in Jakarta. According to one news source, "Australian unions have said that until the company resolves its problems with the independent hotel union members in Indonesia, no hotels will be built . . . at the Melbourne Docklands. In solidarity with the locked out Shangri-La workers, the Victorian Building Workers Union publicly stated that it would boycott the building project if it were awarded to Robert Kuok" (Asia Monitor Resource Centre 2001). Another source reported, "Australian construction unions, as an act of solidarity with the hotel workers . . . threatened bans if

Mr. Kuok's company won the project. . . . The construction workers in Melbourne told the State Government there they would not work co-operatively with the Shangri-La group if they won the project because of the continuing dispute in Jakarta. Victorian unions, backed by the ACTU, lobbied strongly to stop Mr. Kuok winning the tender" (*LaborNet* 2001).

While it is not possible to verify definitively that the union's statement influenced the proceedings of the contract bid, there is evidence that the threat of a building ban had an impact. On April 12, 2001, the *Age* reported that the Victorian Docklands Authority denied Kuok the contract, awarding it instead to Lend Lease, a company known for its cooperative relationship with Australian unions (*Age* 2001). The state government of Victoria would not comment on why Kuok did not win the bid. In any case, it was a lucrative contract to have lost.

DIM SUM OF STRUGGLE: MAINTAINING LABOR'S LOCAL FRONT

The Shangri-La TLA continued its strategy of structural power on both the domestic and international scales. Australian unions' efforts, alongside those of other IUF affiliates, undoubtedly stirred the Kuok Group in Hong Kong. Four months into the conflict, Kuok was already claiming US$14 million in damages due to the Jakarta dispute. Nevertheless, the TLA campaign seemed to do little to deter local owner Osbert Lyman and the on-site managers of the hotel in Jakarta from continuing their strategy of emphasizing the legal process and breaking up local protests. Sources close to the negotiations indicate that Kuok in fact would have liked to settle the dispute much sooner, while Lyman remained recalcitrant.

The SPMS members still seeking to win their jobs back thus became preoccupied with the local front. In addition to daily demonstrations, workers set up a small restaurant staffed by former Shangri-La Hotel waiters, stewards, and cooks, who prepared five-star meals sold at low prices to passersby. Set up under a two-by-five-meter tent furnished with two benches and decorated with campaign photos and union banners, Warung Solidaritas (Solidarity Café) served items named to invoke the spirit of the campaign, such as Siomay Perjuangan (Dim Sum of Struggle) and Nasi Goreng Stop PHK (Stop Dismissal Fried Rice). SPMS also took to the streets. On May 1, SPMS members led a sit-in outside the Jakarta Central Court. Over two thousand workers from several hotels sang, chanted slogans, and distributed flyers to the public.

These local actions generated substantial public support. As an IUF staff member explained, "In Jakarta, the general public, for sure, supported the workers. [The workers] would hold demonstrations in really busy parts of central Jakarta. At a court hearing, there was a Swedish foreign embassy person, someone from the Dutch embassy, someone from the UN, and the ILO . . . so the whole NGO expat community in Jakarta heard about the dispute" (IUF researcher, personal interview, November 1, 2011). Still, it was not clear that this local support would extend much beyond public sympathy, as few outside the labor movement directly challenged management's efforts to induce yet more attrition on the picket line and compel the remaining ninety-four workers to concede. In other words, the Shangri-La workers were not only struggling to exercise context-appropriate power but were also struggling to keep conflict on the international scale.

In early July 2001 the campaign suffered a significant setback when SPMS president Halilintar Nurdin announced his resignation and acceptance of an undisclosed amount of monetary compensation. Shortly thereafter, Shangri-La's lawyers announced to the press that the dispute was officially over (*Jakarta Post* 2001g). Even more shocking to the remaining campaigners, however, was Nurdin's public repudiation of the TLA campaign. On July 10, 2001, the *Jakarta Post* reported that he "regretted the industrial action [and] stressed that the decision to settle was made of his own free will, free from any pressure" (2001g). Although only eighty-two workers remained in the campaign, Valentinus Wagiyo, the new president of SPMS, vowed to continue contesting the dismissals. SPMS deputy secretary Odie Hudiyanto added that "Halilintar does not represent all of the members of the union, and his statement was misleading" (*Jakarta Post* 2001b). On behalf of its affiliates, the IUF also expressed its unwavering support, stressing that it was "duty bound to come to the aid of the SPMS," whose members' families were in need of food and other necessities (*Workers Online* 2001).

For the next four months, stalemate dominated the dispute. Demonstrations continued outside the hotel, while workers waited for their appeal of the P4P decision to move through the state administrative high court. Meanwhile, the IUF waited for the ILO to respond to its charges that Shangri-La's actions were violating core conventions, as when, in late August, a sixty-strong police squad violently dispersed a peaceful protest by eighteen SPMS members before arresting fourteen of them (ILO 2001). Management, union representatives, and government officials met four times between August and November 2001, with the Ministry of Manpower chairing the events. Each time, however, management rejected any possibility of rehiring the remaining workers.

EMPLOYER ACTIONS IN INDONESIA, PART TWO: SCALE RESTRICTED

Near the end of 2001, stalemate gave way to a tug-of-war. On one end, the Shangri-La TLA attempted to maintain the campaign on the international scale by further involving the ILO and the IUF, whose attempts to meet directly with Kuok and Lyman were repeatedly rebuffed. On the other end, local hotel managers redoubled their efforts to sideline the TLA and restrict the conflict to the local scale, attacking workers not only locally but personally as well.

On November 1, 2001, the South Jakarta District Court found six SPMS executives and one IUF staff member "guilty of intimidating the hotel's management," ordering them to pay Rp 20.7 billion (US$2.2 million)—a massive sum—"in compensation for the losses they were accused of causing during their demonstrations against the hotel's management" (*Jakarta Post* 2001f). Additionally, the six union officials—Odie Hudyanto, Isep S. Mubarok, Adeng Surachman, Valentinus Wagiyo, Muhammad Zulrahman, and Hemasari Dharmabumi—were ordered to publish a formal apology in five local newspapers, pay fines for each day the apology failed to appear, and pay the costs of the court hearing. The attack on these six also entailed intimidation tactics meant to pressure them into ending the campaign. One of the defendants described the extent of the intimidation: "They didn't only attack our union but our own personal lives. They spread around our pictures, including me, and said 'three million for their head.' Can you imagine? Because there were a lot of goons in Jakarta, we had to make a system of protection at that time. . . . Fortunately, they didn't kill us" (SPMS union official, personal interview, March 5, 2012).

The IUF released a statement calling the civil suit a "deliberately vindictive" attempt to bankrupt SPMS, noting that "no criminal charges have been brought, nor convictions recorded, against the unionists." To alert the international community, SPMS members Hudiyanto and Mubarok flew to Geneva to join three thousand other participants at an ILO meeting in mid-November. The IUF also submitted official complaints to the ILO. In mid-November the ILO Committee on Freedom of Association released a report criticizing the Indonesian government for failing to protect union rights adequately, citing allegations that workers had been pressured to quit their union as a condition of staying employed and that workers had been dismissed for their union involvement rather than on legitimate grounds. The ILO urged the government to see to the reinstatement the remaining seventy-nine workers and "take the appropriate measures to remedy any effects of the anti-union discrimination for the workers and the union concerned" (ILO 2001).

In response, the Indonesian government was dismissive. Jacob Nuwa Wea, minister of manpower and transmigration, emphasized that labor disputes are a domestic matter; hence, there was no need for any international intervention. "We refuse pressure either from inside or outside the country. . . . There is no need to immediately take the matter to the International Labor Organization," he stated, adding that the Manpower Ministry, not the ILO, is the appropriate mediator in such disputes. Shangri-La's managers concurred. Muljo Rahardjo, a Shangri-La commissioner, remarked that the ILO recommendation "was only a report. We cannot reemploy the former workers because there is not an acceptable argument for it" (*Jakarta Post* 2001d).

Meanwhile, SPMS general secretary Odie Hudyanto, deputy secretary general Indrayani Lobo, treasurer Agus Zainal, and member Timron Nababan visited the United States on invitation from the Solidarity Center to participate in a panel organized by the United States–Indonesia Society (USINDO), a nonprofit organization. After the unionists described the physical attacks and other intimidation tactics used against the protesters, USINDO agreed to relocate a two-hundred-person dinner they had planned away from the Shangri-La Hotel.

This small victory was soon overshadowed by yet another setback for the campaign. In early February 2002 the *Melbourne Age* tipped that the Kuok Group would likely win approval from the Docklands Authority to build office buildings, residential towers, and a fresh-food market in another part of the Docklands. Although Kuok had lost the more valuable contract in 2001, this new, $700 million development contract, awarded to the Kuok Group officially in May 2002, was both a financial and a symbolic victory for Shangri-La.

Australian unions once more rose in solidarity with the workers in Jakarta, though this time they stopped short of threatening industrial intervention. Sharan Burrow announced that ACTU remained "concerned about this group's attitude to working people, particularly given their failure to convince their Indonesian partners to respect freedom of association and the right to collectively bargain," while Brian Boyd of the Victorian Trades Hall Council added that the "building unions in Victoria are ready, willing and able to back the ACTU in sorting out those outstanding international problems" (Bimbauer 2002). Australian Labor Party president Greg Sword wrote a letter to Victorian premier Steve Bracks, while LHMU and other unions in Melbourne, Sydney, and Canberra organized protests on Collins Street, in front of Shangri-La's marketing office, and outside the Indonesian consulate. The IUF posted updates of these efforts on its website, while unions in Toronto, New York, and Washington, DC, staged yet more solidarity protests. Australian unions also posted "click and send" form letters on their websites through which supporters could send protest messages to Robert Kuok.

Rather than engage the TLA, however, the managers in Jakarta maintained their focus on the local scale. When IUF officials, including General Secretary Ron Oswald, joined SPMS in their protests outside the hotel in Jakarta, police attempted to arrest Oswald, who was forced to flee the picket line. The IUF later noted on its website that "the threat was made directly to the IUF in order to deny the IUF its internationally recognised right to meet with and support its members engaged in a legitimate struggle" (IUF 2002). During that same visit, a meeting scheduled with Indonesia's Labour minister—the IUF's third attempt at such a meeting—was canceled once again.

A flash of hope came to the remaining campaigners when the state administrative high court ordered Shangri-La managers to reinstate all 561 workers who had been dismissed after P4P's decision in April 2001. Since 482 workers had already resigned and accepted compensation, however, this effectively meant orders to reinstate the 79 who remained. Yet immediately after the high court announced its ruling, P4P declared it would appeal the case to the Supreme Court. Management likewise launched an appeal and, rather than reinstate any workers, insisted that all parties simply wait for the Supreme Court to process the appeals. Noting that such appeals typically take around eighteen months to be heard, the ILO warned of the situation becoming "a case of 'justice delayed, justice denied'" (ILO 2001).

As the glimmer of a swift resolution to the already drawn-out dispute faded away, the remaining seventy-nine workers and the rest of the TLA braced for another bout of uncertainty. The daily protests in central Jakarta continued, while the TLA staged yet more scattered demonstrations, sent more protest emails, and once more approached the ILO. In late June the ILO again recommended that the Indonesian government investigate allegations of union busting. Management again ignored the ILO, with Widanto even claiming that the ILO had "not yet made any decision" regarding the dispute, despite clear evidence to the contrary (*Media Indonesia* 2002). The *Jakarta Post*, on June 26, 2002, summed up all sides' sentiments well with the headline "Hotel Legal Dispute Drags On."

SPMS members remained mired in court proceedings for nearly all of the rest of the year. On August 27, 2002, the six unionists who had been sued attempted to file an appeal, which the court promptly rejected, claiming the defendants had missed the filing deadline by months. In a press release, the six labor leaders countered that the appeal deadline of November 16, 2001, was unrealistic, considering that the South Jakarta District Court only handed down its decision fifteen days before that deadline. The labor leaders also claimed they needed time to raise the appeal fee of Rp 700,000, expressed "deep concern" about the appeal rejection, and criticized the court's apparent effort to "ignore the principles of justice and subordinate them to legal formality" (Shangri-La Workers' Advocacy Team 2002). While workers criticized the court system, the government "pointed the finger at the IUF, accusing it of being an outside force that has disturbed the situation" (*Tempo Magazine* 2002). Hotel managers echoed this complaint about outside interference. Widanto added that the daily demonstrations were a constant annoyance. "We aren't forbidding their demonstrations, but [we ask that they] don't go so far as to disturb the hotel guests," he remarked. "*We* aren't holding demonstrations because we're waiting for the Supreme Court decision," he added (*Suara Pembaruan* 2002, emphasis in original).

Finally, in mid-December 2002, the Supreme Court announced its decision. Ruling in favor of the Shangri-La Hotel, the Supreme Court backed P4P's original decision and authorized the termination of the seventy-nine remaining protesters, declaring illegal their occupation of the hotel in December 2000. Whatever remained of the hope for reinstatement evaporated, and the Shangri-La workers' campaign ended in defeat. All that was left to do was negotiate a settlement.

"We have endured a long and difficult struggle for justice and for our rights as workers, rights which had been violated," wrote FSPM general secretary Odie Hudiyanto in a press release shortly after the Supreme Court decision, "but we were finally prevented by the mechanisms of an utterly shambolic industrial dispute resolution system in Indonesia." He went on to argue that the legal system could not have been expected to have helped the workers since "justice can only be secured through the strength of workers themselves" (Hudiyanto 2003).

THE OUTCOME: THE SHANGRI-LA CAMPAIGN CONCLUDES
UNSUCCESSFULLY

After two months of negotiations, Shangri-La and the workers reached a confidential settlement in March 2003. Manpower Minister Jacob Nuwa Wea mediated the talks between local managers in Jakarta and leaders of the soon-to-be defunct SPMS, who released a joint press statement announcing the end of the conflict. Robert Kuok and the IUF held separate bipartite talks in Hong Kong to negotiate terms of an agreement officially ceasing the TLA campaign in exchange for compensation for the seventy-nine workers who had held on through the end.

The details of the final settlement are confidential, and parties to the dispute are legally barred from discussing them publicly. Nonetheless, reports from organizations such as the International Centre for Trade Union Rights suggest that although the seventy-nine workers were to receive compensation, reemployment was not discussed. Sources close to the negotiations in both Jakarta and Hong Kong indicate, however, that the initial agreement between Kuok and the IUF called for full reinstatement. As a local Indonesian representative for the IUF explained in an interview, "The original agreement was that these people left will be reinstated. . . . But then, in the local level, the management, the local owner, couldn't accept this settlement. And they had another meeting with our local union, and our local union approached us, and they have a consideration that it's almost impossible for them to be reinstated, to get their jobs back, and then to work in a normal situation. They understand that the situation is not the same inside the company. . . . They don't see how they can have a fair working place" (March 5, 2012). Another interviewee pointed out that, by the end of the ordeal, "99 percent didn't want to go back to those jobs anyway," suggesting that the worker-employer relationship at Shangri-La had been damaged irreparably (AMWU organizer, personal interview, November 8, 2011).

How one assesses the effectiveness of the Shangri-La campaign thus depends on how one weighs the workers' and employer's losses and gains. In terms of material gain, it is clear that tenacity paid off: The seventy-nine workers who campaigned through the end ultimately received financial compensation that was not only far higher than that received by the nearly five hundred other workers who resigned in the months prior but also higher than the amount ordered by the Supreme Court. Although the exact amount is not public knowledge, it was clear that the workers' compensation and severance pay "was enough to be financially secure—enough to buy a house" (IUF researcher, personal interview, November 1, 2011). An IUF official explained that the money was "much higher than they otherwise would have gotten. The workers who gave up [early on] lost out big by taking the small compensation provided by the company" (personal interview, September 16, 2011). These material gains prevented the outcome from being a full failure.

At the same time, one cannot ignore the fact that 561 workers—nearly the entire unionized workforce at the Shangri-La Hotel, Jakarta—lost their jobs. For many, unemployment persisted for years since so many workers were blacklisted and thus unable to secure work at other hotels or even other businesses in Jakarta. Several former Shangri-La workers moved to other cities and even other regions to find new jobs. "Their lives were disrupted. Some had to go back to the villages" (IUF researcher, personal interview, January 1, 2011). Despite the monetary awards, then, it is clear that the TLA campaign failed to achieve its main goal of winning back workers' jobs. This material loss arguably outweighs the workers' material gains. Moreover, if one also considers what workers lost in terms of capacity, the outcome is even more disappointing. The final settlement stipulated that both parties terminate all legal actions, as well as the "examination of the Shangri-La case at the international level" by the ILO and the IUF. The workers and their allies are not allowed to discuss the campaign publicly, and the IUF has deleted all references to the Shangri-La campaign from its website. Perhaps most importantly, the mass dismissal completely destroyed SPMS, a major loss in capacity for the Indonesian labor movement. This capacity loss thus places the campaign's outcome closer to a failure than a success.

As one IUF official summarized in an interview, "You have the curious situation that the Shangri-La workers secured a substantial financial benefit but not their jobs back or their union back in the hotel. . . . Shangri-La is a strange campaign. . . . If you look very objectively at the workers involved, it doesn't look like such a great success. . . . The workers got a hell of a lot more money and therefore could feed their families. Many of them took care of themselves in different ways with the money they got, and by Indonesian standards the money was substantial. But of course, in so far as it's a fight about union rights, the right to have a union and the right to have collective bargaining, on that level, they did not succeed" (September 17, 2011).

Holiday in Cambodia: Scale and Strategy in the Raffles Campaign

Like the Shangri-La TLA, the Raffles TLA relied on local protests, various sorts of demonstrations, and a series of well-coordinated transnational solidarity actions. Local hotel managers in Cambodia meanwhile attempted to force the conflict to play out primarily on the local scale, where management had an advantage, just as the managers did in the Shangri-La case. What differed, however, was the Raffles TLA's exercise of coalitional power, a shift in strategy that occurred only after a realization that structural power was not working.

EMPLOYERS' ACTIONS IN CAMBODIA

Because they are paid so little, most hotel workers in Cambodia rely on service fees to supplement their basic incomes. Service fees typically take the form of a 10 percent gratuity automatically applied to customers' bills. Article 134 of the national Labor Law stipulates that this fee be distributed directly to employees in full. Hotel workers often complain, however, that managers distribute the service fee in an arbitrary manner or even withhold these funds entirely. Managers have responded that workers sometimes receive service fee funds in other forms, such as bonuses, meals, and job training, which they claim is well within the law.

The service fee issue is what caused collective bargaining to break down at the Raffles hotels in late 2003. In January 2004 the Cambodian AC ordered Raffles to pay workers on a monthly basis all service fees collected and increase the basic wage to US$50 a month. The AC also ruled that workers may not claim back pay for previously undistributed service fees, bonuses, or other income. Yet rather than accept the AC's rulings, Raffles simply chose to discontinue their service fee entirely—a unilateral decision made at other luxury hotels as well. There is nothing illegal about not charging a service fee, nor was ignoring the AC of any legal consequence since the AC's decisions are nonbinding. As CTSWF president Ly Korm explained, "The Arbitration Council is just, but it cannot [force] the management to adhere to its decisions" (*Cambodia Daily* 2004e).

What followed were daily demonstrations involving hundreds of workers picketing outside the two hotels, in the streets, in the park, and in tourist areas. As in the Shangri-La case, Raffles' managers pursued a multipronged strategy in an effort to restrict the scale of conflict and induce attrition on the picket line. First, local managers met union militancy with direct retaliation. As the *Financial Times* reported on April 28, 2004, the head of the union at the Raffles Grand Hotel d'Angkor received explicit threats, and workers reported instances of Cambodia's "much-feared elite police unit" visiting the homes of union officials (Burton and Kazmin 2004). On May 7, 2004, several men entered the union office at the Grand and destroyed several important documents. Union leader Pat Sambo "watched as his union office on the hotel's premises was looted and government documents, establishing his union as the sole representative of the workers, were stolen" (*Cambodia Daily* 2004c). According to witnesses, the hotel's personnel manager personally took charge of the incident.

Management's second tactic was an attempt to establish a new union. Immediately after raiding the union office, managers at the Grand created a new bargaining unit with handpicked employee representatives, then announced to international media that the conflict had been settled. The *Business Times Singapore* reported on May 8, 2004, that the hotel "appears to have resolved its problem amicably" with a new twelve-month agreement "strengthening the working partnership between management and workers [and] preventing future labor disputes" (Koh 2004). Raffles Grand Hotel d'Angkor manager Riaz Mahmood declared, "We are delighted to have signed this new collective bargaining agreement, as it enables us and our employees to move forward and build a sustainable future" (*Cambodia Daily* 2004g). Meanwhile, management at both the Grand and the Royal declined to participate in mediated talks, while Royal operations manager Stephan Gnaegi refused to return reporters' phone calls or allow visits to his office. Gnaegi later emerged to announce that another new "union" was set up at the Raffles Le Royal and had negotiated a new yearlong contract. Im Khemara, deputy director of the Labor Inspection Department, backed management's move, stating that both agreements were "within the law" and supported by the Ministry of Social Affairs (*Cambodia Daily* 2004f).

The dismissed workers were not so sanguine. CTSWF filed complaints with the Ministry of Social Affairs and local police. According to Raffles Le Royal union president Sao Vanthein, Raffles' actions were "illegal. The hotel has abused the labor law" (*Cambodia Daily* 2004f). He elaborated: "Owners and managers had a lot of strategies to counter our union. They break [*sic*] my own union to fight each other. They used pro-government unions to break us, and especially, they used the court. . . . Yes, that is effective when we do the legal process because some legal paper is missing" (personal communication, May 14, 2011).

On June 8, 2004, the AC ruled that Raffles Le Royal illegally locked out ninety-seven employees, offered reemployment only to those relinquishing their right to strike, unlawfully appointed new worker delegates, and negotiated an illegitimate collective agreement, all with the "clear intent" of destroying the union (*Cambodia Daily* 2004a). Once more, the AC ordered Raffles to reinstate the dismissed workers and pay them back wages dating from April 2004. Arbitrators also told Raffles to cease bargaining with the handpicked workers' representatives. Predictably, managers again rejected the AC's ruling, and the decision became legally unenforceable. Gnaegi continued to point out, truthfully, that Raffles had not broken any laws by ignoring the AC. Claiming the workers had "caused the company a loss in terms of finances and goodwill and dignity," Gnaegi insisted that his "party requires a settlement based on a just resolution of the independent judicial institutions"; hence, the parties should "move the case to the Municipal Courts of Phnom Penh and Siem Reap" (IUF 2004a). Raffles' managers' third tactic was therefore aimed at restricting the scale of conflict, just as Shangri-La's local managers had, given management's advantages in the courts and other domestic institutions.

Allowing the dispute to play out through the formal court system would have been detrimental to the workers' campaign. They therefore pushed back by expanding the conflict to the international scale, as the TLA took actions to threaten Raffles' business interests and raise public awareness of Raffles' labor practices internationally. Nevertheless, unless the TLA could transform public support into tangible leverage, simply spreading awareness would do little more than allow the dispute to devolve into a tedious public relations war.

With help from the Solidarity Center, the Cambodian workers redoubled their efforts at increasing public awareness locally and abroad. "We started looking for tourists coming in and reaching out to tuk tuk drivers. . . . We made sure the media followed up" (Solidarity Center field director, personal interview, December 15, 2011). An official of the Raffles Grand Hotel union elaborated: "We distributed leaflets to all tourist place [*sic*], at least 250 to 300 pieces per day. Then we sent to the IUF and SEIU more [leaflets] than ever. At that time, the IUF invited us—two person [*sic*] each from Hotels Le Royal and Grand—to do the campaign in Europe and especially the USA" (personal interview, May 16, 2011).

In the United States, the Los Angeles branch of the Hotel Employees and Restaurant Employees Union leafleted the Raffles L'Ermitage in Beverly Hills. In the United Kingdom, the TGWU and Trades Union Council distributed leaflets to guests and passersby at the Raffles Howard Hotel in central London. In Australia, the LHMU led a protest outside the Raffles-owned Swissôtel in Sydney. Local and international media, including a Khmer-language radio station, covered these events. Labor allies held additional demonstrations at Raffles hotels and Cambodian embassies in Bangkok, Chicago, Los Angeles, London, Moscow, San Francisco, Sydney, and Toronto. The TLA also publicized its campaign through the internet. On its website the IUF published a call for "urgent action" alongside a click-and-send email link through which campaign supporters sent over three thousand protest messages to Raffles' headquarters in Singapore. The TLA also ran an advertisement on Google, which appeared when users searched for terms related to Cambodia, tourism, and hotels.

Transnational leafleting, demonstrating, and internet campaigning undoubtedly expanded the scale of conflict. Nonetheless, raising awareness did not by itself compel Raffles' managers to concede. Months into the campaign, it became clear that sustaining protests and other attempts to physically disrupt Raffles' businesses would not win the campaign. A Solidarity Center field director recalled the situation:

> I went to Cambodia in May [2004]. The campaign was actually going downwards, and so we had essentially to revitalize the campaign. The reason it was dying down was because the workers essentially were just doing the regular strike thing, standing in front of the hotel and camping in the parks. . . . See, the model was the garment [industry]. In the garment model, with on-time delivery—basically, you stop the delivery of goods and you create a lot of financial loss for management. Then you have management that would settle for a lot of things . . . because this garment has to be delivered. . . . But we were now realizing that the hotel is just a totally different animal. They can withstand, as Raffles has shown, long periods [of striking and protests]. . . . They hire a scab, do some training, you have a certain buffer. . . . So they could take a loss for a long time. (Personal interview, December 15, 2011)

This revelation marked a major turning point in the campaign. Rather than just physically disrupt Raffles' operations in the short run, the TLA would target the company's long-run business interests on the international scale. This meant not only inflicting financial damage but also, crucially, calling on influential actors beyond the labor movement to threaten serious harm to Raffles' reputation and the longevity of its international brand. American allies would prove essential in helping the hotel workers exercise context-appropriate coalitional power.

CONTEXT-APPROPRIATE POWER: RAFFLES UNRAVELS

Unlike the Shangri-La TLA, the Raffles TLA not only kept the scale of conflict expanded internationally but also switched from a strategy of structural power to one of coalitional power. Through its ties to the Solidarity Center and the AFL-CIO, the Cambodian workers were well equipped to persuade key political leaders to support their cause. These efforts to leverage the influence of actors beyond the labor movement culminated in a high-profile boycott of the Raffles Le Royal and the Raffles Grand d'Angkor.

Framing the campaign in terms of human rights, as opposed to focusing solely on labor issues, helped broaden the TLA's international appeal. Instead of emphasizing freedom of association or collective bargaining, for example, the TLA focused on the hotel workers' hardship and poverty and alluded to the tragic history of this long-suffering country. "Cambodia is emerging from decades of chaos and tragedy that literally destroyed the basic institutions of society," read one open letter. "Two union leaders have been murdered this year and many others . . . have reportedly been beaten, threatened, fired, and intimidated . . . [while workers are still] earning just a dollar a day" (US Fed News 2004). Noting that Cambodia's per capita gross domestic product "is close to the cost of a luxury Raffles suite . . . for one night," an IUF bulletin highlighted the blatant disparity between wealthy tourists and the average Cambodian citizen (IUF 2004a). A segment broadcast on National Public Radio (NPR) in the United States likewise alluded to the injustices of economic inequality. As NPR's Michael Sullivan explained, "That 10 percent tacked onto the hotel bill might not seem like much, especially to guests paying $250 a night, but it's a fortune here in Cambodia where the average worker is lucky to earn $50 a month" (Sullivan 2004). At a press conference outside the Royal, union leader Sao Vanthein emphasized that "the workers are facing poverty, and it is difficult for them to support their families. This is poverty caused by the hotel" (*Cambodia Daily* 2004b).

In addition to portraying the campaign as a battle against poverty and indignity, the TLA and its coalition of outside supporters also stressed Raffles' refusal to abide by "the law." This required some stretching on the part of campaigners since, technically, Raffles' refusal to abide by the AC's nonbinding rulings was irrelevant in terms of Cambodian law. Nonetheless, "the union's message was Raffles is a law breaker. . . . So the message we're putting out is that Raffles is violating the law" (Solidarity Center field director, personal interview, December 15, 2011). Whether the TLA's coalition of supporters understood the distinction is not clear. Since the creation of the AC had been heavily supported by the US government, however, it is not unreasonable to surmise that American political leaders maintained an interest in upholding the AC's integrity regardless of the nonbinding nature of its decisions.

Support for the campaign flooded in from American political leaders. The International Republican Institute (IRI), based in Washington, DC, was among the first organizations to take a stand. IRI country director Jackson Cox explained, "We felt we had to stand up because it is a clear case of right and wrong. Everyone I've talked to in the international community is disappointed and looking to take their business elsewhere" (*Cambodia Daily* 2004g). Cox reiterated his sentiments at a press conference, announcing, "I am here to encourage the international community to continue to boycott Hotel Le Royal. Right and wrong in this case is, of course, clear. You are right and Raffles is wrong" (*Cambodia Daily* 2004b). Also prominent in the campaign was US representative George Miller, who, after a visit to Cambodia, called on the UN, the International Monetary Fund, the World Bank, and the Asian Development Bank to cease patronizing the Raffles hotels in Phnom Penh and Siem Reap. In a letter to World Bank president James Wolfensohn, Miller argued that the "continued use of Raffles hotels by World Bank employees serves to undermine the development and strengthening of those fundamental democratic institutions which are at the core of the World Bank's agenda in Cambodia and around the globe" (US Fed News 2004). The US embassy declined to hold its July 4 reception at the Raffles hotel in Phnom Penh and publicly encouraged delegations to stay elsewhere. Cambodian and foreign tourists also declined to book rooms with Raffles. In early August, three trade union centers in Russia, collectively representing thirty-five million workers, sent a joint letter to the Russian ambassador to Cambodia urging the embassy to avoid the Royal and the Grand. Unions and political officials sent similar letters to the embassies of Australia, Austria, India, the Philippines, and South Korea.

"The boycott seems to be hurting," remarked a diplomat from Singapore, Raffles' home country. "It is so sad. . . . Le Royal is bleeding. . . . It is our biggest investment in Cambodia" (*Far Eastern Economic Review* 2004). While Raffles might have sustained some short-term financial losses over time, the company could not endure long-term losses due to a damaged reputation. Six months after the start of the original dispute, Raffles, under mounting pressure from increasingly bad publicity activated through the TLA's coalitional power, acquiesced.

THE OUTCOME: THE RAFFLES CAMPAIGN CONCLUDES SUCCESSFULLY

On September 12, 2004, CTSWF president Ly Korm, representatives of the two unions at Raffles Le Royal and Raffles Grand d'Angkor, the two hotels' general managers, and Raffles Global Group human resources director Han Hun Juan signed an agreement officially ending the conflict. The outcome was an unambiguous win for the workers. Raffles agreed to reinstate 80 percent of the fired employees, effective September 13, 2004, and pay 75 percent of their wages backdated to April 11, 2004. The remainder would receive full severance pay, 100 percent of back wages, and priority in the hotel's next hiring round. Raffles also agreed to reinstate the service fee and distribute the funds directly to employees. In addition to these material gains, managers agreed to recognize as their exclusive bargaining partners the original unions at the Royal and the Grand and dismantle the "fake unions" set up earlier to replace them. This open acknowledgment of the strength and legitimacy of the unions boosted the workers' capacity substantially.

For its part, Raffles suffered substantial material losses throughout the duration of the dispute. The company also endured a great deal of negative publicity internationally. Nevertheless, Raffles ultimately avoided permanent damage to its corporate image and brand. Hence, the TLA campaign resulted not so much in total defeat as a fresh start under new rules of the game. Today Raffles Hotels and Resorts continues to thrive and remains highly regarded in the global luxury hotel industry.[10]

"My personal opinion is the outcome for this campaign is a great achievement," stated an official of the Raffles Hotel Le Royal union, adding that the union's "relationship with management [is] much, much better if compare [*sic*] from the past" (personal communication, May 14, 2011). The union leader's counterpart at the Raffles Grand Hotel concurred, stating, "Both unions at Raffles in Phnom Penh and Siem Reap still remain the same, unchanged, and we can manage our members. Yes, I consider that a success, the same as my colleagues" (personal communication, May 14, 2011). As one Solidarity Center organizer summarized, "Nothing was left unresolved" (personal interview, May 4, 2011).

Discussion: Explaining the Two Outcomes

Between late 2000 and early 2004, two highly similar TLAs emerged in response to similar disputes at five-star hotels in Southeast Asia. In the Shangri-La case, a well-resourced, strongly supported campaign not only failed to win workers' jobs back but also ended with the dissolution of their local union. In contrast, employee reinstatement, renewed collective bargaining, and full union recognition resulted from the Raffles campaign. Why did only one set of workers succeed?

The case studies show that these campaigns' outcomes hinged on who controlled the scale of conflict and whether the TLA exercised context-appropriate power. At the beginning of both disputes, workers faced a restricted scale of conflict and did not exercise context-appropriate power. Both sets of workers then expanded the scale of conflict through TLA members' international actions but still struggled to exercise the appropriate power type. Although the scale of conflict remained international for some time in both cases, at one stage the two campaigns diverged, with the Shangri-La TLA exercising structural power and the Raffles TLA switching to coalitional power. Finally, the Shangri-La workers lost their opportunity to exercise context-appropriate power, as management effectively restricted the scale to the level of domestic institutions, while the Raffles workers succeeded in full.

Analyzing Employers' Actions: Struggles over Scale

As noted, TLAs in both campaigns sought to rescale the conflict to the international level. Conversely, Shangri-La's and Raffles' local hotel managers strove to restrict the scale of conflict. Because legal institutions in Indonesia and Cambodia tended to give employers an advantage, whether due to overt biases or simply the slow and financially draining nature of the legal process, managers in both cases intentionally steered the conflict into the courts.

Shangri-La's managers turned not only to P4P but also to the formal court system to rule on the legality of the mass dismissal and workers' subsequent protests. Shangri-La also used the courts for retaliation against campaign organizers. Suing six union officials was an especially effective intimidation tactic that not only threatened to drain the TLA of vital resources but also forced key campaigners to focus on the local scale as they struggled in vain to file an appeal. Meanwhile, Supreme Court proceedings kept the seventy-nine remaining protesters mired for months in a state of uncertainty before the court ultimately declared their protests illegal and approved the mass dismissals, ending the dispute. Hence, regardless of the Shangri-La workers' numerous acts of protest both locally and internationally, court battles always seemed to take center stage. The workers lost the campaign in part because managers brought the conflict back to the level of domestic institutions.

Raffles' managers likewise attempted to channel the conflict through the court system and, in doing so, won some small victories, as when judges at the municipal courts of Phnom Penh and Siem Reap declared the workers' protests illegal. Although the Cambodian AC complicated the strategic landscape, Raffles' managers were able simply to ignore its rulings and, in an attempt to deflect public criticism for doing so, continually point to the legally nonbinding nature of the AC's decisions.

In addition to invoking legal arguments and the authority of judicial institutions, both sets of hotel managers also utilized heavy-handed tactics to physically disrupt the workers' campaigns, again in an effort to force workers to focus their energies on the local scale. Sending private security guards to break up demonstrations at the Shangri-La Hotel in Jakarta and ransacking the Raffles unions' offices in Phnom Penh and Siem Reap forced campaigners in both cases to concentrate their attention on the local scale. The attempted arrest by Jakarta police of the president of the IUF, who had flown in from Geneva to support the campaign, also represents an attempt to restrict the scale of the conflict.

Yet despite these similarities, the two employers' strategies differed in two crucial respects. First, Shangri-La's managers played a more sophisticated game when it came to dealing with local protesters. By offering the carrot of monetary compensation for workers willing to abandon the campaign, managers anticipated that a small financial loss on the company's part would induce enough attrition among protesters to stem potentially serious material and reputational losses for the hotel in the future. Meanwhile, workers who clung to the campaign were subjected to increasingly harsh intimidation tactics and the slow, painful grind of ongoing court proceedings. In contrast, Raffles offered no such compromise to local protesters, who responded to managers' blunt tactics by mobilizing further rallies and demonstrations and, eventually, widening their circle of supporters to encompass actors outside the labor movement. Because Raffles' managers failed to restrict the scale of conflict, the TLA could continue to exercise power on the international scale.

While it is tempting to conclude from this analysis that control over the scale of conflict was mainly a matter of choice, it is important to recognize the role that structural factors played in shaping employers' agency. Notably, Shangri-La's local managers had more autonomy than Raffles' local managers due to the complex ownership structure of the Shangri-La Hotel, Jakarta. Although the Kuok Group owned roughly half of the hotel, the remainder was controlled by local owners in Indonesia. This ownership split meant that local managers, who were much more concerned about stemming the rise of independent unionism in Indonesia than about risking the reputation of the global hotel chain, had a certain amount of freedom in deciding how to quell local labor unrest. Osbert Lyman reportedly found the union situation unacceptable, as did Wastu Widanto and the hotel's other local managers, whose approach to labor relations had clearly been shaped by the institutions to which they had become accustomed before the political transition.

"Locally, we faced entrenched anti-unionism," explained one Shangri-La campaign participant. "They were not caring how much money they lost. They wanted to make sure unions do not spread in Indonesia. Local management had the real ideological fight, whereas Robert Kuok is a business man. Robert Kuok had his brand to defend" (IUF researcher, personal interview, November 1, 2011). According to an IUF official, Shangri-La's corporate leaders in Hong Kong were in fact "much more used to unions, versus the local company involved, which was not used to the idea and saw the situation as totally unacceptable. They had never had to face workers fighting back. So their response was to try to tough it out" (personal interview, September 16, 2011). Consequently, according to another IUF representative, "Robert Kuok actually already gave up, very much before the local owner" (personal interview, March 5, 2012). Yet because Kuok had only limited control over the Jakarta hotel, local managers were able to drag the dispute through the courts and otherwise delay compromise in hopes of breaking SPMS.

In contrast to Lyman and Widanto, Stephan Gnaegi and the other Raffles managers in Cambodia had closer ties to the Singapore-based Raffles Hotels and Resorts, which fully owned both the Hotel Le Royal and the Grand Hotel d'Angkor. Whether corporate leaders at Raffles' headquarters in Singapore actively pressured local managers to settle the dispute in Cambodia is unknown. Still, the fact that the Raffles conflict lasted only six months—less than one-quarter the length of the Shangri-La conflict—suggests that Raffles' managers in Phnom Penh and Siem Reap felt a sense of urgency that their counterparts in Jakarta did not.

It is crucial to note, however, that this variation in hotel ownership structures cannot by itself explain why Raffles lost the campaign against it. Even with the conflict rescaled to the international level, the company would have prevailed had the TLA continued to exercise an inappropriate power type. Likewise, if the Shangri-La TLA had pursued a context-appropriate power strategy while the conflict was still focused on the international scale, the hotel managers would not have been able to keep the conflict local, and the workers would have won. Key to this analysis is the fact that the two employers were equally vulnerable to coalitional power. As international companies, Raffles (based in Singapore) and Shangri-La (based in Hong Kong) already had established brand names and multiple hotel properties around the world. Both therefore had a lot to lose from bad publicity, as I show next.

Analyzing Labor's Actions: Strategy Matters

At first glance, both TLAs' strategies seem very similar in substance. Both the Shangri-La and Raffles campaigns entailed significant efforts to channel conflict onto the international scale through rallies and demonstrations, mass emailing and letter writing, and other acts of protest. As the case studies show, however, strategy mattered: once the Raffles TLA switched from a strategy of physical disruption through on-site protest (structural power) to a large-scale, stakeholder-backed, international boycott (coalitional power), managers' efforts to channel the dispute back into domestic institutions proved futile.

What made coalitional power context appropriate in these two cases was the inherent vulnerability of luxury hotels to negative publicity and long-term brand damage. As one Solidarity Center staff member put it, "Raffles has global ambitions. They don't want to have to explain what's happening to investors" (personal interview, May 4, 2011). Shangri-La had an equally valuable brand to protect. "Robert Kuok was painted as an enemy," explained an IUF staff member, "and if he hadn't had a brand to hurt, we would have had very few leverage points" (IUF researcher, personal interview, November 1, 2011).

Hence, the most important factor that distinguished the Shangri-La and Raffles campaigns was the type of power each TLA used on the international scale. While the Shangri-La TLA stuck with structural power, the Raffles TLA switched from structural to coalitional power, a strategy marked by strong support from stakeholders beyond the labor movement. This is not to say that the Shangri-La campaign lacked public support. Marches, speeches, rallies, and the Solidarity Café all garnered considerable public sympathy; the Shangri-La dispute in fact became "the most visible and best-publicized industrial dispute in Indonesia" (*Workers Online* 2002). According to one campaign participant, local support came "not only from other unionists but also other parts of society like artists, newspapers, filmmakers. . . . [The] Shangri-La case is very popular because it's the biggest fight in the early post-Suharto era" (SPMS official, personal interview, March 5, 2012). Nevertheless, while the Indonesian public was generally supportive, most individuals outside the labor movement were hesitant to take direct action. Moreover, in terms of *international* support, the Shangri-La campaign did not extend far beyond the labor movement. Consequently, the TLA failed to exercise coalitional power on the international scale and therefore could not threaten serious damage to Shangri-La's global brand.

Instead, *structural power* remained central to the Shangri-La campaign. On the international scale, Australian unions threatened to physically obstruct construction projects in Melbourne if the Kuok Group were to be awarded the Docklands contract. Kuok lost that valuable contract, yet the incident failed to faze hotel managers back in Jakarta, who continued to use monetary compensation and violent intimidation tactics to induce attrition among local protesters. Even the Kuok Group did not appear excessively concerned about losing the Docklands bid, especially since Kuok later won another (albeit less valuable) contract in Melbourne the following year. Evidently, short-term disruptions to profits did not endanger Shangri-La's long-term viability, so structural power could not win the campaign.

Interestingly, the Shangri-La TLA continued to fall back on protests, rallies, and demonstrations, both locally and internationally, throughout the duration of their two-year, three-month-long campaign—despite these tactics' apparent ineffectiveness. A similar dynamic played out in the Raffles campaign, as managers remained recalcitrant despite workers' attempts to physically disrupt the company's operations locally and internationally through on site protest activities. Shortly into that campaign, however, the Raffles TLA began to realize that these activities had a limited impact at best. Crucially, campaign organizers acknowledged—in the words of the Solidarity Center field director quoted earlier—that the TLA was "just doing the regular strike thing" despite the fact that "the hotel is just a totally different animal" compared to the garment industry and can "take a [financial] loss for a long time" (personal interview, December 15, 2011).

This reference to the garment industry as the original strategic model for the TLA's actions is telling. The director's comment that the time-sensitive nature of garment manufacturing allows labor to "stop the delivery of goods and . . . create a lot of financial loss for management," whereas hotels can "have a certain buffer," summarizes exactly why the use of structural power is only appropriate in certain situations. Simply put, the Raffles TLA con-sciously realized that structural power—the physical disruption of an employer's operations—does not work well in the hotel industry, and this realization prompted the TLA to switch strategies.

As illustrated, the Raffles TLA exercised *coalitional power* by enlisting the assistance of actors beyond the realm of employment relations—particularly potential customers, including business travelers and American political leaders—who in turn persuaded personnel from high-profile inter-national organizations such as the IRI, the World Bank, and the International Monetary Fund and several foreign embassies to cease patronizing the Raf-fles hotels in Cambodia. Through this coalition of supporters, the hotel work-ers and Solidarity Center staff kept the Raffles campaign focused on the international scale, forcing the Raffles managers to assess the implications of the campaign for the company's future globally. This was possible because the wide-scale boycott launched by the TLA's coalitional partners not only cost the company a considerable amount of money but also threatened its reputation. A cascade of negative publicity—including pro-worker com-mentaries in the *Financial Times* and on NPR—amplified these effects. Observers noted that "the dispute was very costly to the Raffles brand" (Adler and Woolcock 2009, 182), a "public relations disaster" (*Agence France Press* 2004), and "a major embarrassment for Raffles" (Mills 2004).

Conclusion: Context-Appropriate Power Is Crucial

Surface-level similarities often obscure significant variations between cases. With respect to the TLA campaigns analyzed here—the relatively unsuccess-ful Shangri-La campaign, launched in Indonesia in late 2000, and the fully suc-cessful Raffles campaign, initiated in Cambodia in early 2004—evidence shows that these cases' differing outcomes can be explained primarily by the strategic interactions of the actors involved. Specifically, both sets of managers attempted to restrict these conflicts to the national and local scales, thereby channeling conflict into institutions of dispute resolution that tended to favor the employers' side. Managers' relative control of scale shaped the dynamics of both campaigns. At the same time, the hotel workers, along with their transnational allies, strove to channel conflict onto the international scale. By both upscaling and expanding the campaign to involve nonlabor stakeholders whose coalitional support threatened the hotel's core, long-term interests, the Raffles TLA succeeded.

Conclusion: Labor's Unwritten Future

Whatever their long-term impact, TLA campaigns are first and foremost about their immediate outcomes for workers, be they those handling cargo on the foggy docks of Liverpool, loading ships on the sun-soaked ports of Melbourne and Sydney, stocking supermarket shelves in San Bernardino, manning cash registers in Manchester, guarding buildings in Delhi and Cape Town, or serving guests at luxury hotels in Siem Reap, Phnom Penh, and Jakarta. No matter the issue, what is most important for the vast majority of workers engaged in a TLA campaign is the direct impact that campaign has on their own well-being and that of the people closest to them. With this in mind, in this book I have sought to explain systematically what causes some TLA campaigns to succeed while others stall, fall short, or simply fail.

The six case studies presented in this book support the predictions of the CCAP theory: intraunion coordination, interunion coordination, and context-appropriate power are individually necessary and jointly sufficient for a TLA campaign to succeed. All three variables are present in

Table 2. Simplified summary of findings

TLA Campaign	Intraunion Coordination?	Interunion Coordination?	Context-Appropriate Power?	Outcome
Liverpool	No	Yes	Yes	Failure
Patrick	Yes	Yes	Yes	Success
Tesco	Yes	No	Yes	Failure
G4S	Yes	Yes	Yes	Success
Shangri-La	Yes	Yes	No	Failure
Raffles	Yes	Yes	Yes	Success

each successful TLA campaign analyzed, while each unsuccessful campaign lacks one of these key variables. Table 2 summarizes these findings, which are also formalized using Boolean algebra in the following equations.

Causal Relationships as Boolean Equations

$$X_1 * X_2 * X_3 = Y$$
$$\sim X_1 + \sim X_2 + \sim X_3 = \sim Y$$

Key

X_1 = intraunion coordination
X_2 = interunion coordination
X_3 = context-appropriate power
$\sim X_1$ = lack of intraunion coordination
$\sim X_2$ = lack of interunion coordination
$\sim X_3$ = lack of context-appropriate power
Y = successful outcome
$\sim Y$ = unsuccessful outcome
$*$ = the logical AND
$+$ = the logical OR

As noted in chapter 1, this basic congruence test—the observation that variables line up as expected with outcomes—is by itself inadequate for establishing causation. So how do we know that each of these three variables really mattered? We know because there is evidence in each case study of the causal mechanisms linking the presence or absence of intraunion coordination, interunion coordination, and context-appropriate power to the success or failure of each campaign.

The first matched pair—comparing the Liverpool and Patrick campaigns—showcased the importance of intraunion coordination. Despite some disagreements between union leaders and members, the MUA overall maintained a united front, as its leaders successfully mobilized the membership to confront Patrick Stevedores and the Howard government in full force. In contrast, TGWU leaders refused to back their own members, leaving the Liverpool dockers to their own devices. The significance of this difference becomes clear when one examines the impact intraunion coordination had on the dockers' abilities to coordinate with other unions internationally and exercise structural power. Although both sets of dockers successfully secured interunion coordination, made possible in part by maritime unions' long history of international solidarity, interunion coordination was weaker in the Liverpool TLA, as TGWU's leaders discouraged the global union ITF from giving the dockers substantial assistance. The Liverpool TLA thus suffered from a lack of resources and limits on logistical support, which made it impossible to maintain the transnational component of the campaign over time. In contrast, the MUA's internal unity proved crucial not only for maintaining their local front but also for securing active support from the ITF, which assisted in the logistics of the transnational campaign. Weak intraunion coordination harmed the Liverpool campaign more directly as well, as TGWU's leaders' backdoor negotiations with MDHC left the Liverpool workers worse off than they were before the campaign.

The second matched pair—the Tesco and G4S campaigns—showed what happens when a TLA fails to attain interunion coordination. Both UFCW and SEIU had leaders committed to the transnational campaign and enough internal unity to mobilize their own members. Both also chose context-appropriate power strategies in combining coalitional and institutional tactics, including appeals to shareholders, the ILO, an EWC, the OECD, and the home union. The Tesco TLA broke down, however, because UFCW could not convince the home union, USDAW, to assist in taking on Tesco.

While the TLA did eventually expand to encompass issues in Thailand and South Korea, the campaign's overall framing remained focused on UFCW's specific goal of unionizing Fresh & Easy grocery stores in the United States, which made interunion coordination hard to attain. In contrast, SEIU secured interunion coordination by broadening the goals of the transnational campaign and making the TLA more genuinely inclusive of others' interests. In doing so, SEIU managed to bridge the gap between itself and home union GMB, which played an indispensable role in exercising institutional power to change the behavior of G4S.

In the third matched pair—Shangri-La and Raffles—we see two TLAs that successfully solved the double coordination problem but only one that exercised context-appropriate power. As militant unions with strong leadership-membership ties, both SPMS and CTSWF easily secured intraunion coordination. Existing transnational relationships with other unions also made interunion coordination relatively easy: SPMS benefited from its ties to the IUF and various Australian unions, while CTSWF had full support from the US-based Solidarity Center and its broader network. What differed in the end was the TLAs' power strategies: The Shangri-La TLA exercised structural power, including protests, demonstrations, and the Australians' threat of a construction ban, none of which posed a serious threat to the hotel company's core interests. The Raffles TLA, in contrast, shifted from structural power to coalitional power by mobilizing stakeholders beyond the labor movement whose actions threatened the company's long-term interests, particularly its global brand.

Taken together, these six case studies demonstrate the vital importance of coordination and power for TLA campaigns' success. In all but two of these six campaigns, TLAs solved the double coordination problem, effectively mobilizing workers to act collectively both within individual unions and across national borders. Moreover, in each campaign analyzed, workers were able to exercise different types of power drawn from their embeddedness in GVCs, national and international institutions, and networks of nonlabor stakeholders. What made the exercise of specific power types effective, however, was each target employer's core, long-term interests. Both MDHC and Patrick were vulnerable to structural power because of the time-sensitive nature of shipping and the location-dependent nature of stevedoring. Both Tesco and G4S had to answer to international institutions as well as their home unions in the United Kingdom. And the two hotel companies, Shangri-La and Raffles, both deeply valued their brand names and sought to protect their public images from long-term reputational damage.

One vital point bears repeating: all power is relational. As emphasized in chapter 1, it is only meaningful to discuss workers' power with reference to that of another actor, which, in the case of TLA campaigns, is more often than not the employer. I now look briefly at what the case studies suggest about employers' strategies in TLA campaigns.

On Scale and Strategy: What Employers Want

Unions, workers, and their allies are not the only actors with agency. In every campaign examined, employers also exercised power and attempted to control the circumstances under which these disputes unfolded. Although employers varied in the specific ways in which they engaged with these TLAs, all sought in some way to restrict conflict to the local or national scale. Managers at the Shangri-La in Jakarta and the Raffles hotels in Phnom Penh and Siem Reap attempted to force their respective labor conflicts to play out through local and national court systems, where employers had an obvious institutional advantage. Tesco ably deflected UFCW's requests for a meeting with corporate leaders in Britain by claiming that issues with Fresh & Easy ought to be dealt with where Fresh & Easy is located: in the relatively union-hostile United States. Tesco also insisted that issues raised concerning South Korea, Thailand, and Turkey would be best addressed through the legal machinery of those particular countries. G4S likewise attempted to keep conflicts local by contending that alleged labor rights abuses in India, the United States, and several African countries should be dealt with by local management in those countries. MDHC's strategy of negotiating with TGWU leaders behind the backs of the rank and file was likewise an effort to restrict conflict to a scale on which the employer had the upper hand. In the Australian waterfront dispute, Patrick Stevedores hardly engaged with the MUA's international allies and instead focused on fighting labor locally and nationally only.

Employers confronted with TLA campaigns thus appear to have an interest in restricting the scale of conflict. They do so by forcing the workers with whom they are in direct conflict to concentrate on court battles, arbitration proceedings, strikebreaking violence, union-busting tactics, backdoor negotiations, or other practices that distract or disadvantage the workers. By keeping labor preoccupied with resource-draining struggles on the local or national scale, and by ignoring or minimizing the actions of TLA members on the international scale, employers make it difficult for TLAs to exercise power effectively. A TLA under these circumstances must therefore first expand the scale of conflict before it can alter an employer's behavior. Expanding scale means more than just forming a TLA or alerting international allies of the existence of a conflict. To expand scale, the TLA must create a situation that compels the employer in question to shift its attention and energy to actions occurring outside the country in which the dispute originated. It is only when the employer feels forced to respond to transnational actors that workers can be said to have expanded scale. This reflection on scale is an extension of the logics of intra- and interunion coordination since expanding the scale of conflict necessitates not only sustained cooperation across national borders (interunion coordination) but also concrete actions carried out by groups of workers with the capacity to mobilize themselves within their own organizations to act collectively (intraunion coordination). Hence, while not the main focus of the present analysis, evidence that actors gain advantages by expanding or restricting the scale of conflict appears in these cases, which, at least at this point, suggests that there is more to be explored along these lines in future research.

A Closer Look at Outcomes: Explaining the Standoff and Partial Cases

Although in this book I consider campaigns mainly on the basis of their general outcome—success or failure—these dichotomous categories are a simplification. A more complete assessment of outcomes would acknowledge that success for the Patrick campaign was only partial, just as the Tesco and Shangri-La campaigns did not fully fail. It may therefore be useful to consider some conceptual revisions to accommodate these more complicated outcomes. One can begin by coding only those cases with unambiguous endings—gains for labor without any losses or losses for labor without any gains—as "full successes" or "full failures," respectively. Instances in which workers neither gain significant benefits nor suffer substantial losses can be coded as "standoffs." Finally, between the extremes of full success and full failure are campaigns that conclude with some mix of losses and gains. One can code these as "partial successes" if gains outweigh the losses and as "partial failures" if losses outweigh gains. Moving from a dichotomous coding of the dependent variable to this reconceptualization makes it possible to refine the CCAP theory. As a first attempt at doing so, I consider here some of the nuances not predicted by the original causal hypothesis yet revealed through the process-tracing analyses of the Patrick, Tesco, and Shangri-La cases.

Partial Success in the Patrick Campaign

Generally speaking, the Patrick TLA met all three conditions necessary for success, as predicted by the CCAP theory. Yet technically the campaign was not fully successful since the gains workers won—including higher wages, back pay, and worker reinstatement—were partially offset by some losses, such as reduced overtime rates, compulsory weekend work, on-call shifts, and lost jobs. The campaign was thus only a partial success. To explain this outcome, it is worth considering that the campaign's intraunion coordination, while sufficiently strong, was not as airtight as it appeared on the surface. As noted in chapter 2, there were disagreements between the MUA's leaders and some of its members. MUA officials refused to authorize what they believed to be overly aggressive and possibly illegal actions against Patrick, whereas more militant MUA members expressed a preference for more direct action. One major point of contention was the TLA's failure to take action against the *Australian Endeavour*, a ship loaded at a Patrick terminal by nonunion labor. MUA leaders refused to call on the TLA to disrupt the *Endeavour*'s operations, and so, with the exception of a few dockers in Japan, the MUA's allies left the scab-loaded ship alone. Hence, one possible explanation for the Patrick campaign's partial success is that imperfect intraunion coordination precluded the full exercise of structural power, which in turn set limits on the TLA's threat to Patrick Stevedores' core interests.

Standoff in the Tesco Campaign

While the Tesco TLA did not succeed, one could argue that it was not actually a failure because none of the workers involved were worse off than they had been before the campaign. Why, then, did the Tesco campaign result in a standoff rather than a partial or full failure? One possible explanation is that the TLA was not completely lacking in interunion coordination, despite the obvious divide between UFCW and USDAW. Leaving aside this divide, UFCW still had the full support of UNI Global Union, which helped solicit the support of unions from a dozen different countries to create the Tesco Global Union Alliance. UNI then helped reframe the campaign to be somewhat less US-centric, particularly by assisting with the production of reports that brought to light labor violations at Tesco-owned workplaces in Thailand and South Korea. There are two problems with this potential explanation, however. First, it is not clear why having weak (but existing) interunion coordination would necessarily prevent an outcome in which workers are worse off than they were before the campaign. Second, and more importantly, as defined in chapter 1, interunion coordination must entail more than just a TLA's existence. Common goals, shared planning, and tangible cooperation in pursuit of those goals must be present and, in most cases, must include the home union; in that case, it might not make sense to say that the Tesco TLA had interunion coordination after all.

An alternative explanation for the Tesco campaign's ending as a standoff rather than a failure is that the TLA truly did lack interunion coordination, but complete lack of interunion coordination in general is not nearly as detrimental to a transnational campaign as the absence of *intra*-union coordination. Even when workers fail to cooperate across national borders, they can still cooperate within their own organizations to take action locally. The reverse is not true; if unions are coordinated internationally but not within their own organizations, then it is nearly impossible to take action, let alone sustain campaign actions over time. This explanation would align with the finding of full failure in the Liverpool campaign, which lacked intraunion coordination despite having interunion coordination and a context-appropriate power strategy. Further research would be needed, however, to test the hypothesis that lacking only interunion coordination is sufficient for an unsuccessful TLA campaign but not a fully failed one.

Partial Failure in the Shangri-La Campaign

The last complex outcome to consider is the Shangri-La campaign. Lack of a context-appropriate power strategy led to partial failure, with the destruc-

tion of the hotel union and massive job losses being somewhat offset by severance pay for seventy-nine of the former employees. One possible explanation for this mixed result is that the campaign was not entirely devoid of
context-appropriate power. As noted in chapter 4, the Shangri-La TLA did
initiate some actions that began to resemble coalitional power, particularly
when four SPMS officials flew to the United States to speak at an event organized by USINDO, subsequently convincing the group to boycott the
Shangri-La Hotel in Jakarta. Moreover, although the TLA did not otherwise exercise coalitional power on the international scale, local solidarity
actions signaled significant support from stakeholders beyond the labor
movement. Alternatively, one could hypothesize that the Shangri-La campaign was not a full failure because structural power (the TLA's main strategy) had enough impact on Shangri-La to extract some concessions from
the employer. As always, however, testing these hypotheses would require
further research.

In short, although the evidence strongly supports the CCAP theory, the
exact contribution of each of the three independent variables to the various types of campaign outcomes has yet to be fully explored. Additional
studies of partial and standoff cases that include combinations of variables
not represented in this book's six cases could shed light on these complexi-
ties. One possible starting point is the hypothesis that TLA campaigns
proceed in stages, with intraunion coordination necessarily preceding interunion coordination, which itself precedes the exercise of power. If sequence matters, then one might hypothesize that intraunion coordination
is the foundation on which all successful TLA campaigns are built; without it, failure is virtually certain. This hypothesis could explain why the
Liverpool campaign failed completely while the Tesco campaign simply
made no progress and the Shangri-La campaign made some progress, but
not enough for the workers to win. Another important hypothesis to explore
could assume instead that standoff and partial cases are not explained by
variation in these three independent variables, and other factors not accounted for in the present analysis play a role in systematically condition-
ing campaigns' outcomes. Either way, additional research based on more
intricate hypotheses than the one examined in this book could greatly enhance our understanding of the causal variables responsible for the full
range of possible outcomes.

Implications for Labor's Agency: What If the Workers Had Acted Differently?

Nothing in the present analysis suggests that solving the double coordination problem and exercising context-appropriate power are entirely in a TLA's control. Path-dependent effects of historical events and shifting political conditions shape the economic structures, institutional frameworks, and stakeholder networks in which workers and employers are embedded. External circumstances therefore condition workers' abilities to exercise power and achieve intra- and interunion coordination. That said, choice still matters. When windows of opportunity open, workers can make decisions that directly affect the trajectories of TLA campaigns.

Because the cases within each matched pair are so similar to one another, each failed campaign suggests an irresistible counterfactual: What if the workers had acted differently? This analysis suggests that if TGWU officials had supported the Liverpool dockers, if UFCW had won USDAW's trust, and if the Shangri-La TLA had exercised coalitional power, then these three unsuccessful campaigns would have had different outcomes.

Counterfactual One: Intraunion Coordination in the Liverpool Campaign

First, TGWU officials could have backed the Liverpool dockers by providing material resources and connecting them with the ITF. As the wealthiest of the global unions, ITF had the capacity to map out key pressure points and optimize dockers' physical disruptions of port operations. Such support could have transformed the transnational campaign into a sustainable, logistically sophisticated series of work stoppages across waterfront workplaces worldwide. In other words, had TGWU's leaders actively encouraged the ITF to continue coordinating and financing the transnational campaign, the Liverpool TLA could have exercised structural power consistently enough to threaten MDHC's core interests.

At the very least, TGWU officials could have refrained from actively undermining the Liverpool campaign. Understandably, union leaders feared the repercussions of officially supporting illegal secondary boycotts. Nevertheless, these fears, while legitimate, did not have to translate into turning the ITF against the TLA. As revealed in chapter 2, TGWU leaders used their clout within the ITF to reverse the global union's initial support for the Liverpool dockers. The ITF then dissuaded its own affiliates from participating in the transnational campaign. As a result, the TLA's solidarity actions remained sporadic and unsystematic, causing only temporary damage to MDHC (Castree 2000). TGWU officials also could have chosen not to cooperate with MDHC in a backdoor deal to end the dispute. Unfortunately, that is exactly what occurred.

As we learned from the Patrick case, a relatively collaborative relationship between union leaders and members enhances not only local collective action but also the coordination of campaign actions on the international scale. MUA officials' full commitment to the fight against Patrick was necessary for sustaining the multiscalar campaign. Had TGWU also enjoyed this level of intraunion coordination, the Liverpool campaign could have concluded differently.

Counterfactual Two: Interunion Coordination in the Tesco Campaign

The second counterfactual to consider is in the Tesco campaign. UFCW made the mistake of expecting solidarity from USDAW without first considering how the British union's precarious position would prevent it from active involvement in the TLA. Moreover, while UFCW deserves credit for forming the Tesco Global Union Alliance, in reality, the transnational campaign was far too US-centric. Had UFCW focused less on its own interests and more on expanding the campaign into a genuinely global one, it could have secured stronger interunion coordination and won USDAW's trust and cooperation over time.

In particular, with the help of global union UNI, the TLA could have invested more resources in other countries, continuing efforts that began with the Thailand and South Korea reports. This would have involved not only producing more country reports but also offering on-the-ground assistance to Tesco employees engaged in workplace conflicts around the world. More genuine attention to issues outside the United States would have helped the TLA organize around interests shared by all unions representing or potentially representing Tesco workers, such as health and safety standards, the sustainability of developing-country markets, and human rights. Having reframed the campaign around big-picture issues with a potential to compromise Tesco's future profitability, UFCW could have then invited US-DAW to engage with Tesco executives in ways that emphasized the unions' shared, long-term interests, instead of insisting that USDAW immediately open the door to direct dialogue with Tesco management. USDAW could not justify risking its good relationship with Tesco to help one union in the United States, but it could have justified approaching Tesco about big-picture issues of legitimate concern to its employees globally.

As we learned from the Alliance for Justice at G4S, gaining the home union's trust, as SEIU did with GMB, meant first making the transnational campaign as inclusive as possible and demonstrating a sincere commitment to assisting workers in several other countries. By investing heavily in UNI Global Union and dispatching dedicated organizers to help workers win workplace conflicts in various countries, SEIU helped produce a series of small but significant victories for G4S workers. This, in turn, boosted the campaign's legitimacy in the eyes of GMB, as the emphasis shifted from SEIU's self-interested aims to the unions' shared strategic interests in building union power and raising labor standards in the security services industry globally. Had UFCW done something similar, the Tesco campaign could have had a different conclusion.

Counterfactual Three: Context-Appropriate Power in the Shangri-La Campaign

Finally, consider what would have happened had SPMS and its transnational allies made different decisions in the Shangri-La campaign. For the duration of the campaign, the TLA relied mainly on structural power when it could have chosen a coalitional power strategy instead, specifically by mobilizing local and international actors to boycott Shangri-La-branded hotels. Since Shangri-La was so deeply invested in its international image, a serious threat to the hotel company's reputation would have also threatened its core interests in remaining profitable over the long run. Evidence suggests that the TLA had good potential to leverage the influence of stakeholders beyond the labor movement, as the hotel workers' conflict was, at the time, the most visible labor dispute in Indonesia. More to the point, there was at least one instance in which the TLA did exercise coalitional power: in January 2002, four SPMS officials flew to the United States to speak at a meeting of USINDO, which subsequently relocated an event previously planned to be held at the Shangri-La Hotel. Clearly, the TLA had the capacity to extend this strategy into a full exercise of transnational coalitional power.

Asked why the TLA did not do more to target the Shangri-La brand and convince nonlabor stakeholders to support an international boycott, IUF general secretary Ron Oswald explained that SPMS and its allies simply did not know what would be most effective. "Well, we did a little bit at the time, but our campaigning—our understanding of campaigning now these days—was not what it is today. We didn't really have a strategic approach going back to the Shangri-La campaign" (personal interview, February 23, 2016). Part of the problem was framing. Exercising coalitional power on the international scale would have first required reframing the campaign to resonate with an international audience of nonlabor actors. One way to do so would have been to portray the Shangri-La dispute less as a labor issue and more as a matter of human rights (Kang 2012, 4), just as the Raffles TLA did in the Cambodian case. To that end, the Shangri-La TLA could have also placed greater emphasis on the campaign as emblematic of the struggle for justice in post-Suharto Indonesia.

As we learned from the successful Raffles campaign, starting out with the wrong power strategy need not be detrimental, as long as the TLA exercises context-appropriate power later on. In the Raffles case, the switch from structural to coalitional power was brought on by a realization that the TLA's tactics had so far been ineffective. The TLA thus became conscious of the need to switch power strategies and did so, which ultimately won the campaign. Had the Shangri-La TLA switched strategies as well, a different outcome would have been possible.

These counterfactual exercises show us that structural factors alone do not fully determine the trajectories of TLA campaigns. While workers cannot control the conditions that make it possible to coordinate and exercise power in the first place, the matched pairs make it clear that workers can consciously choose to take advantage of opportunities for coordination and strategic action that arise within the economic, political, and social environments in which they are embedded. Simply put, no analysis of TLA campaigns can be complete without consideration of labor's agency.

The Bigger Picture

A frequent critique of case study research (and small-N qualitative analyses in general) is that the results of such studies are not generalizable across the broader population of cases. One strength of the present analysis, however, is that the patterns of success and failure found across these six TLA campaigns span four industries, fifteen years, and dozens of countries. As Slater and Ziblatt (2013) argued, confirmatory results from multiple controlled comparisons that maximize variation in background factors (such as a time and place) offer strong evidence that a causal theory can in fact "travel" across a range of contexts. This methodological insight lends credence to the claim that the CCAP theory is potentially generalizable to all TLA campaigns or at least potentially applicable to cases outside this initial sample.

That said, scholars should continue to research what causes TLA campaigns' various outcomes, in terms of both initial results and impacts over the long run. In addition to further developing the CCAP theory, future research could investigate whether successful TLA campaigns benefit workers over time and whether different national contexts are more or less conducive to transforming TLAs' short-run gains into lasting improvements in workers' material well-being and capacity for contestation. Researchers should pay particular attention to the complex implications of partial and standoff outcomes in order to understand their longer-term impact on employment relations. Moreover, the role that employers' interests, structures, and strategies play in shaping the dynamics of TLAs and the outcomes of transnational campaigns deserves greater attention as well. Finally, further exploration of the ways in which economic globalization enhances workers' power would deepen our comprehension of the impact of TLAs on global capitalism overall.

Final Thoughts

A lot has happened since the launch of the Liverpool campaign. TLAs have expanded from a handful of disparate efforts into a series of increasingly sophisticated campaigns spanning scores of countries, industries, and issues. Since the 1990s, TLA campaigns have been propped up and propelled by revitalized global unions, reinvigorated national labor movements, and emboldened local labor activists, all acting in concert to eliminate exploitative practices and protect workers' rights. The most important finding from this book is perhaps the most basic: Workers are not passive victims of economic globalization. Rather, they can actively shape their own working conditions and rights through interactions with TNCs and other employers on the international scale. When TLA campaigns succeed, they help maintain or improve the material well-being and overall capacity of the workers involved. Even when TLA campaigns are not successful, workers can learn from past failures, apply those lessons in future conflicts, and go on to succeed.

NOTES

1. The New Politics of Transnational Labor

1. See McCallum (2013) for a thorough analysis of the G4S agreement's impact in India and South Africa.

2. The full population of TLA campaigns is not known, as systematic research on this subject began only in recent years. In 2015, I launched the Transnational Labor Alliances Database Project in order to document the basic facts of over one hundred TLA campaigns, including both success and failure cases, occurring over the past two decades. The database contains an archive of chronologically ordered sources with relevant information on each campaign and extensive timelines summarizing the chronology and basic facts of each campaign. As of the writing of this book, data collection and analysis are ongoing, with just over half of the cases in the database completed. To date, the data indicate that unsuccessful TLA campaigns outnumber successful campaigns. Moreover, success cases are likely overrepresented in the TLA database due to a reliance on publicly available sources, which document successes more often than failures.

3. The concept of associational power, developed by E. Wright (2000), Silver (2003), and others, will be discussed later in this chapter in the context of intraunion coordination.

4. Some gains can be coded as both material and capacity enhancing, such as the creation of more full-time jobs, which not only affords workers a livelihood but also enhances their bargaining power by decreasing overall unemployment.

5. In order to determine whether a loss is truly significant, however, one must understand the extent to which a particular loss meaningfully reduces workers' material well-being or overall capacity. Some losses are universally significant. Complete destruction of the union on whose behalf a campaign was undertaken in the first place is one obvious example. On the other hand, there are losses that are tangible but trivial, as when the Joy Mining Company eliminated its employees' paid, ten-minute tea break following an otherwise successful transnational campaign that won workers a 12 percent wage increase. Though the Joy workers were reportedly "outraged" by the tea break incident (*Daily Telegraph* 2000), it seems sensible not to regard this as a significant material loss. Of course, most losses are neither undoubtedly devastating nor obviously trivial. For instance, if unions launched a campaign pushing for shorter working hours and more time off, and workers willingly accepted reduced pay in exchange for these requests, then the lower wages might not count as a loss significant enough to render the campaign a failure. Hence, while concessions on things such as wages, hours, medical leave, vacation days, or overtime pay would ordinarily constitute a loss, in the context of some campaigns, these might not be considered significant.

6. Although power can involve open conflict, agenda setting (Bachrach and Baratz 1963), or A's internalization of B's interests (Gaventa 1980)—which Lukes (2005, 1994) referred to as, respectively, the first, second, and third faces of power—of greatest relevance to TLAs is power's first face, manifesting in situations of overt conflict.

2. Dockers, Wharfies, Longshoremen Unite

1. Quoted in Bacon (1998a).

2. Quoted in Erem and Durrenberger (2008, 179).

3. TGWU, also known as T&G, merged with Amicus in 2007 to form the union Unite.

4. In the Liverpool case, the rank-and-file workers acted without official recognition from their union, the TGWU, a situation I will shed light on shortly. Hence, *interunion coordination* need not literally be union to union and can instead refer to effective coordination between any organized groups of workers across national borders.

5. Personal interview, August 18, 2010.

6. An independent arbiter was called in and decided that the health and safety excuse was legitimate. ILWU thus managed to defend itself against legal action.

7. More liberal estimates place the number closer to one hundred thousand (Svensen 1998, 8).

8. The Labour government sold its shares in MDHC after the Liverpool dispute ended (Hughes 1998).

9. Personal interview, April 28, 2010.

10. Emphasis added. The original text in French read, "Les affiliés de l'ITF doivent attendre le signal de l'ITF avant d'organiser toute action de solidarité. N'intervenez

pas contre un navire qui aurait charge or déchargé de cargaisons dans le port de Liverpool sans avoir contacte au préalable le Secrétariat de l'ITF!" The full translation is available in Dropkin (n.d.a).

11. The Australian courts did not have the power to reinstate the wharfies permanently since it was impossible to force the four financially insolvent labor-hire companies, which had technically employed the 1,400 workers, to continue to operate. Thus, the real decision-making and the fate of the wharfies were left to Patrick and the MUA.

3. Service-Sector Solidarity

1. Speech at the Union Network International World Congress, Chicago, IL, August 23, 2005.

2. UNI Commerce is a division of the global union UNI, now called UNI Global Union.

3. UNI Property Services is another division of UNI Global Union.

4. Though the website is now defunct, its contents can be accessed via the Wayback Machine: https://web.archive.org (accessed August 1, 2017).

5. In 2010 G4S rebranded Wackenhut as G4S Secure Solutions (USA).

6. SEIU's 2005 report and related materials were available at http://www.focusong4s .org/violating-american-workers-rights. As of 2009, the URL was defunct; however, its contents can be accessed via the Wayback Machine: https://web.archive.org (accessed August 1, 2017).

7. Though the website is now defunct, its contents can be accessed via the Wayback Machine: https://web.archive.org (accessed August 1, 2017).

8. Australian Council of Trade Unions Organising Conference, workshop C1, "Growing Unions in a Global Perspective," Sydney, Australia, April 28, 2010.

9. Moreover, even if one could argue that SEIU had an edge over UFCW in its potential for interunion coordination, neither outcome was predetermined; SEIU was not sufficient for interunion coordination. This matters because one might argue that interunion coordination (X) is only a proximate variable, and some antecedent cause (Z) related to the characteristics of SEIU might be the truly important causal factor. We can test this alternative explanation using a set theoretic perspective, specifically the method of sequence elaboration, in which we can think of Z (SEIU characteristics) being an antecedent cause of X (interunion coordination), which in turn is necessary for Y (successful campaign). Only when X is almost entirely caused by Z (that is, when Z is nearly sufficient for X) is Z the more important causal variable (Mahoney, Kimball, and Koivu 2009). Because SEIU was not sufficient or nearly sufficient for interunion coordination, X is more causally important than Z.

10. President Obama appointed Hansen to the US Trade Representatives Advisory Committee for Trade Policy in September 2010. In February 2011, Obama appointed Hansen to the President's Council on Jobs and Competitiveness.

11. The CtW Investment Group worked with pension funds sponsored by unions affiliated with the breakaway federation Change to Win.

12. A recording was available online at http://www.parliamentlive.tv/Main/Player .aspx?meetingId=4459&wfs=true until it was archived in mid-2010. However, a copy may be obtained from the Parliamentary Recording Unit. A transcript of the hearing can also be found in UK Parliament, Joint Committee on Human Rights (2009b).

13. According to SEIU, G4S managers declined to meet with the delegations.

14. The Democratic Republic of the Congo, Germany, Greece, Israel, Malawi, Mozambique, Nepal, Panama, Uganda, Uruguay, and the United States.

15. Personal interview, November 18, 2009.

16. Personal interview, September 20, 2009.

17. Personal interview, November 24, 2009.

18. Personal interview, November 30, 2009.

19. This was also true with some countries involved in the Tesco campaign. Tesco workers in South Korea, Thailand, Poland, and Turkey had been attempting to organize before the TLA became involved.

20. SP Securicor Indonesia was affiliated with ASPEK, which, despite being referred to as a "confederation" in Indonesia, more closely resembles an individual union. Thus, SP Securicor Indonesia would be the equivalent of a local.

21. Elements of the Indonesian security guards' strike resemble parts of the Shangri-La Hotel campaign, which also involved hundreds of workers in Indonesia (see chapter 4).

22. For more on the specific capacity-enhancing and material gains made by G4S workers as a result of the GFA, see McCallum (2011, 2013).

4. Struggle in Paradise

1. Quoted in *Agence France Presse* (1997).

2. Personal interview, September 17, 2011.

3. Quoted in Burton and Kazmin (2004).

4. The seven hotels were the Hotel Cambodiana, Hotel Inter-Continental, Sunway Hotel, Sofitel Royal Angkor, Pansea Angkor, Raffles Le Royal, and Raffles Grand d'Angkor.

5. Also known as the American Center for International Labor Solidarity, the Solidarity Center was established in 1997. The relationship between the CTSWF and the Solidarity Center is explained in greater detail later.

6. Formal labor courts (Pengadilan Hubungan Industrial [PHI]), endorsed by the ILO, replaced P4P and P4D (Panitia Penyelesaian Perselisihan Perburuhan Darah [Regional Committee for Settlement of Labor Disputes]) in January 2006.

7. Ranked one of the top fifty richest men in Indonesia, Lyman owned approximately one-quarter of the Shangri-La Hotel, Jakarta, through investments of the Lyman Group of Indonesia, known for its success in the timber industry.

8. SPMS president Halilintar Nurdin contested the figure quoted, arguing that only 250 had quit by early April.

9. While all Indonesian workers, whether laid off or fired, are legally entitled to severance pay, in the Shangri-La case, the longer P4P took to make its decision, the

more attractive an immediate payment became, especially since management offered more money than P4P would likely award.

10. In 2005 Raffles merged with Fairmont Hotels and Resorts Inc. to become Fairmont Raffles Hotels International. As of this writing, the company owned and managed 105 hotels around the world under the Raffles, Fairmont, and Swissôtel brands.

REFERENCES

Abrahamsen, Rita, and Michael C. Williams. 2011. *Security beyond the State: Private Security in International Politics*. Cambridge: Cambridge University Press.

Adler, Daniel, and Michael Woolcock. 2009. "Justice without the Rule of Law? The Challenge of Rights-Based Industrial Relations in Contemporary Cambodia." SSRN Scholarly Paper ID 1445687. Rochester, NY: Social Science Research Network. http://papers.ssrn.com/abstract=1445687.

Age. 2001. "Shangri-La Boss Loses $Bill Project." April 12, 2001.

Agence France Presse. 1997. "Luxury 'Killing Fields' Hotel Opens in War-Weary Cambodia." November 24, 1997.

——. 2004. "Luxury Hotel Group Reinstates Cambodian Workers to End Long-Running Strike." September 13, 2004.

Ahlquist, John S., and Margaret Levi. 2013. *In the Interest of Others: Organizations and Social Activism*. Princeton, NJ: Princeton University Press.

Anderson, Jeremy. 2009. "Labour's Lines of Flight: Rethinking the Vulnerabilities of Transnational Capital." *Geoforum* 40 (6): 959–68.

Anderson, Jeremy, Paula Hamilton, and Jane Wills. 2010. "The Multi-scalarity of Trade Union Practice." In *Handbook of Employment and Society: Working Space*, edited by Susan McGrath-Champ, Andrew Herod, and Al Rainnie, 383–97. Northampton, MA: Edward Elgar.

Anner, Mark S. 2011. *Solidarity Transformed: Labor Responses to Globalization and Crisis in Latin America*. Ithaca, NY: Cornell University Press.

———. 2012. "Corporate Social Responsibility and Freedom of Association Rights: The Precarious Quest for Legitimacy and Control in Global Supply Chains." *Politics and Society*, 40 (4): 609–44. https://doi.org/10.1177/0032329212460983.

———. 2015. "Labor Control Regimes and Worker Resistance in Global Supply Chains." *Labor History* 56 (3): 292–307. https://doi.org/10.1080/0023656X.2015.1042771.

Armbruster-Sandoval, Ralph. 2005. *Globalization and Cross-Border Labor Solidarity in the Americas: The Anti-sweatshop Movement and the Struggle for Social Justice*. New York: Routledge.

Arnold, Wayne. 2002. "The A.F.L.-C.I.O. Organizes in Cambodia." *New York Times*, July 12, 2002.

Asia Monitor Resource Centre. 2001. "Hotel Reopens with Non-union Labour." April 4, 2001. Accessed August 6, 2012. http://www.amrc.org.hk/alu_special/regional_roundup/Indonesia_2.

Bachrach, Peter, and Morton S. Baratz. 1963. "Decisions and Nondecisions: An Analytical Framework." *American Political Science Review* 57 (3): 632–42. https://doi.org/10.2307/1952568.

Bacon, David. 1998a. "The Aftermath of Liverpool: Where Was British Labor? An Interview with Liverpool Dock Striker Mike Carden." David Bacon's website. November 15, 1998. http://dbacon.igc.org/Portrait/08Carden.htm.

———. 1998b. "The War on the Wharfies Hits L.A." David Bacon's website. May 10, 1998. http://dbacon.igc.orgPJust/25WharfieWar.htm.

Bailey, Chris. 2006. "The Liverpool Dockworkers' Strike 1995–98 and the Internet." *EastBound Journal* 1:229–43. http://citeseerx.ist.psu.edu/viewdoc/download?doi=10.1.1.628.3851&rep=rep1&type=pdf.

Banks, Andrew, and John Russo. 1998. "Development of International Campaign-Based Network Structures: A Case Study of the IBT and ITF World Council of UPS Unions." *Comparative Labor Law and Policy Journal* 20:543.

Bartley, Tim, and Curtis Child. 2014. "Shaming the Corporation: The Social Production of Targets and the Anti-sweatshop Movement." *American Sociological Review* 79 (4). Published ahead of print. June 27, 2014. https://doi.org/10.1177/0003122414540653.

Bieler, Andreas, and Ingemar Lindberg. 2010. "Conclusions: A Variable Landscape of Emerging Transnational Solidarities." In *Global Restructuring, Labour, and the Challenges for Transnational Solidarity*, edited by Andreas Bieler and Ingemar Lindberg, 220–231. New York: Routledge.

Bimbauer, William. 2002. "Docklands Boosted by $700m Development." *Age*, May 17, 2002.

Blackburn, Daniel, and K. D. Ewing. 2009. "Memorandum Submitted by International Centre for Trade Union Rights." May 1, 2009. In *Any of Our Business? Human Rights and the UK Private Sector*, first report of session 2009–10, by UK Parliament, Human Rights Joint Committee. November 24, 2009. London: Stationery Office Limited. https://publications.parliament.uk/pa/jt200910/jtselect/jtrights/5/5we53.htm.

Braithwaite, Tom. 2008. "Tesco Under Pressure from US Union." June 4, 2008.

Bramble, Tom. 1998. *War on the Waterfront*. Brisbane: Brisbane Defend Our Unions Committee.

Bronfenbrenner, Kate, ed. 2007. *Global Unions: Challenging Transnational Capital through Cross-Border Campaigns*. Ithaca, NY: Cornell University Press.

———. 2009. "No Holds Barred: The Intensification of Employer Opposition to Organizing." Briefing Paper No. 235, Economic Policy Institute, Washington, DC, May 20, 2009. http://digitalcommons.ilr.cornell.edu/reports/38/.

Bronfenbrenner, Kate, and Robert Hickey. 2004. "Changing to Organize: A National Assessment of Union Organizing Strategies." In *Rebuilding Labor: Organizing and Organizers in the New Union Movement*, edited by Ruth Milkman and Kim Voss, 17–60. Ithaca, NY: Cornell University Press. http://digitalcommons.ilr.cornell.edu/cgi/viewcontent.cgi?article=1050&context=articles.

Brookes, Marissa. 2013. "Varieties of Power in Transnational Labor Alliances An Analysis of Workers' Structural, Institutional, and Coalitional Power in the Global Economy." *Labor Studies Journal* 38 (3): 181–200. https://doi.org/10.1177/0160449X13500147.

———. 2015. "Power, Labour, and Globalisation: How Context-Appropriate Strategies Help Transnational Labour Alliances Succeed." In *Labour and Transnational Action in Times of Crisis*, edited by Andreas Bieler, Roland Erne, Darragh Golden, Idar Helle, Knut Kjeldstadli, Tiago Matos and Sabina Stan. London: Rowman & Littlefield International.

Burton, John, and Amy Kazmin. 2004. "Hospitality at Cambodia's Top Hotels Does Not Extend to Unionised Workers." *Financial Times*, April 28, 2004.

Business Wire. 2006. "SEIU: UK Company Group 4 Securicor That Seeks to Guard the 2012 Olympics, Compromises Security of Major US Ammunitions Plant." September 26, 2006.

Cambodia Daily. 2003. "New HRCT Federation Emerges in Cambodia." September 11, 2003.

———. 2004a. "Council Orders Raffles to Rehire Workers." June 9, 2004.

———. 2004b. "Fired Raffles Staffers Make a Public Appeal." June 21, 2004.

———. 2004c. "Fired Union Leader Says Office Was Looted." May 10, 2004.

———. 2004d. "Hotel's Tactics Killing Workers." May 13, 2004.

———. 2004e. "Labor Arbitrators Challenged by Limitations." March 25, 2004.

———. 2004f. "Raffles Hotel Says Dispute Settled, Workers Disagree." May 17, 2004.

———. 2004g. "Raffles Hotels Puts Best Face on Breaking Unions in Cambodia." May 11, 2004.

Cambodian Tourism and Service Workers Federation. 2004. "Open Letter to Honored Guests of Cambodian Hotels." *Cambodia Daily*, February 19, 2004.

Caraway, Teri L. 2004. "Protective Repression, International Pressure, and Institutional Design: Explaining Labor Reform in Indonesia." *Studies in Comparative International Development* 39 (3): 28–49.

Carnegie, Bob. 2000. "Waterfront: The Battle That Changed Australia: An Opinion." *Workers' Liberty*, August 2000. http://archive.workersliberty.org/australia/Newsletter/August00/review.html.

Carter, Chris, Stewart Clegg, John Hogan, and Martin Kornberger. 2003. "The Polyphonic Spree: The Case of the Liverpool Dockers." *Industrial Relations Journal* 34 (4): 290–304.

Castree, Noel. 2000. "Geographic Scale and Grass-Roots Internationalism: The Liverpool Dock Dispute, 1995–1998." *Economic Geography* 76 (3): 272–92.

Chamberlain, Phil. 2006. "Workers of the World Unite." *Guardian*, August 11.

Champagne, Jessica. 2006. "Unions Act Globally: Workers Unite to Win Severance Pay for Retrenched Securicor Indonesia Employees." *Inside Indonesia* 89. http://www.insideindonesia.org/weekly-articles/unions-act-globally.

Chheang, Vannarith. 2008. "The Political Economy of Tourism in Cambodia." *Asia Pacific Journal of Tourism Research* 13 (3): 281–96.

Chun, Jennifer Jihye. 2005. "Public Dramas and the Politics of Justice." *Work and Occupations* 32 (4): 486–503.

Coe, Neil M., and David C. Jordhus-Lier. 2011. "Constrained Agency? Re-evaluating the Geographies of Labour." *Progress in Human Geography* 35 (2): 211–33.

Costello, Anne, and Les Levidow. 2001. "Flexploitation Strategies: UK Lessons for Europe." October 29, 2001. http://citeseerx.ist.psu.edu/viewdoc/download?doi=10.1.1.459.7634&rep=rep1&type=pdf.

Croucher, Richard, and Elizabeth Cotton. 2009. *Global Unions, Global Business*. London: Middlesex University Press.

CtW Investment Group. 2010. "CtW Investment Group Calls on Tesco Director to Address U.S. Pay and Performance Failures at Friday's AGM." June 29, 2010. https://web.archive.org/web/20100823053520/http://www.ctwinvestmentgroup.com/index.php?id=130.

Cumbers, Andrew. 2004. "Embedded Internationalisms: Building Transnational Solidarity in the British and Norwegian Trade Union Movements." *Antipode* 36 (5): 829–50.

Dahl, Robert Alan. 1961. *Who Governs? Democracy and Power in an American City*. New Haven, CT: Yale University Press.

Daily Telegraph (Sydney). 2000. "Storm over Tea Break." October 27, 2000.

Davies, Steve, Nikolaus Hammer, Glynne Williams, Rajeswari Raman, Clair Siobhan Ruppert, and Lyudmyla Volynets. 2011. "Labour Standards and Capacity in Global Subcontracting Chains: Evidence from a Construction MNC." *Industrial Relations Journal* 42 (2): 124–38. https://doi.org/10.1111/j.1468-2338.2011.00620.x.

den Hond, Frank, and Frank G. A. de Bakker. 2012. "Boomerang Politics: How Transnational Stakeholders Impact Multinational Corporations in the Context of Globalization." In *A Stakeholder Approach to Corporate Social Responsibility: Pressures, Conflicts, Reconciliation*, edited by Adam Lindgreen, Philip Kotler, Joëlle Vanhamme, and François Maon, 275–92. Aldershot, UK: Gower.

Donaghey, Jimmy, Juliane Reinecke, Christina Niforou, and Benn Lawson. 2014. "From Employment Relations to Consumption Relations: Balancing Labor Governance in Global Supply Chains." *Human Resource Management* 53 (2): 229–52. https://doi.org/10.1002/hrm.21552.

Dropkin, Greg. n.d.a. "Comment on ITF Response to LabourNet Article." LabourNet. Accessed May 15, 2018. http://www.labournet.net/docks2/9609/ITFDEB3.HTM.

Dropkin, Greg. n.d.b. "Democracy and the Union: A Reply to Bill Morris." LabourNet. http://www.labournet.net/docks2/9802/GREG.HTM.

Dufour, Christian, and Adelheid Hege. 2010. "The Legitimacy of Collective Actors and Trade Union Renewal." *Transfer: European Review of Labour and Research* 16 (3): 351–67.

Durrenberger, Paul. 2009. "If You Have a Strong Union, You Don't Need a Necktie: U.S. Labor and Global Solidarity." *Dialectical Anthropology* 33 (2): 129–41.

Ellem, Bradon. 2006. "Scaling Labour: Australian Unions and Global Mining." *Work Employment Society* 20 (2): 369–87.

Erem, Suzan, and E. Paul Durrenberger. 2008. *On the Global Waterfront: The Fight to Free the Charleston 5.* New York: Monthly Review Press.

Evans, Peter. 2010. "Is It Labor's Turn to Globalize? Twenty-First Century Opportunities and Strategic Responses." *Global Labour Journal* 1 (3): 352–79.

———. 2014. "National Labor Movements and Transnational Connections: Global Labor's Evolving Architecture under Neoliberalism." *Global Labour Journal* 5 (3): 258–82. https://escarpmentpress.org/globallabour/article/view/2283.

Fairbrother, Peter, Christian Lévesque, and Marc-Antonin Hennebert. 2013. *Transnational Trade Unionism: New Capabilities and Prospects.* New York: Routledge.

Far Eastern Economic Review. 2004. "Boycott Hits Cambodian Hotels." July 8, 2004.

Felsted, Andrea. 2009. "Unions Criticise Tesco." *Financial Times*, June 30, 2009.

Fichter, Michael, and Markus Helfen. 2011. "Going Local with Global Policies: Implementing International Framework Agreements in Brazil and the United States." In *Shaping Global Industrial Relations*, edited by Konstantinos Papadakis, 85–115. International Labour Organization. London: Palgrave Macmillan. https://doi.org/10.1057/9780230319448_5.

Fichter, Michael, Markus Helfen, and Jörg Sydow. 2011. "Regulating Labor Relations in Global Production Networks: Insights on International Framework Agreements." *Internationale Politik und Gesellschaft* 2:69–86.

Finch, Julia. 2008. "Obama Backs Union in Tesco Fight." *Guardian*, June 25, 2008.

Flint, Richard. n.d. "Reply to Replies: Liverpool and ITF." Open letter. LabourNet. Accessed August 1, 2017. http://www.labournet.net/docks2/9609/ITFDEB5.HTM.

Ford, Michele. 2000. "Continuity and Change in Indonesian Labour Relations in the Habibie Interregnum." *Asian Journal of Social Science* 28 (2): 59–88. https://doi.org/10.1163/030382400X00055.

Ford, Michele, and Michael Gillan. 2015. "The Global Union Federations in International Industrial Relations: A Critical Review." *Journal of Industrial Relations* 57 (3). Published ahead of print, April 24, 2015. https://doi.org/10.1177/0022185615574271.

Fougner, Tore, and Ayca Kurtoglu. 2010. "Victory through Solidarity? The Story of a Women Workers' Strike in Turkey's Antalya Free Zone." In *Global Restructuring, Labour, and the Challenges for Transnational Solidarity*, edited by Andreas Bieler and Ingemar Lindberg, 101–15. New York: Routledge.

Fresh & Easy Buzz. 2008a. "Obama Asks Tesco to Meet with Union." June 26, 2008.

———. 2008b. "United Food and Commercial Workers Union Begins Its Spring 2008 Organizing and Communications Campaign Directed at Tesco's Fresh & Easy." March 26, 2008.

G4S (Group 4 Securicor). 2008. "G4S and UNI Sign Global Agreement." December 16, 2008. http://www.g4s.com/en/Media%20Centre/News/2008/12/16/G4S%20and%20UNI%20sign%20global%20agreement/.

G4S (Group 4 Securicor) and UNI Global Union. 2008. "Ethical Employment Partnership." http://www.g4s.com/-/media/g4s/corporate/files/csr/ethical_employment_partnership_signed.ashx?la=en.

Gaventa, John. 1980. *Power and Powerlessness: Quiescence and Rebellion in an Appalachian Valley.* Urbana: University of Illinois Press.

George, Alexander L., and Andrew Bennett. 2005. *Case Studies and Theory Development in the Social Sciences.* Cambridge, MA: MIT Press.

Glanville, Bob, and Adrian Roberts. 2005. "Britain: World's Workers Hammer Group 4." *Morning Star,* July 1, 2005.

Godard, John. 2009. "The Exceptional Decline of the American Labor Movement." *Industrial and Labor Relations Review* 63 (1): 82–108.

Goertz, Gary. 2006. *Social Science Concepts: A User's Guide.* Princeton, NJ: Princeton University Press.

Goodman, James. 2004. "Australia and Beyond: Targeting Rio Tinto." In *Labour and Globalization: Results and Prospects,* edited by Ronaldo Munck, 105–27. Liverpool: Liverpool University Press.

Gordon, Michael E., and Lowell Turner. 2000. *Transnational Cooperation among Labor Unions.* Ithaca, NY: Cornell University Press.

Goss, Jasper. 2001. "Violence Hits Indonesian Dispute." *Workers Online,* no. 85 (February 23, 2001). http://workers.labor.net.au/85/news4_bash.html.

Graham, Dave. 1996. "The Mersey Docks Dispute." *Subversion* 18 (September 20, 1996). http://www.af-north.org/Subversion/subversion_18.htm.

Greer, Ian, and Marco Hauptmeier. 2008. "Political Entrepreneurs and Co-managers: Labour Transnationalism at Four Multinational Auto Companies." *British Journal of Industrial Relations* 46 (1): 76–97.

Greven, Thomas. 2008. "Competition or Cooperation? The Future of Relations between Unions in Europe and the United States." Briefing Paper No. 7, Friedrich-Ebert-Stiftung Briefing Papers—Global Trade Union Program, Bonn, Germany. http://library.fes.de/pdf-files/iez/05444.pdf.

Guardian. 2009. "Tesco Chief Takes Flak from Unions and Investors at Fiery AGM." July 3, 2009.

———. 2010. "Pressure Group Urges Senior Tesco Director to Tackle Concerns over Pay." July 2, 2010.

Hall, Peter. 1986. *Governing the Economy: The Politics of State Intervention in Britain and France.* New York: Oxford University Press.

Hall, Peter, and David Soskice, eds. 2001. *Varieties of Capitalism: The Institutional Foundations of Comparative Advantage.* New York: Oxford University Press.

Hannan, Ewin, and Ben Mitchell. 1998. "Union Wins Control of the Docks." ILWU Local 19 website, June 15, 1998. http://www.ilwu19.com/global/wharfie/unionwins.htm.

Hardy, Jane, and Ian Fitzgerald. 2010. "Negotiating 'Solidarity' and Internationalism: The Response of Polish Trade Unions to Migration." *Industrial Relations Journal* 41 (4): 367–81. https://doi.org/10.1111/j.1468-2338.2010.00574.x.

Harris, Nick. 1997. "Footballer Falls Foul of the Rules as He Shows His Political Colours." *Independent*, March 22, 1997.

Harrod, Jeffrey, and Robert O'Brien. 2002. *Global Unions? Theory and Strategies of Organised Labour in the Global Political Economy*. London: Routledge.

Hathaway, Oona A. 2007. "Why Do Countries Commit to Human Rights Treaties?" *Journal of Conflict Resolution* 51 (4): 588–621. https://doi.org/10.1177/0022002707303046.

Hawker, Dianne. 2007. "Bid to Bar Securicor from 2010 Contracts: Company Accused of Labor Malpractices." *Cape Argus*, May 31, 2007.

Heery, Edmund. 2005. "Sources of Change in Trade Unions." *Work, Employment and Society* 19 (1): 91–106.

Herod, Andrew. 1995. "The Practice of International Labor Solidarity and the Geography of the Global Economy." *Economic Geography* 71 (4): 341–63.

——. 1997. "From a Geography of Labor to a Labor Geography: Labor's Spatial Fix and the Geography of Capitalism." *Antipode* 29 (1): 1–31.

——. 2001. *Labor Geographies: Workers and the Landscapes of Capitalism*. New York: Guilford.

Heyman, Jack. 1996. "ITF Betrayal of the Liverpool Dockers' Strike." Open letter. LabourNet, October 23, 1996. http://www.labournet.net/docks2/9610/HEYMAN.HTM.

——. 2005. "10th Anniversary of the Liverpool Dockers' Sacking: Dockers Gather to Commemorate Liverpool Struggle." LabourNet. http://www.labornet.org/news/1105/dockers.htm.

Hiatt, Jonathan P., and Deborah Greenfield. 2004. "The Importance of Core Labor Rights in World Development." *Michigan Journal of International Law* 26 (1): 39–62.

Hodkinson, Stuart. 2005. "Is There a New Trade Union Internationalism? The International Confederation of Free Trade Unions' Response to Globalization, 1996–2002." *Labour, Capital and Society* 38 (1/2): 36–65.

Hoffman, Christy. 2008. "Global Campaigns: A Case Study with G4S." *Journal of the International Centre for Trade Union Rights* 15 (3): 4–5.

Horowitz, Carl. 2006. "SEIU Campaign against Wackenhut Heats Up." *National Legal and Policy Center*, May 22, 2006. http://nlpc.org/2006/05/22/union%E2%80%99s-corporate-campaign-against-wackenhut-heats/.

Hudiyanto, Odie. 2003. "Labour Dispute at Shangri-La Hotel Resolved." Press release, April 22, 2003.

Hughes, Jack.1998. "Labour Sells Its Shares in Mersey Docks and Harbour Company." *Tribune*, April 2, 1998.

Hurd, Richard, Ruth Milkman, and Lowell Turner. 2003. "Reviving the American Labour Movement: Institutions and Mobilization." *European Journal of Industrial Relations* 9:99–118.

Hyman, Richard. 2010. "Trade Unions, Global Competition and Options for Solidarity." In *Global Restructuring, Labour, and the Challenges for Transnational Solidarity*, edited by Andreas Bieler and Ingemar Lindberg, 16–30. New York: Routledge.

IFSEC Global. 2008. "G4S and UNI Seal Global Employment Deal." December 17, 2008. https://www.ifsecglobal.com/g4s-and-uni-seal-global-employment-deal/.

ILO (International Labour Organization). 2001. Complaint against the Government of Indonesia Presented by the International Union of Food, Agricultural, Hotel,

Restaurant, Catering, Tobacco, and Allied Workers' Associations. Case No. 2116, Report No. 328.

IUF (International Union of Food, Agricultural, Hotel, Restaurant, Catering, Tobacco and Allied Workers' Association). 2002. "Shangri-La Hotel Dispute Continues." March 17, 2002. Accessed August 6, 2012. http://www.amrc.org.hk/text/alu_special /regional_roundup/Indonesia_6.

——. 2004a. "Raffles Refuted: An Anatomy of Union-Busting." July 6, 2004. http://www.iuf.org/cgibin/dbman/db.cgi?db=default&uid=default&ID=1627&view _records=1&ww=1&en=1.

——. 2004b. "Solidarity Now with Cambodian Hotel Workers!" May 3, 2004. http://www .iuf.org/cgi-bin/dbman/db.cgi?db=default&ID=1474&view_ records=1& ww=1&en=1.

Ivens, Joris. 1946. *Indonesia Calling*. Sydney: Waterside Workers Federation Film Unit.

Jackson, Gregory, Sarosh Kuruvilla, and Carola Frege. 2013. "Across Boundaries: The Global Challenges Facing Workers and Employment Research." *British Journal of Industrial Relations* 51 (3): 425–39. https://doi.org/10.1111/bjir.12039.

Jakarta Post. 2000. "Workers Strike Forces Shangri-La to Move Guests." December 23, 2000.

——. 2001a. "Dismissed Workers Threaten to Occupy Shangri-La Hotel." January 26, 2001.

——. 2001b. "Fired Hotel Workers Vow to Fight On." July 12, 2001.

——. 2001c. "Former Shangri-La Workers Threaten to Picket Hotel." March 15, 2001.

——. 2001d. "Minister Rules Out ILO Mediation in Dispute." November 24, 2001.

——. 2001e. "RI Yet to Implement ILO Declaration." January 12, 2001.

——. 2001f. "Shangri-La Employees Fined US$2M." November 2, 2001.

——. 2001g. "Shangri-La Ends Row with Most of Ousted Workers." July 10, 2001.

——. 2001h. "Shangri-La Has Lost RP 18B from Strike." January 13, 2001.

——. 2001i. "Shangri-La Hotel Staff Seek Help from House." January 6, 2001.

——. 2001j. "Shangri-La Hotel Workers Injured during Protest." March 18, 2001.

——. 2001k. "Striking Shangri-La Workers Resign." April 5, 2001.

——. 2001l. "Trouble in Shangri-La." January 6, 2001.

Jensen, Carsten Strøby, Jørgen Steen Madsen, and Jesper Due. 1995. "A Role for a Pan-European Trade Union Movement? Possibilities in European IR-Regulation." *Industrial Relations Journal* 26 (1): 4–18. https://doi.org/10.1111/j.1468-2338.1995.tb00719.x.

Johns, Rebecca A. 1998. "Bridging the Gap between Class and Space: U.S. Worker Solidarity with Guatemala." *Economic Geography* 74 (3): 252–71.

Juravich, Tom. 2007. "Beating Global Capital: A Framework and Method for Union Strategic Corporate Research and Campaigns." In *Global Unions: Challenging Global Capital through Cross-Border Campaigns*, edited by Kate Bronfenbrenner, 16–39. Ithaca, NY: Cornell University Press.

Kang, Susan L. 2012. *Human Rights and Labor Solidarity: Trade Unions in the Global Economy*. Philadelphia: University of Pennsylvania Press.

Keck, Margaret E., and Kathryn Sikkink. 1998. *Activists beyond Borders: Advocacy Networks in International Politics*. Ithaca, NY: Cornell University Press.

Kelly, John. 1998. *Rethinking Industrial Relations: Mobilization, Collectivism and Long Waves*. London: Routledge.

Keohane, Robert O. 1986. "Reciprocity in International Relations." *International Organization* 40 (1): 1–27. https://doi.org/10.1017/S0020818300004458.

Knight, Jack. 1992. *Institutions and Social Conflict*. Cambridge: Cambridge University Press.

Koh, Joyce. 2004. "Raffles Hotels in Cambodia Settles Row." *Business Times Singapore*, May 8, 2004.

LaborNet. 2001. "Shangri-La Boss Loses $Bill Project." April 12, 2001. http://www.labor.net.au/news/935.html.

Lamb, Celia. 2008. "Blue Diamond Workers Reject Union." *Sacramento Business Journal*, November 20, 2008.

Lambert, Rob, and Michael Gillan. 2007. "Spaces of Hope? Fatalism, Trade Unionism and the Uneven Geography of Capital in Whitegoods Manufacturing." *Economic Geography* 83 (1): 75–95.

Lambert, Rob, and Eddie Webster. 2001. "Southern Unionism and the New Labour Internationalism." *Antipode* 33 (3): 337–62.

Larsson, Bengt. 2012. "Obstacles to Transnational Trade Union Cooperation in Europe—Results from a European Survey." *Industrial Relations Journal* 43 (2): 152–70. https://doi.org/10.1111/j.1468-2338.2012.00666.x.

Leeds, Jeff. 1997. "1-Day Job Action Idles Cargo Ships on West Coast." *Los Angeles Times*, January 21, 1997.

Lerner, Stephen. 2007. "A Reply to 'Breaking with the System.'" *New Labor Forum* 16 (3/4): 128–31.

Lerner, Stephen, Jill Hurst, and Glenn Adler. 2008. "Fighting and Winning in the Outsourced Economy: Justice for Janitors at the University of Miami." In *The Gloves-Off Economy: Workplace Standards at the Bottom of America's Labor Market*, edited by Annette Bernhardt, Heather Boushey, Laura Dresser, and Chris Tilly, 243–67. Champaign: Labor and Employment Relations Association, University of Illinois at Urbana-Champaign.

Lévesque, Christian, and Gregor Murray. 2010. "Understanding Union Power: Resources and Capabilities for Renewing Union Capacity." *Transfer: European Review of Labour and Research* 16 (3): 333–50.

Levi, Margaret, and David Olson. 2000. "The Battles in Seattle." *Politics and Society* 28 (3): 309–29. https://doi.org/10.1177/0032329200028003002.

Lillie, Nathan. 2006. *A Global Union for Global Workers: Collective Bargaining and Regulatory Politics in Maritime Shipping*. New York: Routledge.

Lillie, Nathan, and Miguel Martinez Lucio. 2004. "International Trade Union Revitalization: The Role of National Union Approaches." In *Varieties of Unionism: Struggles for Union Revitalization in a Globalizing Economy*, edited by Carola M. Frege and John E. Kelly, 159–80. Oxford: Oxford University Press.

Lindberg, Ingemar. 2010. "Varieties of Solidarity: An Analysis of Cases of Work Action across Borders." In *Global Restructuring, Labour, and the Challenges for Transnational Solidarity*, edited by Andreas Bieler and Ingemar Lindberg, 206–19. New York: Routledge.

Lindblom, C. E. 1977. "The Privileged Position of Business." In *Politics and Markets: The World's Political-Economic Systems*, 170–88. New York: Basic Books.

Locke, Richard M. 2013. *The Promise and Limits of Private Power: Promoting Labor Standards in a Global Economy*. Cambridge: Cambridge University Press.

Locke, Richard M., Ben A. Rissing, and Timea Pal. 2013. "Complements or Substitutes? Private Codes, State Regulation and the Enforcement of Labour Standards in Global Supply Chains." *British Journal of Industrial Relations* 51 (3): 519–52. https://doi.org /10.1111/bjir.12003.

Logan, John. 2006. "The Union Avoidance Industry in the United States." *British Journal of Industrial Relations* 44 (4): 651–75.

Lukes, Steven. 1994. "Power: A Radical View." In *Power: Critical Concepts*, edited by John Scott, 2:233–68. London: Routledge.

———. 2005. *Power: A Radical View*. Hampshire, UK: Palgrave Macmillan.

Macalister, Terry. 2005. "Group 4 Securicor Rebuffs Union Claims of Problems with US Contracts." *Guardian*, March 15, 2005.

Mahoney, James, Erin Kimball, and Kendra L. Koivu. 2009. "The Logic of Historical Explanation in the Social Sciences." *Comparative Political Studies* 42 (1): 114–46. https://doi.org/10.1177/0010414008325433.

Mahoney, James, and Kathleen Thelen, eds. 2010. *Explaining Institutional Change: Ambiguity, Agency, and Power*. Cambridge: Cambridge University Press.

McAteer, Emily, and Simone Pulver. 2009. "The Corporate Boomerang: Shareholder Transnational Advocacy Networks Targeting Oil Companies in the Ecuadorian Amazon." *Global Environmental Politics* 9 (1): 1–30. https://doi.org/10.1162/glep.2009.9.1.1.

McCallum, Jamie K. 2011. "Trade Union Renewal and Labor Transnationalism in South Africa: The Case of SATAWU." *WorkingUSA* 14 (2): 161–76.

———. 2013. *Global Unions, Local Power: The New Spirit of Transnational Labor Organizing*. Ithaca, NY: Cornell University Press.

McConville, Chris. 2000. "The Australian Waterfront Dispute 1998." *Politics and Society* 28 (3): 393–412.

Media Indonesia. 2002. "Supreme Court Urged to Quickly Rule on Shangri-La Hotel Appeal." November 23, 2002.

Merk, Jeroen. 2009. "Jumping Scale and Bridging Space in the Era of Corporate Social Responsibility: Cross-Border Labour Struggles in the Global Garment Industry." *Third World Quarterly* 30:599–615.

Meyerson, Harold. 2009. "Where Are the Workers?" *American Prospect*, February 16, 2009. http://prospect.org/article/where-are-workers.

Milkman, Ruth. 2006. *L.A. Story: Immigrant Workers and the Future of the U.S. Labor Movement*. New York: Russell Sage Foundation.

Mills, Elizabeth. 2004. "Long-Running Cambodian Hotel Strike Ends with Workers' Reinstatement." *World Markets Research Centre*, September 14, 2004.

Moody, Kim. 1997. "Towards an International Social-Movement Unionism." *New Left Review*; *London* 0 (225): 52–72. https://search.proquest.com/docview/1301918838 ?accountid=14521.

Morris, Bill. 1998a. "Letter: More Dispute Over Dockers." *Guardian*, January 30, 1998.

———. 1998b. "Letter: Bill Morris: Why I Was Right." *Guardian*, February 4, 1998.

Munck, Ronaldo. 2002. *Globalisation and Labour: The New Great Transformation*. London: Zed Books.

New Republic. 2004. "Trading Up." August 16, 2004.

New York Times. 2006. "Why Is Everybody Going to Cambodia?" January 22, 2006.

Niforou, Christina. 2014. "Labour Leverage in Global Value Chains: The Role of Inter-dependencies and Multi-level Dynamics." *Journal of Business Ethics* 130 (2): 301–11. https://doi.org/10.1007/s10551-014-2222-8.

Nolan, Jim. 1996. "Letter from Dock Stewards to International Colleagues." Open letter. LabourNet, August 11, 1996. http://www.labournet.net/docks2/9611/8NOVLETT .HTM.

Nolan García, Kimberly A. 2011. "Transnational Advocates and Labor Rights Enforce-ment in the North American Free Trade Agreement." *Latin American Politics and Society* 53 (2): 29–60. https://doi.org/10.1111/j.1548-2456.2011.00116.x.

OECD (Organisation for Economic Co-operation and Development). 2011. *OECD Guidelines for Multinational Enterprises*. OECD Publishing. https://doi.org/10.1787 /9789264115415-en.

Olson, Mancur. 1965. *The Logic of Collective Action: Public Goods and the Theory of Groups*. Cambridge, MA: Harvard University Press.

Parfomak, Paul W. 2004. *The US Contract Security Guard Industry: An Introduction to Services and Firms*. Washington, DC: Congressional Research Service, Library of Congress.

Pierson, Paul. 2001. *The New Politics of the Welfare State*. Oxford: Oxford University Press.

Pilger, John. 1998. "Letter: Workers Done Down." *Guardian*, January 29, 1998.

Piven, Frances Fox. 2008. "Can Power from below Change the World?" *American Sociological Review* 73 (1): 1–14.

Piven, Frances Fox, and Richard A. Cloward. 2000. "Power Repertoires and Globaliza-tion." *Politics and Society* 28 (3): 413–30.

PR Newswire. 2001. "Raffles Holdings Acquires Swissotel Hotels and Resorts." April 23, 2001.

PR Newswire Europe. 2007. "Global Union Solidarity Campaign Brings Victory for G4S Security Workers in Malawi." July 12, 2007.

Raffles Hotels and Resorts. n.d. "The Raffles Story." Accessed August 1, 2017. http:// www.raffles.com/about-raffles/history/history/.

Rainnie, Al, Andrew Herod, and Susan McGrath-Champ. 2007. "Spatialising Indus-trial Relations." *Industrial Relations Journal* 38 (2): 102–18.

——. 2011. "Review and Positions: Global Production Networks and Labour." *Competition and Change* 15 (2): 155–69.

Ramsay, Harvie. 1997. "Solidarity at Last? International Trade Unionism Approaching the Millennium." *Economic and Industrial Democracy* 18 (4): 503–37. https://doi.org /10.1177/0143831X97184002.

Riisgaard, Lone, and Nikolaus Hammer. 2011. "Prospects for Labour in Global Value Chains: Labour Standards in the Cut Flower and Banana Industries." *British Journal of Industrial Relations* 49 (1): 168–90. https://doi.org/10.1111/j.1467-8543.2009.00744.x.

Ruggie, John Gerard, ed. 1993. *Multilateralism Matters: The Theory and Praxis of an In-stitutional Form*. New York: Columbia University Press.

———. 2004. "Reconstituting the Global Public Domain—Issues, Actors, and Practices." *European Journal of International Relations* 10 (4): 499–531. https://doi.org/10.1177/1354066104047847.

Rupidara, Neil Semuel, and Peter McGraw. 2010. "Institutional Change, Continuity, and Decoupling in the Indonesian Industrial Relations System." *Journal of Industrial Relations* 52 (5): 613–30.

Sadler, David. 2004. "Trade Unions, Coalitions and Communities: Australia's Construction, Forestry, Mining and Energy Union and the International Stakeholder Campaign against Rio Tinto." *Geoforum* 35 (1): 35–46.

Sadler, David, and Bob Fagan. 2004. "Australian Trade Unions and the Politics of Scale: Reconstructing the Spatiality of Industrial Relations." *Economic Geography* 80 (1): 23–44.

Schulze-Cleven, Tobias. 2017. "Collective Action and Globalization: Building and Mobilizing Labour Power." *Journal of Industrial Relations* 59 (4): 397–419. https://doi.org/10.1177/0022185617715893.

Seidman, Gay. 2008. "Transnational Labour Campaigns: Can the Logic of the Market Be Turned Against Itself?" *Development and Change* 39 (6): 991–1003. https://doi.org/10.1111/j.1467-7660.2008.00525.x.

SEIU (Service Employees International Union). 2007. *Changing Workers' Lives: SEIU 2007 Annual Report.* https://www.yumpu.com/en/document/view/26208171/changing-workers-lives-seiu-2007-annual-report.

Selwyn, Ben. 2007. "Labour Process and Workers' Bargaining Power in Export Grape Production, North East Brazil." *Journal of Agrarian Change* 7 (4): 526–53.

———. 2011. "Beyond Firm-Centrism: Re-integrating Labour and Capitalism into Global Commodity Chain Analysis." *Journal of Economic Geography* 12 (1): 205–26.

Scharpf, Fritz, and Vivian Schmidt. 2000. *Welfare and Work in the Open Economy.* Oxford: Oxford University Press.

Shangri-La Workers' Advocacy Team. 2002. "Legitimising the Victimisation of Trade Union Activists in the Name of Legal Formality." Press release, August 28, 2002.

Silver, Beverly J. 2003. *Forces of Labor: Workers' Movements and Globalization since 1870.* New York: Cambridge University Press.

Sjolander, Jonas. 2010. "Detours of Solidarity: Experiences from Ericsson in Colombia." In *Global Restructuring, Labour, and the Challenges for Transnational Solidarity*, edited by Andreas Bieler and Ingemar Lindberg, 33–48. New York: Routledge.

Slater, Dan, and Daniel Ziblatt. 2013. "The Enduring Indispensability of the Controlled Comparison." *Comparative Political Studies* 46 (10): 1301–27. https://doi.org/10.1177/0010414012472469.

Smith, Caroline. 2010. "Internationalising Industrial Disputes: The Case of the Maritime Union of Australia." *Employee Relations* 32 (6): 557–73.

Smith, Martin. 2008. "A Critical Look at Global Strategic Campaigns." *International Union Rights* 15(3): 8–9.

Stevens, Michelle. 2010. "Union Relationship Vital for HR, Says G4S's Myles." November 11, 2010. UNI Global Union. http://webcache.googleusercontent.com/search?q=cache:bJBhvtMYmy0J:mail.uniglobalunion.org/apps/iportal.nsf/PrintDoc/20090122_jjylEn+&cd=1&hl=en&ct=clnk&gl=us.

Streeck, Wolfgang, and Kathleen Thelen. 2005. *Beyond Continuity: Institutional Change in Advanced Political Economies.* Oxford: Oxford University Press.

Suara Pembaruan. 2002. "Shangri-La Case Awaits Supreme Court Decision." November 23, 2002.

Sullivan, Michael. 2004. "Labor Dispute Shakes Up Cambodian Tourism." *Morning Edition,* NPR, August 17, 2004. Audio recording, 4:44. http://www.npr.org/templates /story/story.php?storyId=3854503.

Supermarket News. 2007a. "Tesco Selects 31 Sites across the Southwest." January 8, 2007.

———. 2007b. "UFCW Protests 'British Invasion' of Tesco." September 20, 2007.

———. 2011. "Group Asks Tesco to Review Fresh & Easy." June 20, 2011.

Svensen, Stuart. 1998. "The Australian Wharf Lockout." *Capital and Class* 22 (3): 1–11.

Tattersall, Amanda. 2010. *Power in Coalition: Strategies for Strong Unions and Social Change.* Ithaca, NY: Cornell University Press.

Telljohann, Volker. 2009. "UK-Based Multinational Signs First International Framework Agreement." *EurWORK,* March 15, 2009. http://www.eurofound.europa.eu/eiro/2009 /02/articles/eu0902059i.htm.

Tempo Magazine. 2002. "What News of the Shangri-La Workers?" October 20, 2002.

Tesco Union Alliance. n.d. "UNI Tesco Union Alliance Re-Affirms Commitment to Discussion." https://web.archive.org/web/20110811132101/http://www.tescounion-alliance.org/.

Thelen, Kathleen. 1999. "Historical Institutionalism in Comparative Politics." *Annual Review of Political Science* 2 (1): 369–404.

———. 2014. *Varieties of Liberalization and the New Politics of Social Solidarity.* New York: Cambridge University Press.

Townsend, Abigail. 2004. "Democrat Contender Puts Group 4 on its Guard by Backing US Unions." *Independent,* July 18, 2004.

TUAC (Trade Union Advisory Committee). 2008. "UNI Success in G4S OECD Guidelines Case." December 19, 2008. https://members.tuac.org/en/public/e-docs/00/00/03 /C7/document_news.phtml.

Turner, Lowell. 2005. "From Transformation to Revitalization: A New Research Agenda for a Contested Global Economy." *Work and Occupations* 32 (4): 383–99.

UFCW (United Food and Commercial Workers). n.d. "UFCW Leaders: Joseph T. Hansen." Accessed July 15, 2013. http://archive.is/4oYtA.

———. 2008a. *The Two Faces of Tesco.* Washington, DC: United Food and Commercial Workers International Union.

———. 2008b. "UFCW Launches Campaign in Britain against 'the Two Faces of Tesco.'" June 4, 2008. http://www.ufcw.org/2008/06/04/ufcw-launches-campaign-in-britain -against-the-two-faces-of-tesco-2/.

UK Parliament, Joint Committee on Human Rights. 2009a. *Any of Our Business? Human Rights and the UK Private Sector.* First report of session 2009–10, November 24, 2009. Vol. 1, *Report and Formal Minutes.* London: Stationery Office Limited.

———. 2009b. *Any of Our Business? Human Rights and the UK Private Sector.* First report of session 2009–10, November 24, 2009. Vol. 2, *Oral and Written Evidence.* London: Stationery Office Limited. http://www.publications.parliament.uk/pa/jt200910/jtselect /jtrights/5/5ii.pdf.

UNI (Union Network International). 2008a. "Asia Pacific Welcome for Tesco Union Alliance." April 3, 2008. http://www.uniglobalunion.org/news/asia-pacific-welcome-tesco-union-alliance.

———. 2008b. "Sixth Regular Convention of the UFCW, Speech by Philip Jennings." August 22, 2008.

———. 2008c. "UNI Commerce Launches Global Union Alliance for Tesco." July 22, 2008. http://www.uniglobalunion.org/news/uni-commerce-launches-global-union-alliance-tesco.

———. 2009a. "G4S Ghana and G4S Security Services (Ghana) Limited Employees Conclude Their Maiden Collective Agreement with G4S Authorities in Ghana." August 12, 2009. http://www.uniglobalunion.org/apps/UNINews.nsf/vwLkpById/6D8E2DC37768A84DC125761E0048FD44/$FILE/Report%20UNI%20PS.pdf.

———. 2009b. "Tesco to Launch European Works Council." June 16, 2009. http://www.uniglobalunion.org/Apps/UNINews.nsf/vwLkpById/BAF79B82106BC404C12575E60025593B.

———. 2009c. "Tesco under Fire over Foreign Labour Rights." June 30, 2009. http://www.uniglobalunion.org/Apps/UNINews.nsf/vwLkpById/5F2DCFDA3AA34770C12575E500488EB2.

———. 2009d. "Unions in Africa Welcome the UNI-G4S Global Agreement." May 11, 2009. http://www.bankonrights.org/news/unions-africa-welcome-uni-g4s-global-agreement.

———. 2009e. "UNI Reports Reveal Tesco's Labour Practices Abroad." June 30, 2009. http://www.uniglobalunion.org/apps/uninews.nsf/vwLkpById/F46CAA79A53E9061C12575E5002C18A1?OpenDocument.

———. 2009f. "UNI Tesco Global Union Alliance Release Report on Tesco, USA." July 22, 2009. http://www.uniglobalunion.org/Apps/UNINews.nsf/0/6C43C28FE9033E96C12575FB003082AD.

———. 2009w. "Tesco's Employment Practices in South Korea: A UNI Global Union Country Report." Accessed June 12, 2013. http://www.uniglobalunion.org/Apps/UNIFiles.nsf/vwLkpFilesById/0B6164465B267220C12575E50033CAD2/$FILE/UNI_SKOREA_FINAL_LR.pdf.

———. 2009x. "Tesco's Employment Practices in Thailand: A UNI Global Union Country Report." Accessed June 12, 2013. http://www.uniglobalunion.org/Apps/UNIFiles.nsf/vwLkpFilesById/0C2E68B6A50D7855C12575E50033D8D4/$FILE/UNI_Thailand_FINAL_LR.pdf.

———. 2009y. "Tesco's Employment Practices in the United States: A UNI Global Union Country Report." http://laborcenter.berkeley.edu/laborlaw/tesco09.pdf.

———. 2010a. "UNI Tesco Union Alliance Re-affirms Commitment to Dialogue." March 5, 2010. http://www.uniglobalunion.org/Apps/UNINews.nsf/vwLkpById/07CD430F743B3620C12576EE005EA6B6.

———. 2010b. "Human Rights Watch: European Companies Deny US Workers Union Rights." September 7, 2010. http://www.uniglobalunion.org/Apps/UNINews.nsf/0/1288ABFF869FACFEC1257796003EBA6?OpenDocument.

UNI Property Services. 2007. "Who Protects the Guards? The Facts Behind G4S in Southern Africa." https://waronwant.org/sites/default/files/Who%20Protects%20the%20Guards.pdf.

Urata, Mac. 2010. "Building Rank and File Activism: A Study of the Global Action Day Campaign in the History of the International Transport Workers' Federation." In *Global Restructuring, Labour, and the Challenges for Transnational Solidarity*, edited by Andreas Bieler and Ingemar Lindberg, 58–72. New York: Routledge.

USDAW (Union of Shop Distributive and Allied Workers). 2009. *Newsletter for Tesco Reps*. October 2009.

US Fed News. 2004. "Rep. Miller Urges Major International Organizations to Stop Patronizing Two Raffles Hotels in Cambodia." July 16, 2004.

Vanden Eyde, Arno, Margaret Sutherland, and Dal Dio. 2008. "Final Statement by the UK National Contact Point for the OECD Guidelines for Multinational Enterprises: G4S and Union Network International." http://www.oecd.org/daf/inv/mne/43750644.pdf.

Vogel, David. 2010. "The Private Regulation of Global Corporate Conduct Achievements and Limitations." *Business and Society* 49 (1): 68–87. https://doi.org/10.1177/0007650309343407.

Voss, Kim, and Rachel Sherman. 2000. "Breaking the Iron Law of Oligarchy: Union Revitalization in the American Labor Movement." *American Journal of Sociology* 106 (2): 303–49.

——. 2003. "You Just Can't Do It Automatically: The Transition to Social Movement Unionism in the United States." In *Trade Unions in Renewal: A Comparative Study*, edited by Peter Fairbrother and Charlotte Yates, 51–77. London: Taylor and Francis.

Waterman, Peter. 2001. *Globalization, Social Movements and the New Internationalisms*. London: Continuum International.

Webster, Edward. 2015. "Labour after Globalisation: Old and New Sources of Power." In *Labour and Transnational Action in Times of Crisis*, edited by Andreas Bieler, Roland Erne, Darragh Golden, Idar Helle, Knut Kjeldstadli, Tiago Matos, and Sabina Stan, 115–27. London: Rowman and Littlefield International.

Williams, Glynne, Steve Davies, and Crispen Chinguno. 2015. "Subcontracting and Labour Standards: Reassessing the Potential of International Framework Agreements." *British Journal of Industrial Relations* 53 (2): 181–203. https://doi.org/10.1111/bjir.12011.

Wills, Jane. 2008. "Making Class Politics Possible: Organizing Contract Cleaners in London." *International Journal of Urban and Regional Research* 32 (2): 305–23.

Wilson, Shaun. 1998. "Union Mobilisation and the 1998 Maritime Dispute." *Journal of Australian Political Economy* 41 (June): 23–36.

Wilton, Nick. 2010. *An Introduction to Human Resource Management*. London: SAGE.

Workers Online. 2001. "Fears Grow over Shangri-La Protests." July 11, 2001. http://workers.labor.net.au/102/news9_shangri.html.

——. 2002. "Shangri-La Workers Still Fighting." July 5, 2002. http://workers.labor.net.au/143/news84_shangrila.html.

Wright, Chris F., and Sarah Kaine. 2015. "Supply Chains, Production Networks and the Employment Relationship." *Journal of Industrial Relations* 57 (4). Published ahead of print, July 8, 2015. https://doi.org/10.1177/0022185615589447.

Wright, Erik Olin. 2000. "Working-Class Power, Capitalist-Class Interests, and Class Compromise." *American Journal of Sociology* 105 (4): 957–1002.

Young, Kevin, and Diana C. Sierra Becerra. 2014. "How 'Partnership' Weakens Solidarity: Colombian GM Workers and the Limits of UAW Internationalism." *WorkingUSA* 17 (2): 239–60. https://doi.org/10.1111/wusa.12109.

Zajak, Sabrina. 2017. *Transnational Activism, Global Labor Governance, and China.* New York: Springer.

Zwiebach, Elliot. 2007a. "Obama, Edwards Endorse Efforts for Tesco Talks." *Supermarket News*, November 9, 2007.

——. 2007b. "Phoenix Local Protests Tesco Liquor Licenses." *Supermarket News*, March 5, 2007.

——. 2008. "Obama Asks Tesco to Meet with Union." *Supermarket News*, June 26, 2008.

Index

Page numbers in italics refer to figures and tables.